'00

RETHINKING AFRICAN
DEVELOPMENT

RETHINKING AFRICAN DEVELOPMENT

Toward A Framework For Social Integration and Ecological Harmony

LUAL A. DENG

Africa World Press, Inc.

P.O. Box 1892
Trenton, NJ 08607

P.O. Box 48
Asmara, ERITREA

Africa World Press, Inc.

P.O. Box 1892
Trenton, NJ 08607

P.O. Box 48
Asmara, ERITREA

Cover design: Jonathan Gullery
Bood design: Wanjiku Ngugi

Library of Congress Cataloging-in-Publication Data

Deng, Lual Acuek Lual.
    Rethinking African development : toward a framework for social integration and ecological harmony / by Lual A. Deng.
        p. cm.
    Includes bibliographical references and index.
    ISBN 0-86543-607-X (cloth). -- ISBN 0-86543-608-8 (pbk)
    1. Africa--Economic conditions--1960- 2. Africa--Economic policy.
    3. Sustainable development--Africa. 4. Democracy--Africa.
    5. Africa--Social policy.   I. Title.
HC800.D455 1997
338.96--dc21   97-36477
                                                              CIP

*This book is dedicated to my
daughter Achol, her mom and sisters
with love*

CONTENTS

TABLES

ACKNOWLEDGEMENTS

◆

The research project for this book was completed at the Christian Michelsen Institute (CMI) in Bergen, Norway where I was a visiting scholar on a leave of absence (1995/96) from the African Development Bank (ADB). I am particularly grateful for a modest grant from the Norwegian Ministry of Foreign Affairs (MFA) and the Norwegian Research Council, which made my stay at CMI quite productive. Special thanks go to: former president of the African Development Bank, Mr. Babacar Nidaye, Gunnar Sorbo of CMI, Knut Opsal of ADB and Aud Kolberg of MFA for their encouragement and support in undertaking this research project. Many colleagues at both the Bank and CMI provided valuable comments on various drafts of the manuscript of this book, but I would particularly like to express my gratitude to the following: Arild Anglesen, Turid Boe, Just Faaland, Charles Lufumpa, Gilbert Mbesherubusa, Richard Moorsom, Brave Ndisale, Ole David Koht Norbye, and Siegfried Pausewang.

I would like to express my appreciation and thanks to Professor Crawford Young of the University of Wisconsin-Madison, Dr. Philip English of the World Bank and Mr. Robert Molteno of ZED books for their critical comments on earlier drafts of the manuscript and subsequent valuable suggestions which have greatly contributed to the present volume. Needless to say, none of them are responsible for any shortcomings of this book. I should add that the views expressed in this book are entirely my own and I am therefore fully accountable for them. Ruth Wanjiku Mwathi for secretarial support, my daughter Aguil for assisting in finding missing references, Wanjiku Ngugi and the entire Editorial Department of Africa World Press for ensuring timely publication of this book.

My dear wife Margaret Angeth and our daughters Achol, Aguil, Nyandeng and Abiol deserve a special mention for it was their valuable time that I took during the course of my writing this book. Their continued support and appreciation of the crucial role of African scholars in the quest for sustainable development in Africa has been an important source of inspiration for me. I am ever grateful to them for their love, encouragement and sacrifices they have made in support of my service of Africa.

Lual A. Deng
Nairobi, Kenya
September 1997

CHAPTER ONE

INTRODUCTION

◆

If we journey backwards to the hour of African independence, in 1960, we may summon from remote corners of our collective memory perspectives and visions of radically different content. "Seek ye first the political kingdom," enjoined Ghanaian independence leader Kwame Nkrumah in his celebrated aphorism. Axiomatic to this widely-shared vision of the times was a sense of unlimited possibilities, with the political kingdom — the state — as macrohistorical agent of progress. Theologian of nationhood, architect of development, manager as well as proprietor of the economy, Mother Theresa to the less fortunate citizens, the state was invested with a breath-taking but at the time entirely credible historical mandate to fulfill dreams, even expectations, of civil society for a life more abundant.

-Crawford Young (1996:2)

After a decade of economic structural adjustment programs (ESAPs), Africa continues to be the 'sick man' of the world with multiple signs of economic decay; civil strife resulting from social disintegration and exclusion; delegitimation of the state; indebtedness; rising poverty; and threats of a creeping desert as well as recurrent drought. These signs have recently triggered a call for a broad-front liberalization of economy and politics in Africa. But the drive to undertake simultaneously economic and political reforms has raised legitimate concerns, within the African policy community, about the feasibility of a broad-front liberalization. Moreover, given the seemingly overloaded agenda of African development, it is unlikely that a meaningful economic growth could be achieved at the turn of the century without a comprehensive policy framework that would guide decision-makers and other stakeholders in formulating appropriate strategies for economic development and social progress in Africa. However, a quick look at the leading issues in African development — economic reform, democratization, protecting the environment, reducing poverty, controlling indebtedness, and resolving internal conflicts — shows that designing such a framework is a complex undertaking, which requires critical thinking as well as moving away from the manner in which public policy has been formulated in the past. It essentially calls for a revisiting of Kwame Nkrumah's celebrated aphorism cited in the above epigraph. This is because the current situation in Africa necessitates going beyond policy prescriptions, to begin addressing the very nature of African state upon which the implementation of appropriate strategies for economic development and social progress in Africa would depend.

In addition to the situation depicted by the preceding paragraph, this book — *Rethinking African Development* — emanates from two general concerns about the process of policy formulation and its application in Africa. First, issues of sustainable development in Africa, in my view, have not yet received the attention needed, especially within the policy-oriented research and academic communities. The numerous world summits organized by the United Nations over the last four years — the Earth Summit, the Population Conference, the Social Summit, the Women's Conference, and so forth — seem not to have created an adequate level of awareness and/or research interest among African development analysts and researchers about the policy implications of the delicate population, poverty, and environment nexus. Second, the nature of the leading issues in African development calls for a critical examination of the past development strategies, and a search for a comprehensive macro-policy framework that would enable Africa to address these issues simultaneously. Such a framework would in turn ensure the developmental impact of a public policy on ordinary Africans at the turn of the century. Therefore, the overall objective in writing this book is to generate research interest in issues of sustainability, and to provoke and motivate critical thinking within the development policy community. A secondary objective has been to contribute to the enhancement of the quality of the contemporary discourse on African development in the 1990s and beyond. I strongly believe that for African intellectuals to make a substantial contribution in the service of Africa, they will have to think more critically and work harder than their contemporaries in the rest of the world. It is our moral duty and social obligation to utilize our accumulated knowledge and lead the quest for quality in the management of African development, so as to restore human dignity to ordinary Africans and then to ourselves. This, I think, is to be done through a systematic intellectual dialogue among those concern with the current state of development on the continent. I also believe that nobody has a monopoly of knowledge. Some people may have control over information pertaining to Africa and financial resources that tend to perpetuate their hegemony over African development policy formulation. Yet, these do not necessarily give them the monopoly on knowledge about African development. Knowledge is power, which we must apply to enhance the quality of life of our fellow Africans. This would be our intellectual contribution to humanity.

By way of revitalizing critical thinking with respect to the above general concerns, the book calls for rethinking

African policy formulation for sustainable development. The cornerstone of this rethinking process is the integration of social, ecological, and growth concerns into a single conceptual framework for macro-policy formulation. Sustainable development is used in this book to imply a balanced combination of economic growth with effective poverty reduction, integration of the dynamic features of social institutions and values, and protection of the environment. A fifth dimension — capacity building/utilization and institutional strengthening for effective internalization of macroeconomic policies — should be added, however, to ensure sustainable development in Africa. It would also assure consistency of development policy with African institutions, systems of thought, and beliefs. In this regard, the view taken here is that there are four tenets of development policy in Africa in the 1990s and beyond: economic growth, poverty reduction, protection of the environment, and integration of social values and institutions into macroeconomic strategies. But all these four tenets presuppose that a broadly based political organ (movement/party) is effectively in charge of the state. That is, a consensus-based system of government is urgently needed in Africa to ensure the design and implementation of a comprehensive macro-policy framework which is commensurate with the multiplicity of African development problems.

The rest of the book is organized into four chapters. Chapter two presents a general overview of development theories and practices in Africa during the first three decades (1965–1994) of political independence. This overview provides an important point of departure for rethinking African policy formulation for sustainable development. The dominant development theory during the first decade (1965–1974) was greatly influenced by W. Arthur Lewis's economic growth theory, which had been practiced as a 'modernization' paradigm. Tanzania, however, pursued its own philosophy of *ujamaa* in guiding her development efforts, something from which this research project has particularly benefited. The focus of the 'modernization' paradigm was primarily on industrialization with corresponding neglect of the important role of agriculture as the engine of growth at this critical stage of African development. Moreover, there was a remarkable convergence of views between the modernization school and socialist thinkers with respect to industry as defining modernity. In addition, the colonial economic structures and institutions were inherited by the newly independent African states. These structures and institutions planted, in my view, the seeds of the development crisis that hit Africa during the early part of the 1980s.

The second period (1975 - 84) is considered here as a decade of 'paradigmatic vacuum,' stemming from ideological differentiation among the African states. One of the main contributing factors to this vacuum is the oil crisis, which subsequently triggered series of economic downturns in the industrialized world during the second half (1980 – 84) of this period. These downturns in the world economy in turn accelerated the economic decline and political decay in Africa. And the inability of African development policy to adjust to a changing world during the decade compounded the crisis. The only possible outlet, then, was the adoption of structural adjustment programs (SAPs) by a majority of African countries, during the third decade (1985–94). These programs were founded on the basic principles of neoclassical economics. Moreover, this period witnessed a strong global wind of change calling for the liberalization of politics as a result, I would argue, of Gorbachev's *glasnost*.

The third chapter identifies six leading issues that are likely to dominate the African development agenda in the 1990s and beyond. These are economic reform, democratization, protection of the environment, poverty reduction, controlling indebtedness, and conflict resolution. These leading issues, in my view, will be competing for the limited resources available to Africa from both domestic and external sources. They are also likely to overload the development agenda, especially in light of weak institutions as well as the lack of an appropriate institutional capacity for policy analysis and internalization. There is therefore a need for sequencing of policy measures both within and between the leading issues themselves. It will, moreover, require an appropriate mix of policy instruments. In the two areas, for instance, of economic reform and democratization, the question that needs to be addressed concerns the order and timing of SAPs and multi-party democracy agenda. Should the political reform program be implemented before or after SAP? Could they be implemented concurrently? And are there appropriate structures and institutions for the timely as well as smooth implementation of economic and political reforms in Africa? These questions and more are the focus of analysis in chapter three. Moreover, issues of the consistency of African institutions and value systems with those underlying SAP and multi-party democracy are raised in the chapter. In addition, the evolution of African institutions, structures, and beliefs is examined with a view to ensuring their eventual harmonization as well as compatibility with the contemporary economic and political reforms.

The fourth chapter, which is the main chapter of the book, presents a conceptual framework for rethinking African development. Here, the overall objective of a development policy is conceived as human progress and betterment, based on freedom, dignity, and the pursuit of individual happiness within the overall community or society's prosperity and welfare. From the perspective of a development policy analyst/formulator, this is essentially an optimization problem. Stated differently, the objective function of a development policy is to improve human well-being and social progress subject to four general constraints. These are the nature of African state; the structure of the economy; the state of physical environment; and the dynamism of social institutions, systems of thought and beliefs. Such a formulation of a development policy problem is intended to facilitate as well as accelerate the search for the most appropriate African model(s) of sustainable development. In this regard, I have identified an African model of sustainable development that consists of four key elements — a consensus-based democratic system of government; an agriculture-led economic growth; social integration; and ecological harmony. Such a model, which is a comprehensive framework, would enable Africa to address simultaneously the six leading issues in African development stated at the beginning of this introduction.

Each of the above four elements of an African model of sustainable development is discussed extensively in the chapter. For the first element, two contrasting models have recently emerged. These are the Mandela's South Africa and Museveni's Uganda, which could in my view provide the range of possibilities for the rise of a sustainable developmental state in Africa. The South African Government of National Unity (GNU) is seen in the book as constituting a consensus-based system of government which exhibits features of a likely African traditional model of governance. The Ugandan National Resistance Movement (NRM) is viewed as a consensus-building political organization that has produced a model of an African state which is able to confront simultaneously the six leading issues of African development, even though there are still pockets of internal conflict in the northern part of Uganda. But the most important lesson to be drawn from Mandela's South Africa and Museveni's Uganda is the necessity as well as the centrality of a national political movement in finding solutions to Africa's development problems. There are, at last, African examples of countries governed by broad-based political organizations of extraordinary caliber — in their leadership, their style of political work, and their consensus-building approaches to public policy formulation and execution.

The second key element of the proposed African model of sustainable development, which is examined in this chapter, is an agriculture-led economic growth. Initial conditions for sustainable economic growth are considered to be inherent in agriculture. Therefore, agricultural transformation with emphasis on the role of farmers, especially women farmers and regional economic integration are the key to sustained growth in Africa by the year 2020. For analytical exposition, Africa is divided into six agro-ecological zones that are envisaged to encourage production of goods and services that a zone or region has a clear comparative advantage to produce. This would also facilitate adoption, by farmers and others, of production techniques that are economically feasible, environmentally sound and consistent with the social fabric of the community. Moreover, the harmonization of macroeconomic, social and environmental policies within each zone would be central, more than before, to the quest for regional economic integration in Africa.

Social integration is the third element of the proposed model. The analysis, seeks to incorporate the cultural pluralism dimension of African societies in the design of sustainable development strategies. This is to be done through the economic, political and social empowerment of Africa's poor. Recent studies have shown this group to constitute the majority of ordinary African people. This triple empowerment is intended to enable the poor and other vulnerable groups in the African society to fully participate in the productive activities of their respective national economies. It would also provide them with an opportunity to take active part in the political process at the community level, which should in turn enhance social cohesion, tolerance, and mutual respect. However, the emphasis here is on the integration of African institutions, systems of thought, and beliefs, into the process of policy formulation, so as to ensure their consistency and compatibility with economic fundamentals as well as global development imperatives.

Ecological harmony is the fourth key element. The view taken here is that African economic man maintained, in the distant past, a symbiotic relation and co-existence with his surrounding environment. However, this relationship started to deteriorate with the introduction, in recent years, of alien production techniques and associated institutions, systems of thought and beliefs. Furthermore, Africa is the only region in the world where the rate of population growth is faster than that of the economy. This situation exacerbates an unbearable stress on Africa's natural resources. Alternative approaches to natural resource management are discussed with a view to integrating the best practices into the process of policy formulation for sustainable development. But, the central theme is to break the vicious circle of rapid population growth, poverty and environmental degradation.

The book concludes with a hopeful note and optimistic outlook for Africa in chapter five. The current quest for economic reform and political pluralism in Africa is one of the three sources identified in the book as constituting the basis for hope and optimism in the rethinking of African development. The other two are the prevailing mode in the donor community with respect to so-called 'development aid' and resource endowment. A recent study by the Washington-based World Resources Institute (WRI) shows that less than one-third of Africa's arable land is currently being utilized. Similar trends are shown with respect to the utilization of natural resources in Africa, which, if properly used, should enable African countries to achieve their objectives of sustainable development by the year 2020.

CHAPTER TWO

THEORY AND PRACTICE OF DEVELOPMENT IN AFRICA: AN OVERVIEW

◆

Most of Africa is not developing. Three decades of effort have yielded largely stagnation, regression or worse. The tragic consequences of this are increasingly clear: a rising tide of poverty, decaying public utilities and collapsing infrastructure, social tensions and political turmoil, and now, premonitions of inevitable drift into conflict and violence.

-Claude Ake (1995:1)

By way of a prelude, a brief review of the theory and practice of development in Africa during the last thirty years (1965 - 1994) is undertaken, so as to appreciate and put in a proper context the urgent need for rethinking African policy formulation. As articulated by the above epigraph, various attempts at African development have not significantly improved the livelihood of ordinary people in Africa. On the contrary, they seem to have impoverished many ordinary African people, witnessed and magnified by the economic crisis of the mid-1980s. This is, despite impressive growth rates of the African economies prior to the first oil shock of the mid-1970s. The review here of the prevailing development theories and practices, then, should hopefully enable us to rationalize the call for the rethinking of African policy formulation with a view to ensuring sustainable development at the turn of the century.

Syed Naqvi (1993), Tony Killick (1992), Bjorn Hettne (1990), David Apter (1987), and W. P. Preston (1982, 1987, 1995) have provided, from my perspective, excellent critiques of development theory then and now. Similarly, Crawford Young (1982) has eloquently analyzed development policy and practice in Africa during the first two decades of independence. I have, therefore, relied heavily in this overview on their respective works. In addition, use is made of some of the recent literature on structural adjustment (see for instance Deng and Oshikoya, 1991; Bromley, 1991; Elbadawi, 1992, 1995a; World Bank, 1994a; Killick, 1993; Helleiner, 1986; Cornia and Helleiner, 1993; Kofi, 1994; Deng, 1995; African Development Bank, 1995) in this brief review of the various attempts at African development. A useful point of entry is a journey backward in search of the African vision of development during the early years of independence. I would think that such a vision was largely reflected in the writings, statements, manifestos, programs, and actions of some governments led by the first generation of African leaders that came to power immediately after political independence. A comparative analysis of this literature tends to show that most of the African states were essentially, or at least claimed to be, benevolent social guardians at the time of political independence. But with the passage of time and/or change of leadership, a majority of these states deviated from the path of social guardianism and disintegrated into various forms. These forms have been described in the political science literature as: neocolonialism, integralism, prebendalism, patriomonialism, bureaucratic-authoritarianism, revolutionary-socialism, and so forth. It would seem to me, however,

that these differences started to appear over the years due
to variations in the ideological orientation pursued by each
country. This point is elucidated by Crawford Young:

> Ideological preference does influence, in significant
> ways, the matrix of policy. At the time of independ-
> ence, there was little to differentiate Ivory Coast and
> Guinea or Kenya and Tanzania. The cumulative im-
> pact over two decades of sharply divergent visions
> of the future has made Ivory Coast and Kenya very
> different from Guinea and Tanzania. (1982:326)

But why should we be concerned with the nature of the
post-colonial state? A correct identification of the post-colonial African state is non-trivial from the perspective of development policy analysis and formulation[1]. As pointed out
by Mahmood Mamdani (1993), the development problem
in Africa centers on the form of the state and the absence of
mass participation in its affairs. Basil Davidson also thinks
"that the whole issue of the postcolonial (or neocolonial?)
state is one that richly merits thorough discussion at this
time" (1993:49). In this regard, a development policy analyst needs to know the behavior of the state — being it a
social guardian, a liberal democratic, a neocolonial, an integral, a prebendal, a patrimonial, a bureaucratic-authoritar-
ian, or a revolutionary socialist — if s/he were to prescribe
and/or recommend an appropriate public policy. This should
in turn make "development economics to view the justness
of the basic institutions - social, economic and political - as
linked both to the maximization of the welfare of the least-
privileged individuals in society and to a net reduction in
their numbers" (Naqvi, 1993:105).

There is no uniformity, however, among policy analysts
in categorizing the post-colonial African states according to
their political philosophy, which guides their economic and
social development. Crawford Young (1982) for instance, has,

provided a useful interpretative framework for analyzing development policy with respect to ideological orientation of the state. He has grouped countries according to "three streams of development philosophy categorized as Afro-Marxism, populist socialism, and market-economy capitalism" (1982:297). The Afro-Marxist group is represented by the following eight countries: Angola, Benin, Congo, Ethiopia, Madagascar, Mozambique, Sao Tome and Somalia. The populist socialist group could be exemplified by seven countries: Algeria, Egypt, Ghana, Guinea, Libya, Mali and Tanzania. While the Afro-capitalist was symbolized by the following seven countries: Cameroon, Cote d'Ivoire, Kenya, Malawi, Morocco, Nigeria and Zaire. On the other hand, Bjorn Hettne (1990) has identified four variant types of African political systems. Based on his classification, we have the following four groups of countries:

a) Afro-Marxist, which emphasizes Marxist-Leninist ideas of economic development and political structure (e.g. Ghana under Nkrumah and Guinea under Sekou Toure);

b) Moderate-socialist, which favors a socialist command economy, but tolerates foreign investment (e.g. Kenya of Kenyatta and Zambia of Kaunda);

c) Pro-Western social democrat (e.g. Senegal under Senghor); and

d) Agrarian-socialist emphasizing models of socialism derived from traditional African social values and institutions (e.g. Tanzania under Nyerere).

Furthermore, Christian Potholm (1970) has defined four African political systems by establishing "four major categories of inquiry which take into account the unity of the political system and the way in which international politics impinge upon that system" (1970:3). The four criteria were i) participation in the decision-making process of the political system; ii) the ability of the political system to organize its human and natural resources and to implement its goals; iii) the goals chosen and their relation to the international environment; and iv) the changing styles and structures of domestic and international decision making. On the basis of these criteria, he then, identified the following four systems: i) the South African political system, representing undemocratic multiparty system that is often found in areas under colonialism; ii) the Tanzanian political system, symbolizing a single-party democracy; iii) the Somali political system, representing a multiparty democracy[2]; and iv) the Ivoirian political system, representing "a modernizing oligarchy and a tendency toward the no-party state."

For the sake of analysis and clarity, development policy in the post colonial era is examined over three decades. These are: i) the decade of political and economic euphoria (1965-74); ii) the period of oil shock and crisis (1975-84); and iii) the decade of structural adjustment and *glasnost* (1985-94). The influence of development models on these countries could be analyzed comparatively over the three decades, using one of the above classification of countries according to their publicly pronounced ideological inclination. However, the concern here is not, *per se*, about the impact of these development theories on the performance of the different categories of African states. In fact, their impact is already common knowledge as illustrated by Claude Ake at the beginning of this chapter. The main objective of this overview is to determine what types of development theory were dominant in Africa during the period (1965-1994). This is intended to guide us in the process of rethinking African policy formulation as well as its implementation.

The Period of Political and Economic Euphoria (1965-74)

When most of the African countries attained their political independence during the early part of the 1960s, they inherited economies which were, generally speaking, transitional, open, small and dependent on the production of raw materials. They were transitional in that more than 75% of the population lived on subsistence agriculture. Open, because of their participation in international trade. Small in economic terms, because they were price-takers and not price-setters in the global economy as well as their low income levels and limited resource-base. Moreover, these economies were and still are dependent on primary goods for their export earnings. These characteristics give a certain uniformity of structure to African economies. While there may be structural diversity in the economies (Taylor, 1983) and cultural pluralism in the politics (Young, 1976) of African countries, they are nevertheless assumed to be facing similar problems and constraints. In addition, the Lagos Plan of Action (LPA) advocates a general development strategy that would enable the continent to face external factors. Hence, for the purpose of analysis and following Jaime de Melo and Sherman Robinson (1982), one could subject African economies to identical development objectives and strategies; to external shocks; and to similar policy reform measures.

The overall objective of the post-colonial African state was the attainment of human progress and betterment. There is nothing *per se* euphoric about this objective, but what is rather elusive is the prevailing popular conviction then, that thought prosperity was to be achieved, literally overnight, once colonialists left. Two forces were at work in most of the African states in the immediate aftermath of the colonial period. The first is the euphoria brought about by the political independence, which led to unreasonable optimism, expectations and over-confidence on what the new state could do. But, "it was the European legacy that" the new leaders "mechanically transplanted onto African soil that was to be their, and Africa's, undoing" (Mamdani, 1993:30), and not necessarily the rising popular expectations of the post-colonial era.

The second is the successful application of Keynesian economics in the United States and in the reconstruction of the war ragged Europe through the Marshall Plan, which in turn created a sense of illusion among economists in believing that economic problems of the "underdeveloped" world could be solved using the same techniques. According to Michael Hogan (1987), Marshall planners blended market forces with new tools of macroeconomic management to rebuild war-torn Europe.[3] These planners mainly used a hybrid economic model, which was an "American brand of cooperative neo-capitalism that went beyond the laissez-faire political economy of classical theory but stopped short of a statist syndicalism" (Hogan, 1987:3). This is because, according to Hogan, the "Marshall planners were far more interested than their predecessors in cutting the web of exchange controls, quotas and import licenses and the tangled network of over two hundred bilateral trade payments agreements that stifled intra-European commerce and prevented the most efficient use of local resources. But they echoed the arguments of their predecessors in attacking these and other restrictions as tantamount to the sort of economic autarky that generated conflict and discouraged growth" (1987:19). In this regard, we should keep in mind the types of economic structures and institutions that existed in the pre-Marshall Plan or the pre-World War Two Europe, for these were inherited by the newly independent African states with dare consequences two decades later on.

I would, therefore, argue that the above two factors reinforced each other in undermining the development process in the post-colonial era. In this regard, the question that needs to be asked is what kind of development philosophy guided policy formulation in the newly independent African states? Development policy should undoubtedly have embraced and guided the nation-building project as an integral part of its strategy. Most of these countries, if not all, were multi-ethnic states, and to this extent nation-building should have been a genuine priority. This is because traditional structures and institutions of various ethnic groups would have been incorporated in the development philosophy as by way of guaranteeing the nation-state. There is now a general agreement within the development policy community that modernization was the dominant development school of thought in the 1960s and early 1970s (Hettne, 1990; Toye, 1987; Riddell, 1981; Preston, 1982, 1987; Kothari, 1988; Apter, 1987; Meier and Seers, 1984; Meier, 1987; Deng and Mou, 1985, and so forth). However, development theory at the time, as shown by Hettne, "ignored the ethnic question and failed to integrate it meaningfully into any analytical framework" (1990:26). This is because the modernization school saw ethnicity as among "the traditional obstacles to development which were supposed to disappear in the course of development" (Hettne, 1990:26).

Moreover, Pierre Landell-Mills has recently concluded that the "first three decades of African independence have been an economic, political and social disaster...because the prevailing development paradigm was fundamentally flawed. This paradigm was based on the erroneous proposition that state institutions derived from metropolitan models could be made the engine of development once colonial governmental superstructure was withdrawn" (1992:1). Mamdani echoes the same sentiment in describing the African elite at the time as "wanting to erase this history in the name of development; it argued for Africa's independence, but could not brook any thought of a development rooted in Africa's own history"(1993:29). I would think that Nyerere's Tanzania was the exception, for her development paradigm was founded on African social values and structures, which were themselves evolving with changing circumstances. I will therefore treat it here as the `African alternative' paradigm. These two models are examined below.

Let us first briefly look at the modernization model of development. What is the theoretical underpinning and/or the origin of the modernization paradigm? According to Preston (1987), "modernization theory" is the ideological child of the Cold War, which replaced the growth theory. I would, nevertheless, argue that modernization is not a theory *per se*, but rather a model, which was essentially an application of the growth theory as advanced by Arthur Lewis (1955) and others. This is because Lewis conceived economic growth as synonymous with development, a point which he illustrates as follows: "Most often we shall refer only to `growth' or to `output' or even occasionally, for the sake of variety, to `progress' or to `development'..." (1955:10). Furthermore, in introducing his oft-cited book — *The Theory of Economic Growth* — Lewis writes:

> The subject matter of this book is the growth of output per head of population...First it should be noted that our subject matter is growth, and not distribution. It is possible that output may be growing, and yet that the mass of the people may be becoming poorer...Secondly, our concern is not primarily with consumption but with output. Output may be growing while consumption is declining, either because saving is increasing, or because the government is using up more output for its own purposes. We shall certainly have to consider the relationships between output, consumption, saving and government activity, but we shall be doing this from the angle of growth of output, and not from the angle of the growth of consumption. (1955:9)

The above passage from Lewis is, in my view, the foundation for the development theory as practiced in Africa during this period. It is also the seed of the demise of the "modernization" model in Africa, since "development economics is nothing if it is not relevant to policy, if it is not sensitive to social suffering, and if it is not explicitly geared to raising social welfare" (Naqvi, 1993:177). Furthermore, Syed Naqvi concurs that: "There are problems with the original development model, due to Lewis and others" (1993:174), and states five main weaknesses of this paradigm. I will come to these weaknesses shortly, but let me first present the core of the growth theory as advanced by Lewis.

According to Arthur Lewis (1955), there are three proximate causes of growth. These are the effort to economize, the increase and application of knowledge, and capital formation. The effort to economize "shows itself in various ways; in experimentation, or risk-taking; in mobility, occupational or geographical; and in specialization...if the effort is not made, either because the desire to economize does not exist, or else because either custom or institutions discourage its expression, then economic growth will not occur" (Lewis, 1955:11). And for growth to occur, from the perspective of the modernization school of thought, African traditional value systems and institutions were to be substituted and replaced by imported[4] structures and foreign beliefs that were seen to be consistent with economic growth. Hence, we find that the development discourse during this period revolved around traditionalism versus modernism within the overall framework of a quest for social change and modernization. Moreover, the effort to economize is essentially a characteristic of human behavior, which depends on the physical, political, economic, and social conditions or surrounding environment of any given society. This is what Naqvi calls "the relativity of economics vis-a-vis the nature of society" (1993:16). Of particular interest to our analysis here are people's attitudes toward work, wealth, and social relations. In agreement with Arthur Lewis, "it is the habit of productive investment that distinguishes rich from poor nations, rather than differences in equality of income, or differences in the respect accorded to wealthy men" (1955:28). In this regard, "the turning point in the life of a society is not when it begins to respect wealth, as such, but when it places in the forefront productive investment and the wealth associated therewith" (Lewis, 1955:28).

Regarding the second proximate cause of economic growth — the increase of knowledge and its application — Lewis acknowledges it as cultural capital, which is knowledge accumulated by a society and "has occurred throughout the human history, but the more rapid growth of output in recent centuries is associated obviously with the more rapid accumulation and application of knowledge in production" (1955:11). This acknowledgement is important because the failure of development policy to integrate African traditional value systems basically deprived it of the cultural capital — knowledge accumulated by African societies over centuries — which was necessary to create initial conditions for sustainable economic growth in the post-colonial era. In retrospect, it is the imported institutions and structures which restricted the increase of knowledge and its application in favor of growth, and not the African traditional value systems. As Mahmood Mamdani put it, "to import European institutions was the same as denying Africa's own legacy" (1993).

The third proximate cause of growth is capital formation. Most of the economic modeling and planning during this period (1965-74) was premised on the belief that factor shares and rates of growth showed that capital accumulation was a more important source of growth in poor countries than in rich ones (Taylor, 1979). This conviction, I would argue, led to another erroneous notion, which stated that there is no growth without capital formation or investment. It is true that there is no growth without investment in the effort to economize, in knowledge (or human capital formation), and in capital accumulation. Stated differently, investment in my view is not synonymous with increasing the amount of capital only, it is a function of the three proximate causes of growth. But what matters to growth, according to Arthur Lewis, "is the formation of productive capital, which is not necessarily associated either with willingness to work or with willingness to save. There is in fact no evidence that

hard work and productive investment necessarily go together" (1955:41). Nevertheless, "hard work and capital formation are an excellent formula for economic growth, but
whereas capital formation without hard work will also produce substantial growth, hard work without capital formation makes little contribution to development" (1955:42).
Hence, I would think that the legitimating model of development, as conceived by the modernization school of
thought, was grounded in the theory of economic growth. It
was nevertheless influenced by the socialist models of development — thus, there is a remarkable convergence of
views between capitalism and socialism with respect to the
importance of industry as defining modernity and subsequently rapid economic growth.

From the preceding analysis, it should be obvious why
industrialization was the dominant theme as well as the strategy of development policy during this period (1965-74). This,
according to Naqvi (1993), is one of the five weaknesses of
development theory at the time. It arose because of the two-
sector model of Lewis (1954), which "led to a frame of thinking in which the growth potentialities of the agricultural sector were grossly underestimated" (Naqvi, 1993: 154). I
would also argue that the modernization philosophy led to
a development paradigm that was fundamentally flawed
because of its emphasis on industrialization with a corresponding neglect to the important role of agriculture as the
engine of growth at this critical stage of development. From
the perspective of this paradigm, the growth of output per
unit of time and/or factor of production is normally greater
in industry than in agriculture. And since there were `un-
limited supplies' of labor[5] from the agricultural sector to
industry, industrialization was a `logical' strategy, which
was recommended by expatriate economic planners to most
African states, irrespective of their ideological orientation.
In fact, modernization became synonymous with industrialization, which was in turn used interchangeably with

progress and/or development. But, as argued by Rostow, "it takes more than industry to industrialize" (1962:22). According to Rostow (1962), the substance of an economic development strategy in a situation where a vast majority of the population still lives on agriculture is to bring about revolutionary changes in agriculture and infrastructure.

There was also a set of convictions, especially from more progressive African states and/or leaders, about industry as defining modernity to which all aspired at the time.[6] For instance, this group was convinced that an agricultural strategy essentially condemned African states to marginality. Moreover, there was the conventional class question — the belief that industrialization was a political necessity for creating a social class that would support the development project in Africa. Two factors were instrumental in reinforcing this conviction. The Soviet model was seen during this period as having found the secret to exceptionally high rapid economic growth, which in turn enabled the Soviet bloc economies to escape from "backwardness" and "underdevelopment." The other contributing factor was the thesis popularized by the economists of the UN Economic Commission for Latin America (ECLA) that there was a secular decline in the terms of trade between agricultural and industrial commodities.[7] In this regard, institutions and structures of both market economy and `state capitalism' were to be transplanted where colonial superstructures did not exist. A point which led Pierre Landell-Mills to conclude:

In retrospect, it is all too obvious that underlying cultural premises of these institutions were alien to the majority of Africans. Consequently the institutions started to crumble the moment the colonial administration left. After independence, both donors and many Western educated African leaders acted as though they were convinced that development could be achieved by the systematic application of rational "modern" techniques and concepts using state institutions based on Weberian bureaucratic principles. (1992:1)

The second shortcoming of the development model as applied during this period is what Naqvi calls its 'bloody-mindedness' with respect to equity and distribution of growth. As shown earlier in this chapter, the focus was on the growth of output and "not to some such concept as welfare, satisfaction or happiness" (Lewis, 1955:9). I consider this to be an unfortunate statement from one of the pioneers of development economics, because the main objective of economic policy is the attainment of happiness, human progress, and betterment through the production of goods and services for all the people in a given society, and not only for a privileged few. In addition, the growth of output cannot be sustained without an effective demand, not from the producers of this output, but from consumers, who use it for satisfying their needs, which essentially translates into welfare and happiness. For, in most cases, people consume goods and services in order to derive satisfaction — and hopefully happiness — that is utility maximization. Moreover, Adelman and Morris (1973) and Leontief (1983) have shown that growth with equity can be achieved. In fact, they are not necessarily incompatible objectives of a public policy.

The third weakness is the over-emphasis on the "centrality of savings rate in the process of economic growth — an aspect of the Harrod-Domar model that development economists accepted uncritically" (Naqvi, 1993:153). It was generally believed that savings and productive investment were peculiar to a capitalist economy, and by extension, to industry. For instance, Arthur Lewis states: "As capitalism develops within a backward economy, the proportion of the national income accruing as capitalist profits increases all the time, and so the share of the national income saved and invested grows automatically all the time, until the economy is fully converted to capitalism, when the share of profits in the national income is stabilised. All the countries now developed have gone through this process, except the U.S.S.R.; and the countries now in line for development can tread the same path if they so desire."[8] In this regard, the emergence and proliferation, for instance, of five/ten-year development plans and parastatal bodies, such as marketing boards, industrial banks, and so on, during this decade, were all aimed at achieving industrialization, and therefore rapid economic growth. These institutions were envisaged to accelerate the process of capital formation by making "saving and productive investment a religion of life" (Lewis, 1960).

Furthermore, growth models, such as Harrod-Domar model,[9] made economic planners think that "capital investment is something like a development vending machine: you put in the money, press the button and get growth" (Preston, 1987:9). This is further articulated by Gerald Meier, who concludes: "One of the logical ways to start planning the general rate of economic development is first to estimate the amount of domestic savings and capital imports that could be expected with no change in economic policies; then to calculate the rate of growth that this level of savings and investment would provide, and finally to compare it with the desired rate of growth"(1976:253). Preston also reminds us that the "social world is a realm of lived human experience and that this is where discussion should begin. . .The social sciences do not, as do the natural sciences, confront a realm of objects (having physical causes), they confront a realm of persons (having beliefs, institutions, and reasons)" (1987:44). However, this realm was not very much appreciated by development economists at the time.

The fourth limitation of the development paradigm during this period, according to Naqvi, is the neglect of the human factor, especially education, which "was not assigned the importance it deserved in these models" (1993:154). But this is quite strange, since the second proximate cause of growth, according to Lewis, is the increase and application of knowledge. The problem in Africa was, however, the failure of these models to incorporate African knowledge in their design. The inability and/or failure of the modernization school of thought to integrate African knowledge into its development models and strategies is therefore seen by this author as one of the contributing factors to the lack of significant human betterment and progress in Africa today. But, according to Claude Ake, "there is a failure of development to be sure, but then it is a development project which never quite started because of inclement political and social conditions" (1995:2). Basic economic and social indicators during the period under review would tend to contradict Ake's statement that the development project did not start in the first place. I would argue that the development project did indeed start and gained momentum, especially during the first half of the decade. It was a decade of large public investment projects, financed from both domestic and international sources. For instance, one of the major achievements of this period is the establishment of the African Development Bank (ADB) with a view to financing these public investment projects. The founding fathers of the Bank envisioned it as financing economic development and social progress in Africa. The Bank might have failed to contribute toward the enhancement of African knowledge asset and its application in the service of Africa, but this should not lead us to deny the fact that development project did start in the earlier days of the political independence.

The fifth and final weakness is the indifference of the development models at the time to the crucial role of technological process "in generating a sufficiently high (ex-ante) rate of investment to raise output on a permanent, rather than on a transitory, basis" (Naqvi, 1993:153). This is a surprising omission, according to Naqvi, "because Solow's classic article (1957) showed clearly whatever is involved in correcting the built-in instability of the Harrod-Domar model,...is to let the capital/output ratio to vary due to technological change" (1993:153-154). Naqvi further points out that there is "yet a deeper reason why technological change must be brought into the picture: without it, the per capita income will at best grow at a constant rate, along the steady-state growth path. But this is not what development economics is concerned about; instead, it is concerned primarily with the ways and means of raising the per capita income (output) over time" (1993:154). This can be further qualified and reformulated to reflect the new realities, and concerns about, the sustainability of development. In this regard, it could be stated that this technological change should be environmentally sound and socially viable.

Let us now look at the alternative development paradigm that was attempted in Julius Nyerere's Tanzania. In the early days of independence, the Tanganyika African National Union (TANU) adopted socialism as a philosophy to guide the development efforts of the newly independent state. It later culminated in the Arusha Declaration in 1967. This was on the conviction that "socialism is about people, and people are the products of their history, education and environment" (Nyerere, 1968:20). The basic principles underlying the Tanzanian model were rooted in African systems of thought, and the paradigm became popularly known as *ujamaa*. Traditional African societies developed these systems of thought into effective strategies for coping with their ecology and the world around them. The choice of the word *ujamaa* was made, according to Nyerere, for two special reasons. "First, it is an African word and thus emphasizes the African-ness of the policies we intend to follow. Second, its literal meaning is 'family-hood', so that it brings to the mind of our people the idea of mutual involvement in the family as we know it" (Nyerere, 1968:2).

President Nyerere then identified seven general characteristics of socialism as: i) the centrality of 'man' in all social activity; ii) the equality of all members of the society; iii) the

upholding of human dignity; iv) the upholding of democratic principles; v) all members of the society are workers;
vi) public ownership of the means of production and exchange; and vii) the centrality of social values in a socialist
society. These were features of the ideal socialist society and
it was now the task of TANU to see to it that the Tanzanian
state steered society toward this goal. It was recognized,
however, that there was "no 'socialist road map' which de-
picts all obstacles and provides a path through or around
them" (Nyerere, 1968:19). Tanzania was therefore to chart
the course of her destiny anew, using relevant points from
other development paths. This is well articulated by the following passage:

> We in Tanzania are a part of mankind. We have to
> take our place in the world. We would be stupid to
> reject everything or everyone coming out of the West
> because that is the home of capitalism; we would
> be stupid to reject everything the communists do.
> We are trying to build ujamaa - socialism - which is
> neither of these things. We can learn from both -
> and from other political systems - without trying to
> copy or seeking for their approval. Our task is to
> look first at our own position and our own needs,
> and then to consider other experience and other
> suggestions in the light of our requirements. We
> should not put ourselves into blinkers as though we
> were a horse which could not be trusted to see what
> is going on elsewhere. We should be willing to learn
> from our fellow men, and we should contribute to
> the common pool of knowledge and experience. We
> can do this if we use our brains - that is, if we THINK.
> (Nyerere, 1968:22)

In retrospect, African socialism with its home in Dar es
Salam, under both intellectual and political patronage of

President Julius Nyerere, had a better chance of spreading to the rest of Africa. An alternative paradigm for a real African development guided by ujamaa could have been adopted widely, if the liberation wars in Southern Africa had not bogged it down. Tanzania had to play a leading role — first, in the liberation of Angola, Mozambique and Zimbabwe, and later with the Front-line states in the war against the apartheid regime in South Africa. All these efforts meant diversion of the most needed resources (including time) from the development of an African role-model, which could have been followed and/or copied by others. Yet, Tanzania was able to make a significant progress in the home front against illiteracy and tribalism that are still haunting a number of African states. For instance, one of the strengths of what I would called Nyerereism is its ability to address the ethnic question by forging a sense of oneness among the Tanzania people, especially on the mainland. The development of Kiswahili as a national language contributed greatly to this.

There were, nevertheless, gross mistakes in the application of the model in Tanzania when ujamaa was translated into villagization. In the words of Wole Soyinka, "by uprooting cohesive communities, relocating them in comparatively modernist villages...centuries old and tested modes of production were abruptly interrupted; the result was, even in Nyerere's admission, not the developmental model it was expected to be" (from Serageldin and Taboroff, 1994:205). But President Nyerere was supported at the time by genuine Africanist scholars, such as Basil Davidson and Reginald Green. As shown by Crawford Young, "Reginald Green, an expatriate adviser to the Tanzanian treasury, noted with satisfaction that by the mid-1970s 80 percent of the medium-and large-scale economic activity lay in the public sector...figures that exceeded those of Eastern Europe at a comparable period after the imposition of Stalinist socialism" (1994:289). Describing the waGogo people of Tanzania, Davidson (1974) has this to say:

> ...the way of life of the waGogo, for want of any suitable alternative, has remained almost exactly as it was before. They have continued to live within the patterns of their ancient settlement and tradition, inhabiting small and isolated homestead groups spread far and wide across their plains. Living like this, they have found it difficult, or impossible, to combine together in any way which would enable them to share in such meager modernizing facilities as have become available, whether in the form of schools, clinics, or mechanically improved water facilities. The colonial authorities of the Trusteeship era-the period from 1919 to 1961-found it unnecessary to do much or anything about the problems of the waGogo...But in 1971 the waGogo decided to begin living in a different way. They had been lately offered an alternative that might help them, and they were to give it a try. (1974:7)

It is ironic that the above passage is from a master piece of work that was intended to provide arguments against growth without development by Basil Davidson through his book: *Can Africa Survive?* It is ironic, because Davidson's diagnosis of the waGogo's problem and its cure are familiar and/ or identical to those of the modernization school, which considers economic growth as synonymous with development. By Soyinka's analysis, the "total way of productive life" of the waGogo people was thus destroyed, and they were offered a new one in the name of growth with development, as shown below:

> The government and its national party, the Tanzanian African National Union, had urged upon them

the advantages that might accrue from ceasing to live in scattered homesteads or little hamlets lost in the bush, and from starting to live in more or less large villages-ujamaa villages, self-help villages which, they were promised, the government would help them to build and furnish with water wells and other community facilities. (Davidson, 1974:8)

Basil Davidson was right then, by asking: can Africa survive? He was also right to warn that Africans "must make their saving revolution, or see their continent reduced to an object of charity and worse." But, he was wrong in asserting that the "development of people" would be achieved through a "forced march to a new culture." Moreover, this is contrary to one of the basic principles of *ujamaa*, which states that "try to build socialism by evolution — by dealing with the problems one by one in accordance with the consensus of opinion and our capacity at any one time" (Nyerere, 1968:25).

The Period of Oil Shocks and Crisis (1975 - 84)

The October 1973 Arab-Israeli war and subsequent oil crisis marked the beginning of the end of development planning and the return of neo-classical theorizing in the form, for example, of supply-side economics in the early part of the 1980s and neo-liberalism at the beginning of the 1990s. But the transition between development planning and neo-liberalism was too long in Africa, for it took about ten years for both policy-makers and experts to comprehend the nature and magnitude of the crisis. This is because economic institutions and structures installed and/or transplanted either by the colonial governments or by apostles of 'modernization' were weak, but at the same time too rigid and inflexible to adjust to changing circumstances in the global economy. There was also the combined effect of petrodol-

31

lars and the commodity boom, which led to a double-digit economic growth rates during the first half of this period (1975-80), as illustrated by table 3.3 in the third chapter of the book. This combined effect largely caused a number of African countries to not recognize the impending economic crisis in the first half of the 1980s.

It is now an acknowledged fact that the basic causes of Africa's economic problems during the second half (1980-84) of this period were multivariate: incompatible development strategies and/or inconsistent macroeconomic policies that led to structural imbalances (Deng, 1988); the rise in oil prices; world recession; and drought. However, I would assign more weight to the role of public policy in the continent's development crisis during this period. Africa's present development problems are the result of the inability of various national governments to transform the structure of their economies in a changing international economic environment. In my view, African governments had not put in place a consistent set of policy tools to deal with the crisis at its very early stages. Yet, a strong argument can be made that there were factors beyond the control of African governments and which have impacted on the performance of their economies. In this respect, three waves of exogenous factors can be identified as the most important external elements that contributed to the African development crisis during this decade.

The first wave of external factors is associated with the successive development strategies that were applied on the economies of Africa during the first decade (1965-74) of independence. These strategies, as shown in the previous section of this chapter, sought to apply linear and similar development models that were incompatible with African economic structures, social values, and institutions. Nevertheless, Rostow's stages of economic development should have had enabled these models to incorporate African structures and institutions, thus ensuring their compatibility. For instance, W. Rostow (1962) emphasizes both economic and non-economic changes as essential factors in bringing about a sound development process. However, the modernization model was founded on the security interests of the ruling elite, which led development, according to Hettne, to mean "a strengthening of the material base of the state, mainly through industrialization, adhering to a pattern that has been remarkably similar from one country to another" (1990:29). Furthermore, these strategies were influenced by what Nyerere has referred to earlier as alien doctrines, which failed to examine the nature and characteristics of the African state and the dynamism of public policies that stem from it (Deng and Mou, 1985). A point which led the Organization of African Unity (OAU) to conclude that:

> The effect of the unfulfilled promises of global development strategies has been more sharply felt in Africa than in the other continents of the world. Indeed, rather than result in an improvement in the economic situation of the continent, successive strategies have made the continent stagnate and become more susceptible than other regions to the economic and social crisis suffered by the industrialised countries...Faced with this situation and determined to undertake measures for the basic restructuring of the economic base of our continent, we resolved to adopt a far reaching regional approach based primarily on collective self-reliance. The Lagos Plan of Action (1980)[11]

The second wave of exogenous shocks that hit most of the African economies is essentially associated with the oil crisis of the 1970s and the subsequent world recessions. This hurt the African states, in particular the non-oil producers, in three ways:

a) Africa found itself paying more for its imports as a direct result of rising oil prices. In addition, most of the African countries were unable to curb the rapidly growing domestic demand, particularly in view of the inelastic demand for imports;

b) Recession in the world economy led to a downturn in the demand for the primary products that Africa exported. Hence, the ability of the African economies to earn foreign exchange through non-oil exports was greatly reduced;

c) Given the rising cost of imports and falling foreign exchange earnings from exports, African economies should have adjusted, other things being equal, to reduce the balance of payments disequilibria. However, other things were not equal. Paradoxically, with easy access to foreign capital through the availability of the petrodollars, Africa was lured into borrowing from various international sources[12] (for example, commercial banks, bilateral and multilateral financial institutions) to finance the rising cost of imports. At the same time, as Bela Balassa (1983) showed, increases in the export prices of some primary commodities (for example coffee and cocoa), offset temporarily the negative effect of high oil prices. In this regard, the negative consequences of the second wave of external shocks were minimized, or even temporarily averted, through the recycling of petrodollars into some of these economies. Hence, most economies continued to grow, albeit slower than during the first decade of the political independence.

The third wave of external shocks during the first half of 1980s was, however, very powerful both in magnitude and intensity. African economies, constrained by the lack of foreign exchange, were already operating below capacity and under the stress of earlier shocks. The third wave consisted of three main elements: rising oil prices; the Sahelian drought; and the higher cost of external borrowing. The hike in world oil prices in 1980 triggered stagflation in most of the countries of the Organization for Economic Cooperation and Development (OECD). This situation led to a severe recession in the developed world with the subsequent downturn in the demand for crude oil and primary commodities. At this time, African economies were severely hit by both climatic and 'financial' droughts.

In addition to these external shocks, there were also internal elements that contributed to the economic difficulties of the 1980s. These internal factors were caused by domestic public policy failure. Among these endogenous factors, which resulted from inconsistent macroeconomic policies, are the imbalances in the structures of production, price, employment, and ownership. These structural imbalances imposed institutional constraints on the market which was therefore unable to send correct signals to the various economic agents in the economy. The inability of market forces to convey appropriate messages to various economic agents in the economy is largely related to what the IMF calls "policy-related distortions - arising from price controls, exchange and trade restrictions, overvalued exchange rates, and official ceilings on interest," (IMF, 1987). In this regard, one would argue that there was essentially a failure of both public policy and market in Africa during the first half of the 1980s.

The interaction of these exogenous and endogenous factors on African economies produced a severe situation characterized by worsening terms of trade on the one hand, and on the other by acute shortages of foreign exchange, which resulted into chronic financial and balance of payments difficulties. The end result was inevitably the inability of African economies to sustain rates of economic growth that had been achieved during the first decade and half of independence. But the poor performance of the African economies during the second half of this period is due mainly to public policy failure. African governments have had no consistent set of policy tools in place to deal with the worsening situation, with the result that domestic consumption, and particularly government expenditures, proved difficult to restrain.

In retrospect, the easy access to petrodollars and commodity boom were instrumental in delaying adjustment, since countries continued to maintain their pre-oil crisis consumption patterns under the illusion that the hike in the prices of imports was a temporary phenomenon. Moreover, the length of the transition led, in my view, to a 'paradigmatic vacuum' in Africa, on the one hand, and paradoxically to a differentiation in the political systems as articulated by Crawford Young's three ideological orientations on the other. It is paradoxical, since a development paradigm practiced in any given country and/or economy is a function of a political ideology. I would think that this arose due to the inability of alternative schools of thought, such as the dependency school, to make a substantial influence on development policy formulation, even though it had effectively shown the inherent structural weaknesses of the modernization paradigm.

One of the limitations of the dependency paradigm was its implicit conclusion that only a world socialist revolution would allow developing countries to break the vicious circle of underdevelopment and achieve economic development[13]. It is true that the liberation struggle in Southern Africa — especially in Angola, Mozambique and Zimbabwe — accelerated the attainment of political independence, mainly through the support of world socialist states. But, the world socialist revolution failed to deliver economic development, since its basic assumption was not different from that of the modernization paradigm — industry as defining modernity.

Besides Nyerereism, however, there were several attempts at alternative paradigms that are capable of addressing some of the weaknesses of the modernization model. For instance, the first half of this period saw emphasis on new approaches, such as integrated rural development, basic needs, growth with equity, and so forth. Moreover, catch-phrases such as popular participation, appropriate technology, and so on, characterized some of the earlier attempts at addressing the general issues of poverty and underdevelopment. But these new approaches were not grounded on a single theoretical underpinning and/or a political philosophy — as was the case with *ujamaa* — for them to produce a viable development paradigm. This assertion can be challenged, however, since "a broadly capitalist framework" guided "the majority of African countries' attempts at growth" (Sandbrook, 1985:10). Nevertheless, Richard Sandbrook seems to contradict his statement: "African states are not, in any real sense, capitalist states" (1985:12). And part of the problem, according to Sandbrook, is that: "The peculiar conditions of postcolonial Africa impel an adaptation of colonial inspired political structures and processes in a patrimonial, or rather neopatrimonial, direction. The omnipresent danger in this adaptation is a degeneration of neopatrimonialism into an economically irrational form of `personal rule.' This decay, manifest in political instability, systematic corruption and maladministration, introduces irrationalities into economic life, but nevertheless is shaped by a particular political logic" (1985:12-13). I have argued elsewhere (see Deng, 1988) that these irrationalities are essentially features of a `policed economy' in a number of African countries, which have further generated and reinforced the growth of parallel economies. Seen within the logic of a neopatrimonial state, systematic corruption, maladministration, moonlighting, smuggling, capital flight and `black-marketeering' are rational behavior in a `policed economy.'

The rise of a "policed economy" came about in Africa when the post-colonial state ceased to pursue the objective of benevolent social guardianism — an agent of development — and began to seek the interest of the ruler and the ruling elite. This in turn, necessitated the establishment of control structures and administrative mechanisms (e.g.

market boards and parastatal financial institutions) for enforcing price and domestic credit ceilings, foreign exchange
restrictions, import and export licenses, and so forth. Some
of these institutions were, however, inherited from the colonial states, but with different objectives. In a "policed
economy," the control structures and administrative mechanisms are used on the one hand to eliminate political oppo-
nents, and on the other to accumulate wealth for the ruling elite[14]. In this regard, the function of resources allocation is performed neither by price-mechanism as in the free
market economies, nor by a central planning agency as in
economies that are centrally managed. Rather, resources
allocation in a "policed economy" is performed by an administrative rationing mechanism to ensure the interest of
the ruling group, but this breeds and institutionalizes corruption. While price and domestic credit control, exchange
and import restrictions could be seen as a rational response
to temporary balance of payments difficulties (Rwegasira,
1987), these measures tend to become institutionalized with
time and have negative effects on growth in the longer term
(Deng, 1988).

The most important feature of this era is that the onset of
crisis seems to have initially accelerated the process of ideological differentiation among African countries. Ethiopia, for
instance, moved from monarchy to an Afro-Marxist-Leninist
system at the commencement of this period. This ideological divergence between African countries should not be a
surprise, since crisis essentially make people take different
routes and adopt varied coping mechanisms for survival.
By the middle of this period, political systems and philo-
sophical differences among the African countries became
evident. Crawford Young explains this as follows:

> By way of recapitulation, I suggest that African po-
> litical economies, in two decades of independence,
> had become widely differentiated along two axes: one

defined by ideology and the other by performance. At the point of departure, there were broad similarities in the economies resulting from the common legacies of mercantile colonial capitalism pursued by the different metropolitan states. Over the two decades, major differences both in ideology and performance appeared. The ideological contrast in 1957 between the fraternal association of Ivoirian dependent capitalism with France and the nationalist but liberal economy proposed by Nkrumah looks in retrospect not very great; the distance between Ivory Coast today and the extremely nationalist Marxism-Leninism Ethiopia is immense. Not until the 1970s did the really calamitous cases of mismanagement become evident, while the basic competence and probity of the state were in large measure sustained in *Algeria, Tanzania, and Cameroon.* (1982:7)

The Era of Structural Adjustment and *Glasnost* (1985 - 94)[15]

Students of African economic history will always remember 1985 as the year in which African leaders made a real attempt to face their public responsibilities forthrightly. This desire was articulated by President Abdou Diouf of Senegal at the 21st OAU Summit when he stated, in an apparent quotation of Frantz Fanon: "What is at stake is our credibility in the face of history. Each generation must discover its mission and either fulfill or betray it."[16]

This reality was brought home by the extremely poor economic growth rates in Africa during the period (1980-85). In this regard, most of the African leaders recognized by mid-1985 that Africa must internalize its economic policies and find a development path capable of leading African peoples out of the triple crises — debt, food, and ethnic — of the state. A sizeable number of, if not all, African countries have since then adopted far-reaching measures aimed at overcoming the rapidly deteriorating external debt situation and revitalizing the economy. By 1988, twenty-eight African countries, accounting for about 75% of the total African population, were implementing comprehensive Economic Recovery Programs (ERPs) at considerable political and social cost. These programs, which consisted of stabilization and structural adjustment measures, were necessary to restore macroeconomic stability, but insufficient to generate sustained economic growth (Deng, 1995; Elbadawi, 1995a, 1995b, 1996; Ndulu, 1995; Elbadawi and Ndulu, 1995).

The challenge, then, was to "live up both to people's expectations, raised by old and new populist policies, and to IMF conditionalities at the same time" (Hettne, 1990:22). In this sense ERPs were essentially overdue logical responses by the African states to the objective conditions in the global economy. Consistent with this line of reasoning, Elliot Berg states:

> Reformers, both external and domestic, may claim credit for these kinds of reforms, but many of them represent no more than a response by African Governments to one compelling reality: economies cannot consume more resources than they produce, borrow or are given. In this sense reform has a logic of its own, internally inspired. (1986:5)

The compelling reality in the above citation — that every country must match its domestic absorption or expenditures to its productive capacity — is one of the fundamental propositions in economics (Grubel, 1981). Failure to observe this economic fundamental leads to macroeconomic disequilibria (internal and external imbalances). For the sake of simplicity, internal balance means that the domestic economy is at full-employment level, while external balance refers to a trade balance. This basic economic fundamental was obviously disregarded during the 1970s as capital flows from foreign borrowing made it possible to overcome, without a major adjustment, the discrepancy between absorptive and productive capacities. In retrospect, most African countries borrowed to finance consumption spending in most instances instead of productive domestic investment. This of necessity led to an increase in imports while domestic output declined. The consequence was a deepening of internal and external imbalances.

By mid-1985 African policy-makers had, as stated earlier, seen the writing on the wall. Continued financing of current account deficits indefinitely was neither viable nor conceivable. African creditworthiness and the flow of aid disbursements needed to be restored through bold economic reform decisions. Economic recovery programs were the only viable alternative exit for Africa.

Many analysts (this author included) have singled out the inappropriateness of macroeconomic policies pursued by African countries during the first two decades of political independence as one of the major causes of the development crisis in Africa. However, a second look at the macroeconomic strategies as well as GDP growth rates of many countries in the 1960s and 1970s would seem to contradict the above statement on the inappropriateness of policies pursued then. Recent surveys by Anne Krueger (1991, 1993), on *Ideas Underlying Development Policy in the 1950s* and on *Political Economy of Policy Reform in Developing Countries*, have revealed that macroeconomic policies in the developing countries were consistent with the development thought of that decade. This is articulated as follows:

> The initial decisions to encourage import substitution therefore were undertaken by leadership of governments, many of which were acting in their role as benevolent guardians at least regarding infant

industries. Economic theory at the time embraced a similar view of government, and the policies that were adopted were regarded as consistent with economic theory. (Krueger, 1993:77)

By extension, economic practices of the 1960s, 1970s and 1980s in Africa should have been consistent with the development thought of these decades. It would therefore be incorrect, by Krueger's analysis, to say that most of the African countries pursued inappropriate macroeconomic practices during the two decades prior to the onset of the development crisis in the 1980s. As shown in the preceding sections, development policies in Africa were consistent with the contemporary development thought in the 1960s and 1970s. Moreover, African economies seemed to have responded positively during these decades to what Krueger terms "two central tenets of development policy: import-substitution and the role of government" (1991:8). This is illustrated by some of the basic economic indicators, which tend to show that the performance of African economies was somewhat impressive in the 1960s and early 1970s[17]. But as the subsequent crisis will show, this growth was basically unsustainable to the extent that it was artificial.

The central tenets of development policy in the 1980s shifted away, however, from import-substitution (i.e., protectionism) and the active (i.e., interventionist) role of the state to the *laissez-faire* system, with emphasis on export-promotion (i.e., free trade) and the private sector (i.e., less role for government). This was mainly due to political changes in the West, which triggered an ideological shift to the right, especially in Washington and London. The theoretical underpinning of the new doctrine of the decade was "supply-side" economics, or neoliberalism, and was articulated by Thatcherism in the United Kingdom and Reaganomics in the United States of America. This new development paradigm, which Benno Ndulu calls the "new consensus on macroeconomics, emphasizes more the threat of inflation over employment, focuses on supply side factors than effective demand for promoting growth, delinks monetary policies from production and highlights the negative effects of fiscal deficits on private investments and price instability rather than proactive role for engendering and supporting growth" (1995:4). In this regard, macroeconomic policies were consistent with the new doctrine in the developed world. As for developing countries, especially in Africa, the response to the new development thought of the decade was slow. Hence, their macroeconomic policies were seen by experts in the World Bank, the International Monetary Fund, and the donor community to be inconsistent with the new development thought and therefore inappropriate. It is in this context, one would argue, that most African countries were made to embark on comprehensive programs of economic adjustment in the mid-1980s.

The consistency between development thought and policy (i.e., practice) was to be ensured, from the perspective of the international experts, through market-oriented economic reform measures. One of the main features of the new paradigm is the minimalist role assigned to the state in the management of the economy. But this seems to ignore or downplay the interventionist role of the state in the attainment of the so-called South East Asia "miracle." This has led Benno Ndulu to conclude:

> In spite of the qualifications to this thrust arising from the great success of SE Asian economies in judicious use of government direction to complement a market-oriented approach, the shift in the development paradigm appears to hold its ground. There is little doubt that this shift has had considerable influence in the current global liberalization wave. More specifically, the reform programmes pursued in SSA over the last decade and a half have been predicated

43

> on this new paradigm, often uncritically since ac-
> cess to multilateral and bilateral assistance was/is
> tied to good behavior as defined by the principles of
> this paradigm. (1995:4)

Good behavior has not been confined only to the domain
of economic rationality, it has of late included such things
as accountability, transparency, and political pluralism. In
sum, good governance! However, the relevant institutions
of multi-party democracy and of free market — which are
embedded in the new development paradigm — were not
in place in most of the African countries undertaking economic reforms during this period. In this regard, I would
argue that adjustment programs in the 1980s — like the
modernization paradigm — were inconsistent with African development thought. The cornerstones of this development thought are family-hood, sharing, and consensus-
building, which SAPs tend to undermine through their
emphasis on individualism and self-seeking motives. With
the exception of Nigeria, I am not aware of any other African country in which SAP was subjected to a consensus-
building process through public debates. And in the absence of a consensus, thousands of workers were usually
retrenched without any credible strategy for 'recycling'
them back into productive activities in the restructuring
economy. This, in turn, put additional stress on the family
and subsequently on the community. From my personal experience with the design and implementation of SAPs in
The Gambia, Malawi, Nigeria, Somalia, Uganda, and Zimbabwe, I would generally agree with the popular view about
the 'SAP paradigm' in Africa. The popular view in Africa
and among the non-governmental organizations (NGOs)
is that structural adjustment programs have tended to ignore the social fabric and objective conditions of the Afri
can society, and to this extent they are inconsistent with
African thought and culture.

Moreover, those who designed adjustment programs assumed that institutions of the market economy could easily be transferred and adapted to the African situation. In addition, the African state has not been able to establish itself as an agent of development as was/is the case for its counterpart in East Asia. I would think that the interventionist role of the Asian state was essentially facilitated by efficient public institutions. The contemporary literature on adjustment in Africa lends support to this line of reasoning. For instance, many scholars — Africans and non-Africans — have often argued that adjustment measures were being imposed on weak, corrupt, and bankrupt governments that have lost their legitimacy to govern.

It is now common knowledge that institutions, even if they were easily transferable across cultures, are not enough to create markets and make them function efficiently. One needs the legal foundations of exchange (Bromley, 1991), cultural values, and social norms as the basis for institutional development of market mechanisms (Platteau, 1993). Daniel Bromley reminds us that "those who regard markets as wondrous arenas in which `anything goes' are sadly misinformed. Markets are `efficient' only when the legal foundations exist to hold down the costs of transacting across time and space" (1991:44). Moreover, two important issues of ethics and morality can be raised with respect to the application of free market-based adjustment programs to African economies in which the individual economic agent is not necessarily what Gay Meeks (1991) calls "a crudely calculating self-interested maximiser." I would think that what is needed here is a "view of human motivation which does not rely exclusively on self-interest maximization, but which also models economic agents as responding as much to moral values — like impartiality, universality, sympathy, commitment — as egotistical drives" (Naqvi, 1993:108). And as argued by Naqvi, "Mainstream economics, and especially growth theory, does not help either in fully understanding the nature of the development problem or in diagnosing any meaningful remedial policies" (1993:17). This notwithstanding, I strongly believe that economics holds the key to a comprehensive understanding of the nature and magnitude of development problems in Africa. There is nothing terribly wrong with the free market principles underlying SAPs. The problem has been the way in which they have been formulated and applied without any due attention to the prevailing objective conditions in most of the African countries. These objective conditions should have been reflected in the design of these programs, by fine-tuning some of the underlying assumptions of adjustment policies in Africa. Again, my personal experience with the design and application of adjustment programs — in Nigeria, The Gambia, Somalia, Malawi, Uganda, and Zimbabwe — will attest to the fact that there was a "genuine ignorance" on the part of those (Africans and non-Africans) who designed economic reform measures, usually expressed in a policy matrix, about the realities as well as complexities of African development problems.

For instance, our failure to assign crucial roles — in the process of policy formulation — to the community (civil society) and its social and cultural institutions and structures, was in my view the problem, and not the economic principles that guided the adjustment exercise. We should have realized by then that the function of economic policy "must be to understand the successes and failures of the market and the government in the wider context of social justice in a growing economy" (Naqvi, 1993:102). This justice could only be achieved, according to Naqvi, "by creating institutions which can translate the longing for a better world into a set of policies that aim at changing the status quo in the developing countries" (1993:102). I will return to this point in chapter four, as this is one of the "building blocks" in the process of rethinking development policy in Africa. In this regard, reforming the economy in order to restore growth is one of the leading issues in African development, which is examined in chapter three.

Africa is now in her second decade of economic reform consisting of stabilization and structural adjustment programs. The overall objective of the former is to restore macroeconomic stability, that is, macroeconomic balances — internal and external — to the economy in the short-run. The central aim of the latter is the restoration of economic growth in the medium-to-long-term, by altering the structure of production, of price, of employment, and of ownership. According to Ibrahim Elbadawi, "SAPs are also designed to enhance the flexibility of the economic system to accommodate adverse exogenous shocks in the short-to-medium term, and to lay the foundation for restoring growth and for further deepening of the articulation of the economy. In turn, they should improve the economy's capability to manage adverse shocks such as droughts" (1995:3). The nature of these programs has now evolved significantly and several lessons have emerged from more than ten years of accumulated experiences of success and failure. But can we from these accumulated experiences state unambiguously that these programs have improved the economic performance and raised living standards in Africa?

Early attempts to evaluate the performance of reforming economies were not conclusive. For instance, the World Bank and the Regional Bureau for Africa of the United Nations Development Program (UNDP) concluded in 1989 that adjusting economies out-performed the non-adjusting ones in the 1980s. This view was, however, challenged by the United Nations Economic Commission for Africa (ECA)[18]. Besides these institutional views, there are also conflicting findings from empirical work of individual researchers. For instance, a number of policy analysts and researchers have found that economic reform measures implemented by a majority of African countries during the last decade have not brought about the expected growth (see for instance, Elbadawi, 1992,

1995a, 1995b; Elbadawi and Ndulu, 1995). As articulated by Elbadawi and Ndulu, "Sub-Saharan Africa (SSA) has the dubious distinction of being the only developing region of the world that experienced zero average per capita growth over the last thirty years, including negative growth rates over the last two decades (at average annual rate of -0.35%)" (1995:1). This finding substantiates the ECA view that adjustment programs have paradoxically hurt investment, which is the foundation of economic growth. The following passage further enunciates this point:

> Structural adjustment programs in Sub-Saharan African [sic] have not significantly improved growth in the second half of the 1980s, and they have hurt investment. They have significantly improved export performance but the perceived increases in export competitiveness and in the efficiency of investment (supposed to be generated by reform programs) have not been sufficient to counterbalance the decline in investment and to restore economic growth. (Elbadawi, 1992:1)

Deng and Oshikoya (1991), using a "before-after" methodology to evaluate the economic performance of a group of ten countries[19] between 1980-84 (before adjustment) and 1985-88 (after adjustment), arrived at a different conclusion from Elbadawi with respect to growth. Our findings were paradoxically supportive of the opposing views in the adjustment debate. They confirmed improvement in economic growth, on the one hand, and decline in living standards, on the other.[20]

To put adjustment programs in their proper context, it may be appropriate to restate the prevailing general conditions in these economies just before they adopted reform measures in the mid-1980s. Besides graphic pictures of victims of both famine and civil wars in the Horn of Africa, aggregate economic statistics also painted a more gloomy picture of African development during the first half of the 1980s. Between 1980 and 1985, for instance, the real per capita GDP for the sub-Saharan African region declined nearly 20 percent; export earnings dropped by about 40 percent; import purchases fell by about 40 percent; and the region's external debt, which stood at US$6 billion in 1970, reached an alarming figure of more than US$120 billion.

The economic crisis confronting these countries during the period was also reflected as well as compounded by a deterioration in a range of physical infrastructure and social indicators. These included crumbling roads, impoverished health facilities, falling educational standards, idle factories, growing unemployment, and falling nutritional intakes.

In light of the above gloomy picture and bleak economic outlook, it would seem to me, then, that African countries did not have many choices before them other than swallowing the bitter pills of SAP. For what was at stake was their very survival. This reality is often missed in the ensuing debate on adjustment in Africa. Let us briefly examine some of our findings at the time, which are still valid today with respect to SAPs. However, the observed results of our study in 1991 on economic performance were tentative at the time due to the following:

a)   time lag involved in response of performance indicators to program measures;

b)   the difficulty in isolating the effects of adjustment lending from other factors, such as initial conditions and external shocks;

c)   varied choice of base years; and

d)   lack of a single agreed-upon methodology for evaluating the effectiveness of structural adjustment programs.

First, the economic performance of most African countries undertaking structural adjustment programs during 1985-90, as measured by gross domestic product (GDP) growth rate, inflation rate, fiscal deficit/GDP ratio, current account deficit/GDP ratio, export/GDP ratio, did improve. The most important indicator of improved economic performance, from our perspective, was the GDP growth rate. And from the viewpoint of the Harrod-Domar model, "each increase in output provides the basis for further growth because part of the increased output is reinvested" (Hettne, 1990:50). Our finding was consistent with the World Bank's and the UNDP's earlier view, which stated that those economies implementing SAPs were doing better than the non-adjusting ones, in terms of growth in the short run[21]. This interpretation of adjusting economies registering growth in the short-term is also supported by Jean-Philippe Platteau (1993) in comparing 43 African countries with respect to agricultural performance between reforming and non-reforming countries. He states that: "As a matter of fact, as table 10 below shows, things rather appear as though the impact of SAPs is more effective in the short than in longer term, generating once-for-all effects that get quickly dissipated" (1993:14)[22]. Mwega (1996) has also shown that the saving-investment gap widened during the period (1982-1992), which implies that the registered growth did not increase domestic savings either. But then why does this growth get dissipated quickly?

Two reasons come to mind in explaining this phenomenon. The first concerns the debt-service of the reforming economies during the period under review. Although the reforming economies had initially registered some growth, it was neither sustained nor translated into improvement in living standards and/or investment, since part of it went toward debt repayment instead of reinvestment or consumption. In this regard, a quick analysis of the resource flows shows that there was a net outflow of resources from adjusting economies to the creditors, especially to the IMF and the World Bank, during the second half of the 1980s and early 1990s. For instance, the 1995 African Development Report, indicated that there was a negative net capital inflows (i.e., capital outflows) for Africa, in the order of -$4.58 billion, -$1.62 billion and -$1.9 billion for 1990, 1991, and 1992 respectively[23]. It would therefore seem to me that ECA, Elbadawi, and others might have been right in pointing out that adjustment programs have actually hurt investment, which in turn led to low levels of economic growth. Nevertheless, I would argue that it was not SAP *per se* which undermined investment, but rather the insistence on repaying debts owed to the multilateral financial institutions at this early stages of economic recovery. In retrospect, it was the designers of SAPs who undermined the adjustment efforts, for these experts seemed to have overlooked the basic principles of the growth theory according to Arthur Lewis and others. This raises an important question about the conflicting role of IMF and the World Bank as both lenders and policy advisers. There is clearly a conflict of interest between these two functions — money lending and policy advice, which is often dictated. Recipient governments do not have a second opinion on SAP policies as presented to them by the two institutions. I go to a money lender to get a credit to buy a car or a house or to pay the tuition of my children. But the money lender does not dictate my choice with respect to a brand name or color of my car, the size and type of my house, or the school to be attended by my children! The money lender is only concerned with my ability to pay back on the basis of my creditworthiness. I will come to this point chapter three in the context of debt as one of the leading issues in African development.

Another explanation, which constitutes my second reason for the quick evaporation of growth, is the possibility of the increased output being saved through non-conventional methods. For instance, higher profits accruing to farmers as a result of the liberalization of the agricultural prices, might have been "saved" by farmers in the forms of more cows, "wives," and/or other traditional saving methods that are not easily captured by the conventional techniques of measuring domestic savings within the African economies.

Our second finding was that the improvement in GDP growth did not, however, translate into better standards of living within the reforming economies. Significant decline in the levels of real per capita consumption and gross national product (GNP) per capita were recorded among the reforming countries. This finding confirmed the view of ECA and the prevailing popular opinion in Africa then: Adjustment programs were hurting a majority of the population, especially the poor in the reforming economies. In agreement with Syed Naqvi: "One does not have to be a Marxist to insist that an essential building block for a useful development theory is an overarching vision about socio-economic change leading to a more just social order, in which the needs of the least-privileged section in society are looked after in the best possible fashion, where unemployment, inequitable distribution of income and wealth, extreme poverty, and social degradation are seen as problem areas deserving the highest priority in a programme for change, and in which human freedom is incomplete without some measure of equality" (1993:22-23).

The apparent lack of improvement in the standards of living in spite of growth is due to this growth not being distributed equitably among the population. That is, most of the increased output went to a few, who in turn might have channelled it out of the country — capital flight (Brown, 1992) — instead of reinvesting it in the domestic economy. But as shown in the preceding paragraphs, the growth generated by SAP in the short run was not sustained, due partly to some of the reasons I have given above. However, the phenomenon of growth without distribution, as shown earlier by Adelman and Morris (1973) and Chenery et al (1974), is not unique to Africa. The lack of improvement in living standards in the reforming economies prompted UNICEF to call for "adjustment with a human face." This in turn led African governments and donors to recognize that the poor and vulnerable groups could not wait for the benefits of adjustment to 'trickle down' to them and that they would need various kinds of assistance during the process. Hence, a social dimension of adjustment (SDA) project was launched in 1987 to address, on the one hand, the problems of protecting the poor and vulnerable groups from bearing undue hardships resulting from economic reforms, and on the other to integrate these groups into the emerging economic environment.[24] The major outcomes of the SDA project have been the integration of poverty reduction measures into the design of structural adjustment programs; the reorientation of public expenditure programs in favor of the poor; and the call for empowerment of the poor and vulnerable groups to actively participate in the productive activities of their respective economies.

Third, the analysis of the principal debt indicators suggests that the burden of external debt might have weakened the sustainability of adjustment programs and constrained long-term economic growth among reforming countries. This reinforces my argument, under the first finding above, that high debt-service ratios tend to undermine the very objective of SAP — restoring growth and macroeconomic stability to the economy in the medium and long terms (more on this is given in chapter three under the section dealing with controlling indebtedness as a leading issue in African development).

Fourth, many African governments did not really internalize and/or own the adjustment programs. The internalization of policies and programs was weak because African governments depended heavily on the international donor community and foreign consultants for the analytical work on which key policy decisions had been based. But this is not unique to adjustment programs. As shown by Bjorn Hettne, this has always been the case as "theories were rather mechanically tried on Third World countries, of which many were colonies and of course never consulted about what kind of development they needed or wanted" (1990:5). In this respect, the momentum and sense of purpose for the programs were diminished especially at the lower echelons of public administration in the reforming economies. I would, therefore, argue that all the stakeholders must participate in all aspects of an economic reform program for it to be successful.

Fifth, policy overload was witnessed during the implementation of structural adjustment programs in several African countries. Experience suggests that sequencing of policies should be based on the prioritization of policy targets over the program period (Deng, 1988). Successful stabilization would pave the way for effective implementation of structural and sectoral reform measures aimed at improving resource allocation and achieving equitable and sustainable growth. This has, however, generated additional preconditions — institutional strengthening and capacity building in the reforming economies. Moreover, the policy overload was intended as a shock therapy, but this was unrealistic and inappropriate given weak economic structures and shaky institutions in most of the African countries.

Sixth, the design, implementation, and evaluation of structural adjustment programs focussed narrowly on economic issues and ignored the political economy aspects of the African development crisis. Here, one can speak of pervasive crisis as used by Hettne to include "a crisis of efficiency and rationality on the level of the system, a crisis of legitimacy on the sociocultural level, and a crisis of motivation on the individual level" (Hettne, 1990:15). These three levels or types of crises imply that economic reform is not simply a technical exercise. It demands the building of partnerships and coalitions among all the stakeholders in order to ensure a broad-based support for "swallowing" IMF (in)famous "medicine." Stated differently, it requires profound political reforms and governance, which involves effective democratization, tolerance, popular participation, and empowerment of the citizenry. In this sense, political reform, which is also one of the leading issues in African development, may be a prerequisite for SAP (more on this in the next chapter).

Finally, structural adjustment programs were designed to reduce distortions and improve the efficiency and productivity of investment. However, the ultimate success of adjustment and growth restoration depends not only on creating enabling environment for the productive use of resources, but also on increasing long-term investment and on building African capacities. This requires public investment in economic, physical, and social infrastructures. In this regard, public investment should be restored and sustained in areas that expand infrastructure and human capital as well as in those that strengthen the legal foundations of exchange and institutional frameworks within which long-term development can take place.

Conclusion

This review of the theory and practice of development in Africa during the last thirty years (1965-1994), has shown that African policy formulation had primarily been dominated by two paradigms — the modernization model and the neoliberalism in the form of SAPs. The alternative paradigm of African socialism as practiced in Nyerere's Tanzania was prevented from spreading mainly by the wars of liberation in Southern Africa, including the struggle against *apartheid*. The wars of liberation have now been won, but African socialism as a development school of thought is dead, at least for now. Moreover, the death of communism in the former Soviet Union and Eastern Europe appears to have closed the doors for an earlier resurrection of the African socialism paradigm. In fact, it is almost a taboo these days to talk about Marxist-Leninist analysis or even African socialism. But, researchers and scholars should not become prisoners of the contemporary global political environment.

An objective analysis of the failure of the Soviet model of dis-development and its replica in Africa is needed in order to avoid similar mistakes in the future. Hence, rethinking African development is an attempt to generate and motivate critical thinking and systematic enquiry into the nature of Africa's problems with a view to finding a dynamic framework for sustainable development. Moreover, this would ensure the inclusion of African intellectual input, which has been so far an important missing link in the process of development policy theorizing and its practice in Africa. Here, the underlying premise is that development will not be sustainable if it ignores African intellectual input. This is due to two main reasons. The first concerns the economics of depending on a large number of foreign 'experts.' There are about 100,000 foreign experts involved in the development management activities in Africa (Ndulu and van de Walle, 1996). We can easily estimate the financial implications of these experts. I would think that their annual total salaries alone cost Africa about US$12.0 billion, which is not at all a small amount of money, especially in light of the current debt over-hang in the continent. The second reason is about the importance of, as well as the need for, Africa to internalize and own her development policy. In this regard, African intellectuals must take the lead in the design, implementation, and management of development strategies so as to ensure not only their ownership but also their impact on the ordinary African people. The African intellectual is accountable to the society and country; the foreign 'expert' is not accountable to the African society for what s/he does.

The role of African scholars in the analysis of the causes of the continent's malaise and its treatment cannot be over-emphasized. Such statements would have been labeled as polemic, if not communistic, in the context of the competitive security politics of the Cold War. But in this time and age of *glasnost* and *perestroika*, sweeping and ideologically loaded statements belong to the annals of the world of yesterday. As pointed out by Edward Jaycox (1991), ". . . .the world is in the midst of fundamental change and the ideological blinkers which so greatly hampered economic development for so long have been taken off. It is universally agreed that people are the means and ends of development — and the potential to improve people's lives the world over is enormous".[25] Improving the lives of African people would, however, require their empowerment so as to fully participate in the design and management of the national development project. Their effective participation would guarantee their stakeholding in the process of development policy formulation. This would in turn reduce and eventually eliminate Africa's reliance "on outside capabilities for initiating and managing" development strategies — a practice which "has not helped the long-term prospects for growth" (Ndulu and van de Walle, 1996:11). Above all, it would minimize the imposition of externally derived and received wisdom whose local application has often remained largely untested. And for this to be a reality, a new generation of broadly based political movements must emerge. The new political leadership that is currently in charge in South Africa and Uganda are some of the examples of this new generation of broadly based political movements. They have provided an acceptable political authority that is making economics more relevant to public policy, more sensitive to social suffering, and more focused on raising the well-being of ordinary people without necessarily reducing that privileges of the well-to-do few of their country men, women, and children. Certainly, both South Africa and Uganda are facing problems of national reconciliation, massive reconstruction, and development — more so more than most African countries. They are blessed, however, with visionary leadership and political movements that derive their legitimacy from their difficult and long walk to freedom as lively told by President Nelson Mandela (1994) in his autobiography.

By way of discovering our own mission, I would argue that we have to revisit the concept of a development paradigm rooted in African systems of thought. One of these is the Tanzanian model. This is due to the fact that the *ujamaa* — or family-hood, which was the foundation of the African development school of thought or Nyerereism[26] — is embedded in the social fabric of every African traditional society. This is vividly illustrated by the following passage from Nyerere:

> Even in our urban areas, the social expectation of sharing what you have with your kinsfolk is still very strong - and causes great problems for individuals! These things have nothing to do with Marx; the people have never heard of him. Yet they provide a basis on which modern socialism can be built. To reject this base is to accept the idea that Africa has nothing to contribute to the march of mankind; it is to argue that the only way progress can be achieved in Africa is if we reject our own past and impose on ourselves the doctrines of some other society. (1968:16).

Moreover, family values and social cohesion have resurfaced as among the major issues on the political agenda of both developed and developing countries in the 1990s. They are likely to continue to dominate the development policy debate in the 21st Century. This is evidenced by the recent global consensus on the core issues — eradication of poverty, expansion of productive employment, and social integration — of sustainable human development. The new consensus was particularly articulated by 118 Heads of State and Government at the World Summit for Social Development, when they stated[27]:

We can continue to hold the trust of the people of
the world only if we make their needs our priority.
We know that poverty, lack of productive employment and social disintegration are an offence to
human dignity. We also know that they are negatively reinforcing and represent a waste of human
resources and a manifestation of ineffectiveness in
the functioning of markets and economic and social
institutions and processes.

In light of the above, an African development school of
thought along the lines of *ujamaa* can be revitalized. This
should now be feasible given the current global call, especially in the United States of America, for a return to family
values and social harmony. In the words of Julius Nyerere,
the pioneer of this school of thought, "Our first step, therefore, must be to re-educate ourselves; to regain our former
attitude of mind. In our traditional African society we were
individuals within a community. We took care of the community, and the community took care of us. We neither
needed nor wished to exploit our fellow men" (1967:166).
This is the basic philosophy of *ujamaa*, and it should provide a solid point of departure for the resurrection and the
advancement of an African development alternative. Africa, thank God, is no longer an ideological battleground
between capitalism and communism, and to this extent,
African intellectuals must begin a thorough and critical
examination of Africa's development malaise. But first, this
process of critical thinking must begin with self-examination among the African intellectuals. What is wrong with
us, individually and collectively? Frantz Fanon reminds us
of our mission, but do we know what our mission is in life
and society? Why is poverty still pervasive in Africa? Have
we tried our best to put our knowledge, experience, and
above all conviction and sense of duty in combating this
menace? Moreover, Francis Deng tells us that "it is not the

dead who suffer, it is those who cause their death, and those who watch them die![28]" CNN's graphic and shocking pictures of famine victims seem to be proving him right. They should, therefore, reinforce our resolve to find lasting solutions for eradicating absolute poverty in Africa. Our grand-children and their children's-children will not, and should not, forgive us for our lack of critical thinking and creativity with respect to the social well-being of African peoples. We have the necessary and sufficient training to make our countries in Africa join the community of developed nations in their consistent quest for prosperity and human dignity. This process of critical thinking seems to have began already, as illustrated by Serageldin in the following passage:

> To many outside observers, SSA shows remarkable strength in terms of social solidarity and mutual support in the face of adversity. This capacity was amply demonstrated in the 1980s when the extended family support system was able to provide a social safety net during severe economic crisis. On the other hand, the difficulty of various institutional models to be either adapted or adopted leaves these same societies unable to benefit more fully from the advantages of the economic incentive structures they put in place to respond swiftly and effectively to a rapidly changing international landscape. The causes of such phenomena are to be studied and understood in the context of a broadened analytical perspective that transcends economics, but does not abandon it. (1994:1)

The difficulty, however, of various institutional models in being adapted and/or adopted in Africa is precisely the point I am trying to make here. That is, such models are doomed to fail not because of lack of good will on the part of those who design them, but rather for their being conceived without full regard to African cultural values and social institutions. This would not have been the case if African intellectuals, especially those in the African Development Bank (this author included) and the ECA, had taken a more proactive role in the ensuing debate on Africa's problems[29]. A careful reading of the three preceding citations from the World Summit for Social Development, Nyerere, and Serageldin, respectively, tends to show that an African development paradigm could be resurrected or nurtured if one believes that it was not dead. In fact, the central point in Serageldin's *Culture and Development in Africa* is not different from Nyerere's African development school of thought reflected in *Freedom and Socialism and Freedom and Unity*. The exigency for such a paradigm will become more appreciated when we look, in the next chapter, at the six key leading issues in African development.

NOTES

1. Even the World Bank is moving toward this direction of trying to understand the behavior of the state. This is articulated by the envisaged focus of the 1997 Development Report, The State in a Changing World.
2. This should tell us how often our projections, we development experts, are wrong. Potholm in the preface of his book has this to say: "Somalia, on the other hand, was for nearly a decade a vibrant, multiparty democracy whose grinding poverty and significant accomplishments in the area of political development combined to offer a substantial amendment to several major assumptions of developmental theory. It also continues to cast into sharp relief the factors necessary to sustain polyarchal decision making. . . ."

3.   This is a good example of a mixed-economy in which
        the government and market complement each other
        in ensuring a smooth functioning of the economy.

4.   Mamadou Dia of the World Bank refers to these as
        transplanted institutions in his recent book: *Africa's
        Management in the 1990s and Beyond — Reconciling
        Indigenous and Transplanted Institutions.*

5.   There was a general belief that the marginal product of
        labor in agriculture was zero.

6.   I thank Crawford Young for pointing our for me this
        important point.

7.   For more on this, see A. Hirshcman(1971). "The Political
        E conomy of Import-Substituting Industrialization in
        Latin America," in his *Bias For Hope.* New Haven:
        Yale University Press.

8.   Quoted fomr *Leading Issues in Economic Development,*
        by Gerald Meier (1976) third edition, p. 257

9.   See for instance, R.F. Harrod (1939), "An Essay in
        Dynamic Theory". In *Economical Journal*, Vol. 49:193,
        pp. 14-33, and D. Domar (1957), *Essays in theTheory
        of Economic Growth.* Westport, CT.:Greenwood.

10.   Emphasis by the author.

11.   Quoted from Robert S. Browne and Robert J.
        Cummings. (1984). *The Lagos Plan of Action Vs.
        The Berg Report — Contemporary Issues in
        African Development.* Washington, D.C.: The African
        Studies and Research Program,   Howard University.

12.   It's a point well articulated by Crawford Young: "Debt
        burdens for a number of states grew rapidly, facilitated
        by a period in the first half of the decade when major
        international banks aggressively sought lending oppor-
        tunities in Africa, with industrial economies stagnant and
        huge volumes of petrodollars to recycle" (1996:7).

13.   I am once more grateful to Crawford Young for pointing
        out this point to me while he was reviewing a draft
        manuscript of this book.

14.   A good example, which is somewhat extreme, is provided
        by the National Islamic Front (NIF) government of
        General Al-Bashir in the Sudan, where some Sudanese have
        been summarily executed for possessing foreign
        currencies. The policy of execution for possessing a foreign
        currency achieved its twin objectives of oppressing
        political opponents and of allowing the members of NIF to
        enrich themselves by having the sole control of trading in
        the now more scarcer foreign currencies and thereby selling
        at very high prices.

15.   Most of this section is taken from my earlier writings on
        structural adjustment programs in Africa.

16.   Excerpts from a speech delivered at the OAU 21st
        Summit by President Diouf of Senegal. Published by
        Africa Economic Digest (AED), Vol.6, No. 30, 27
        July-2 August, 1985.

17.   With the exception of the years of the oil shocks (i.e., 1973
        and 1980), the Gross Domestic Product (GDP) for sub-
        Saharan Africa grew in real terms by 6% during 1965-73
        compared to about 2% in the 1980s.

18.   For a summary of these two opposing views, see Deng
        and Oshikoya (1991), "Structural Adjustment Programs
        in Africa in the 1980s: An Overview of the Performance
        of Restructuring Economies," in *Democratization and
        Structural Adjustment in Africa in the 1990s*. Edited by
        Lual Deng, Markus Kostner, and Crawford Young: Afri
        can Studies Program, University of Wisconsin-Madison,
        USA, 1991.

19.   These were Cote d'Ivoire, Ethiopia, Ghana, Kenya, Nige-
        ria, Somalia, Sudan, Tanzania, Zaire, and Zambia.

20.   These are concluding remarks from "Structural Adjust
        ment Programs in Africa in the 1980s: An Overview of
        the Performance of Restructuring Economies," in *Demo-
        cratization and Structural Adjustment in Africa in the
        1990s*. Edited by Lual Deng, Markus Kostner, and
        Crawford Young.

21. For more on this see *Africa's Adjustment and Growth in the 1980s,* issued by the World Bank and UNDP, 1989.

22. Platteau warns us not to read too much into this: "....The contingency test is again statistically nonsignificant in all the cases constructed, so that this interpretation must not be taken too seriously."

23. See the 1995 African Development Report, table 2.15, page 31. African Development Bank: Abidjan, Cote d'Ivoire.

24. This was initially co-sponsored by the African Develop ment Bank (ADB), the World Bank, and the Regional Bureau for Africa of the UNDP. Several bilateral donors later joined the SDA project, with the World Bank as the imple menting agency.

25.. From a statement to the African-American Institute, New York (USA), July 1991.

26. Hettne argues that "the concept of African socialism, which, even if it should be looked upon primarily as a political and ideological concept, nevertheless, did have theoretical significance" (1990:109).

27. The World Summit for Social Development was held in Copenhagen, Denmark on 6-12 March 1995.

28. Quoted from Lual A.L. Deng (1984:58). *The Abyei Devel-opment Project: A Case Study of Cattle Herders in the Sudan.* Ph.D Dissertation, University of Wisconsin-Madison. Some of my earlier publications have appeared under Lual A.L. Deng, Lual Deng and/or Lual A. Deng. From 1995, only Lual A. Deng will be used.

29. The Abidjan-based African Development Bank has about 500 professional staff of which more than 90% are Afric ans. It thus makes ADB the only institution in Africa with a large concentration of highly qualified and relatively well-paid Africans. Yet, ADB has not been able to make itself felt intellectually. Hence, the intellectual hegemony of the World Bank on African development.

CHAPTER THREE

LEADING ISSUES IN AFRICAN DEVELOPMENT

◆

At the beginning of the 1990s, Africa from Algiers to Capetown faced a common conjuncture, although reached by different trajectories: an imperative of democratization, broadly defined. Battered by economic decline, weakened by political decay, the African state faced narrowed choices; political opening was no longer an option but an obligation. A political economy where, in the oft-cited aphorism, political man ruled the economy, and economic man ruled politics, had finally produced an impasse whose sole exit was a broad-front liberalization, political as well as economic.

-Crawford Young (1991:13)

The above citation enunciates the current trend in African economic and political development. Such a trend is undoubtedly a product of the theory and practice of development in Africa during the last thirty years (1965-1994), and of the subsequent crisis that resulted mainly from the inherent contradictions between transplanted institutions and indigenous social structures, systems of thought, and beliefs. As shown by Mamadou Dia: "Formal institutions, not being rooted in local culture, generally fail to command society's loyalty or to trigger local ownership, both of which are important catalysts for sustainability and enforcement. These formal institutions are at odds with societal behavior, expectations, and incentive systems and therefore face a crisis of legitimacy and enforcement" (1996:1). In this regard, the drive to undertake simultaneously economic and political reforms has raised legitimate concerns, within the African policy community, about the feasibility of a broad-front liberalization. This is because the process of reconciling indigenous and transplanted institutions has just began. Moreover, given the seemingly overloaded agenda of African development, it is unlikely that a meaningful harmonization of these institutions would be achieved at the turn of the century, without a critical inquiry into the nature of Africa's development problems. This inquiry should by necessity involve African intellectuals, so as to generate a comprehensive policy framework that would guide decision-makers and other stakeholders in formulating appropriate strategies for economic progress and the social well-being of African people. Such a framework will have to address the issues of reconciling indigenous and transplanted institutions and value systems; sequencing of reform measures and policy mix; prioritization of actions; and internalization as well as the ownership of macroeconomic policies themselves.

By way of revitalizing a process of critical inquiry, this chapter identifies six leading issues in African development that are likely to dominate both the research and policy agenda as Africa approaches the 21st century. These issues are: economic reform; democratization; protecting the environment; controlling indebtedness; poverty reduction; and conflict resolution. The nature and complexity of these issues requires serious reflection as well as moving away from the manner in which public policy has been formulated in the past. Furthermore, a brief examination of these leading issues is an important point of departure for rethinking African policy formulation for sustainable development.

Economic Reform

The overview, in the preceding chapter, of the theory and practice of development in Africa during the last three decades (1965-1994) shows that the 1980s were, by all accounts, the years of the African development crisis (Deng, 1985, 1988; World Bank, 1989; Deng and Oshikoya, 1991; Elbadawi, 1992, 1996). Some analysts, however, argue that the entire post-colonial era has been a period of stagnation (see, for instance, Claude Ake, 1995). There is, nevertheless, a general agreement within the development policy community that external as well as internal factors were responsible for the crisis and that adjustment was necessary, but insufficient, to restore and/or generate sustained economic growth.

The search for sufficient conditions that would make SAPs or macroeconomic adjustment to generate sustained economic growth will undoubtedly continue to center, in my view, on three general but important concerns. These are (i) the need for sequencing adjustment measures as well as the desire for appropriate policy mix and assignment; (ii) the consistency between adjustment measures and African social institutions and value systems; and (iii) the evolution of these systems and institutions. All three concerns make economic reform one of the leading issues in African development in the 1990s and beyond. Moreover, Benno Ndulu (1995) has recently identified six global changes that are likely to face Africa as it attempts to consolidate its economic recovery programs in the form of SAPs. These global changes are (i) the move toward freer trade; (ii) the globalization of financial markets; (iii) flexible factor mobility, particularly of capital, through foreign direct investment; (iv) a new development paradigm; (v) a shift in the approaches to "development aid;" and (vi) the technological revolution, especially in the informatics, as exemplified by the Internet or information super highway. Such global changes would unquestionably influence the process of economic reform in Africa, and should therefore constitute one of the concerns. In addition, there is still the likelihood of policy reversal in light of the current quest for democratization and multiparty politics.

I have argued in the preceding chapter and elsewhere (Deng, 1988) for an appropriate sequencing between stabilization measures and adjustment programs. Ideally, stability must be restored to the economy before a full structural adjustment program is undertaken. My point of view then and now is that one cannot meaningfully adjust an unstable system -- any system, let alone an economy, which is more complex. In this regard, the sequencing and phasing out of policies within, say, an ERP, should be based on the prioritization of policy targets over the program time-frame. Stability is to be achieved first, followed by adjustment measures. The sequencing and phasing over time of policies would avoid possible conflicts between the differing objectives of stabilization and adjustment programs. For instance, conventional stabilization approaches would normally emphasize the reduction of current account deficits, while adjustment programs would usually aim at the expansion of total output. But, since a majority of African states import capital for productive investment, a desire for a simultaneous expansion of their total outputs and reduction of their current account deficits may not be feasible in the short run.

Furthermore, the importance of sequencing and timing stabilization and adjustment measures is that it facilitates a gradual as well as orderly reform that is socially harmonious and politically acceptable, thus enuring the sustainability of economic reform. This point is supported by the IMF: "A fundamental objective of a fund-supported adjustment program is to provide for an orderly adjustment of both macroeconomic and structural imbalances so as to foster economic growth while bringing about a balance of payments position that is sustainable in the medium term" (1987:1). The importance of sequencing reform measures over a period of time has also been recognized by Williamson (1983): "External balance, interpreted as a current account balance calculated to maximize welfare in the light of national thrift and productivity and foreign borrowing and lending opportunities, should be a high priority but a medium-term objective""(1983:139).

In order to articulate the issue of sequencing and timing (phasing), one can conceptualize a typical economic reform program in such a way that it is implementable over a well-defined time-frame of five to six years. Moreover, this time-frame could be divided into short, medium, and long term segments.

Short term. This could range between 12 and 24 months, during which the focus should be on the elimination of price distortions; balance of payments stability; and rationalization of the public sector. The realization of these targets depends on a national institutional capacity to carry out a number of reform measures in the following five key areas: (a) exchange rate and pricing policies; (b) monetary and credit policies; (c) financial sector rehabilitation; (d) trade liberalization; and (e) fiscal policy.

It must be pointed out here that the immediate objective of a typical economic reform in the short run is the restoration of macroeconomic equilibria through stabilization measures that emphasize mainly expenditure switching and expenditure reducing policies. Here, traditional demand-management measures (for example, fiscal and monetary) are used to enforce discipline on an economy which is out of balance. These measures are supplemented by limited supply-side policies to remove exchange rate and price distortions. Therefore, the preoccupation of policy-makers during the first phase of ERP is how to restore stability to the economy through the use of appropriate monetary and fiscal instruments. That is, the growth of real output in the short run should not be the focus of economic policy per se; a distorted economy needs first to be brought back to normalcy through stringent monetary and fiscal policies.

But, according to Mundell (1968), and Genberg and Swoboda (1987), the conflict between the twin objectives of restoring internal and external balances to the economy arises irrespective of sequencing because of an assignment problem. That is, the conflict results from an inappropriate policy mix. In a world of imperfect information such as Africa, Mundell's solution assigns, under a fixed exchange rate regime, monetary policy to combat the current account imbalances, and fiscal instruments to restore internal balances. However, with a flexible exchange rate regime, Genberg and Swoboda (1987) have found that "fiscal policy has comparative advantage in dealing with the current account, monetary policy with internal balance, and that this assignment will be stable for the case of a single small open economy." Hence, in the event of a current account deficit, reducing government spending will be the most appropriate policy instrument to correct the external imbalance. Similarly, in a situation of internal imbalance characterized by a low level of domestic output relative to aggregate demand, increasing the money stock to enhance the productive capacity of the economy will be the best policy instrument.

In light of the nature of Africa's development problems and given the present state of our empirical knowledge about the African economic policy reform program, there are two main points which need to be mentioned. The first point concerns the conflict of objectives arising when the policy target is to achieve internal and external balances simultaneously (Khan, 1987). Alternatively, the conflict arises when stabilization and adjustment programs are implemented as two separate programs. In either case, the sequencing of policies within the framework of ERP seems to be the most viable solution. The second point relates to the assignment problem, which I consider to be more problematic than the question of timing and sequencing. The assignment problem, since it concerns the appropriateness of policy instruments, arises at all times and in all circumstances. Hence, the critical point here is how to assign appropriate policy instruments (that is, monetary and fiscal) to their respective short-term targets. Failure to provide an appropriate assignment of policies in pursuit of their targets could render the objective of macroeconomic stability unattainable. In this regard, Genberg and Swoboda (1987) think that the breakdown of the Bretton Woods System in 1972 "can be attributed not only to a shortage of instruments, but also to an inappropriate assignment (under fixed exchange rates) of monetary policy to the pursuit of internal balance." Accordingly, the assignment problem should, therefore, be crucial when evaluating the performance of the African economies under ERP. That is, to what extent can the program's success or failure be explained by an appropriate or inappropriate assignment of policy instruments to their respective targets?

Medium term. Following a successful stabilization program, the medium term could vary between 24 and 48 months, in order for adjustment measures to have the desired and significant impact on economic growth. In the absence of major distortions and structural constraints, the economy is generally assumed to have a dynamic and self-propelling tendency to move toward an equilibrium in the following markets: the domestic goods market; the money market; and the foreign exchange market. And in the event of macroeconomic disequilibria, the economy is expected to arrive at equilibrium through the 'invisible hand' of Adam Smith -- producers and consumers, behaving rationally, should switch their expenditures in reaction to changes in relative prices. Moreover, macroeconomic policies that were already in place, if consistent, should facilitate a cost-effective adjustment process. Any persistence in macroeconomic disequilibria is therefore attributable to government policies that prevent the adjustment mechanism from correcting the imbalances.

The adjustment mechanism will, therefore, be assumed to operate in the medium-to-longer term only after the structural constraints have been removed. In this regard, the objective of economic reform in the medium term is to expand the productive capacity of the economy through the use of adjustment measures that constitute what is popularly known as SAP. A typical SAP, in addition to consolidating reforms implemented during the short-term period, centers on five key areas of reform that are usually of a supply-side nature. The five areas are: (a) agricultural policy; (b) incentives for other productive sectors; (c) public enterprise reform; (d) public investment programming; and (e) management of external debt.

Long term. Economic reform measures aimed at restoring macroeconomic stability in the short run, and at generating a reasonable growth in the medium term, are usually expected to lay the basis for a sustainable development in the long term. From the perspective of neoliberalism, the market forces of supply and demand are envisaged to determine what is to be produced, by whom, and for whose consumption. That is, correct signals of what consumers desire will be translated, other things being equal, by producers into economic goods and services through the price-mechanism. At the highest level of abstraction, Adam Smith's 'invisible hand' would create dynamic adjustments that cause prices to move toward their equilibrium values with consumers willing to pay for the products, and producers ready to produce and to sell them. As new patterns of consumption and life-style determine what is to be produced, an economy without distortions would normally react by producing the desired products. This implies that industries (firms) -- publicly or privately owned -- would have to adjust to the new consumers' taste by producing the new products, and those firms that do not adjust will have to give way to new ones. In this way, the process of adjustment becomes dynamic and to the extent that economic reform is imperative. Moreover, the adjustment process requires that government performs an explicit role in the economy as an organ of economic policy and not a producer of goods and services that can be produced efficiently by the private sector. The role of the public policy should then focus, among other things, on the following: provision of legal, social, and business environments for a stable growth of the economy; promotion of competitive markets; reallocation of resources in order to maintain efficiency in the economy when the price-mechanism fails to send correct signals to both consumers and producers; stabilization of employment, income, and prices; and redistribution of income and wealth in an equitable manner (this is of recent emphasis, and it is problematic).

From the preceding analysis, it is obvious that the underlying principles of the recent economic reform in Africa are those of the free market economy. This model of development assumes, of course, that appropriate institutions for a stable growth of a free market economy do indeed exist, or can be established. But the harmony between the institutions of the market economy and African social structures and value systems has been of great concern to many analysts within the development policy community on Africa. It was shown in chapter two that the concepts of family-hood, sharing, and consensus-building constitute a solid base for the African social system, which the new development paradigm tends to undermine. For instance, Michael Prowse argues that "nothing promotes social mobility faster than free markets. What matters in market exchange is the ability of participants to perform specific tasks today: school, class and family background are strictly irrelevant. But in societies that suppress market mechanisms, everything depends on status and rank: on who you are and on whom you know.[1]" I would therefore argue that the designers of public policy and economic reform in Africa have both the mandate and moral obligation to ensure that the social mobility being brought about by free markets does not unduly lead to a breakdown in family values and self-respect. This is because, as articulated by John Stuart Mackenzie: "Economic conditions are made for man, not man for economic conditions; and wherever the conditions of industrial life are found to interfere with the development of men as men, attempts must be made to readjust them" (1894:305). Moreover, President Julius Nyerere has earlier recognized the need for consistency: "We have deliberately decided to grow, as a society, out of our own roots, but in a particular direction and towards a particular kind of objective. We are doing this by emphasizing certain characteristics of our traditional organization and extending them so that they can embrace the possibilities of modern technology and enable us to meet the challenge of life in the twentieth century world" (1968:2). Arthur Lewis has further acknowledged that "much technological progress springs from an attitude that everything in this world is here for the convenience of man, and can be altered by man in his own interest" (1955:102).

In light of the preceding paragraph, economic reform measures would only be for the convenience of ordinary African people, when these are internalized and made to be in harmony with the social institutions and value systems. This further raises the important question of capacity building and institutional strengthening for policy analysis in Africa. The lack of an appropriate institutional capacity for policy analysis leads, in my view, to the seeming inconsistency between the imperatives of economic reform, on the one hand, and African social institutions and values, on the other.

History has shown that it is African institutions that normally bear the brunt of this inconsistency.

The final concern and preoccupation with the current African economic reform is, in my view, the evolutionary process that would facilitate as well as accelerate a change of attitudes, beliefs, and institutions toward the salient features of the market economy. The recent global consensus on the role of the civil society[2] (community in the African sense) in general, and NGOs in particular with respect to public policy formulation, is opportune. A positive social change will only come about through the active participation of various elements of the community (civil society) in the development process. In this regard, the evolution of African institutions and beliefs should be seen from a historical perspective of those societies that have gone through similar processes. Pierre Landell-Mills, for instance, draws important lessons from Asia: "The lesson of recent Japanese and Korean history seems to be that new institutions which grow out of, or integrate with traditional ones, are more likely to be successful. There will, of course, be considerable adaptation and development. Indeed, some may need to be completely new, yet conceived by the local people themselves, borrowing from both local and foreign forms. For example, there is no indigenous Wolof, Igbo or Tswana financial institution which can be the basis for a modern African commercial bank. But a new institutional form is needed" (1992:5). There are, however, indigenous structures that could be the basis for a modern community bank. There are traditional African savings associations that can evolve into credit unions, for instance, and subsequently into community banks.

Democratization

The combined effect of Gorbachev's *glasnost* and *perestroika* not only led to the fall of the Berlin Wall and the disintegration of the Soviet Union and her empire, but also to the emergence of multi-party movements in Africa and the fall of *apartheid* regime in South Africa. Some countries initially resisted the call for multi-party politics. However, many of them caved in under international pressure. This pressure was in most cases through threats and/or suspension of aid (for example, Zambia, Kenya, Zaire, Central African Republic, Malawi, and so forth). I would therefore argue that for a democratic transition to succeed, a set of internal and external factors should exist. These are a core of genuine national democrats that is willing to accept political defeat and, a diversity of political views, cultures, and ethnicity, on the one hand, and strong international support for a democratic process that takes account of the domestic objective conditions, on the other. Hence, these internal and external factors would respectively constitute necessary and sufficient conditions for the liberalization of the political culture, which would in turn foster development of democratic forces, structures, and institutions. The current model of democracy that is being advocated in Africa is essentially a Westminster type of democracy, though some are similar to the American presidential style of politics. However, this model of democracy will need to be adapted to African conditions, so that it is in harmony with social institutions and cultural values, which in turn would ensure its sustainability.

The traditional African method of consensus-building and persuasion, to arrive at major decisions concerning the well-being of the community, has been fruitfully utilized in South Africa. This is illustrated by the Government of National Unity (GNU), which governed South Africa during the first year of multi-party democracy. The principle of 'winner-take-all' that is the backbone of liberal democracy (or multi-party democracy) was not used during the first year. It was seen by the political leadership, especially the African National Congress (ANC), not to be appropriate for a multi-ethnic society, one which needed a reasonable period for national reconciliation and healing. By allocating cabinet portfolios to all political parties that have some seats in parliament, President Mandela has adapted and applied liberal democracy to the objective realities of the new South Africa, but which is a product of a long history of struggle. And Basil Davidson reminds us that "in seeking to re-legitimize the state in Africa, it may be that Africa's own history can be called to aid" (1993:54).

Another useful example, from an African perspective, is the National Resistance Movement (NRM) in Uganda. The NRM is a broadly based political movement rooted in Ugandan social structures that is organized down from the village level up to the national one. It includes all segments of the Ugandan society. If tolerated and allowed to mature by the apostles of multi-party politics, it is likely to provide a blended model of democracy that is both gender and ethnic sensitive. Blended, because it combines elements of Western democracy with African ones. In fact, a careful analysis of the NRM system of government would tend to show that there is an 'invisible hand' of Julius Nyerere beneath Uganda's type of democracy under Museveni. The following passage about democracy by Nyerere may clarify this point:

> . . . .the people's equality must be reflected in the political organization; everyone must be an equal participant in the government of his society. Whatever devices are used to implement this principle, the people (meaning all members of the society equally) must be sovereign, and they must be able to exert their sovereignty without causing a breakdown of the law and order, or of the administration in their society. There must, in other words, be some mechanisms by which the people exert their will peacefully, and achieve changes in the laws which govern them; they must be able to change the per-

sonnel in positions of leadership within the framework of the normal workings of the social system. . . .And none of these things is possible unless every other aspect of society -- its economic, social and legal organization -- is such as to emphasize and serve man's equality. A political democracy which exists in a society of gross economic inequalities, or of social inequality, is at best imperfect, and at worst a hollow sham. (1968:5)

In light of the above, I would agree with Basil Davidson (1993) that democratic structures and institutions should be "capable of being legitimized by African history and its capacities for self-adjustment." This would ensure that the new democratic institutions are instruments of empowerment and the decentralization of the decision-making, rather than of alienation and marginalization. Describing a typical post-colonial African state, Basil Davidson has this to say:

This centralism has again reproduced the alienation of state from people, of government from governed, that characterized the colonial state; and this is the alienation that has robbed the postcolonial state of its legitimacy in the eyes of its subjects. And thus the state's capacity to defend a civil society of accepted law and order is made forfeit and is lost. (1993:52)

History could repeat itself with respect to the African state in the post-Cold War era, if Africa does not avoid what Mahmood Mamdani (1993) calls "a slavish acceptance of models drawn from entirely different histories." In this regard, a rigorous analysis of the current models of democratic development is needed from the African policy community, especially from academic and "think-tank" centers.

Moreover, a correct understanding of what is meant by democracy would facilitate the development of appropriate democratic forces, structures, and institutions that are capable of amalgamating positive aspects of both African traditional values and "modernization" norms. According to Gerald Schmitz and David Gillies (1992), democracy is a "system of coexistence in diversity." I would qualify this by restating it as a harmonious coexistence in diversity. They further state that democracy "is a process and a goal in which the values of plurality, liberty, and equality are paramount," and one is tempted to say Amen! By including more women and involving all the ethnic groups at various levels of the legislative institutions, Uganda would be able to meet these three -- plurality, liberty, and equality -- attributes of democracy.[4] Here, plurality in the African context is understood to be synonymous with ethnicity or what Crawford Young calls "cultural pluralism." In the distant past and long before colonialism, African societies respected and tolerated plurality. There were of course ethnic conflicts, but not on the scale of today's strife in Liberia, southern Sudan, Somalia, and Rwanda. But, what is the origin of this seemingly new intolerance of ethnicity? I will turn to Crawford Young for a possible explanation in the case of Zaire:

Pende and Mbala were not historical enemies whose endemic strife had only been temporarily halted by the enforced truce of colonial rule; chroniclers who visited this area in the nineteenth century make no mention of any such conflict. Ambitious young men from both groups during the colonial period sought urban employment in the regional center of Kikwit, or in the nearest major city of Kinshasa (then Leopoldville); they competed for places in the district secondary schools. However, before the coming of politics in 1959 no one would have thought that

> Pende-Mbala rivalry was a critical factor in the district. Political mobilization was swift and massive in 1960. . . .Only very close scrutiny into the internal factions of the regional party and voting patterns would reveal the first sign of ethnic tensions, inter alia, between Pende and Mbala. (Young, 1976:3-4)

Let us now turn to the recent African experience with democratization. It would appear from a few cases over the last five years that countries which are on course with respect to their political reforms have the necessary and sufficient conditions for a smooth democratic transition. And where these conditions do not prevail, the results are quite shocking. For instance, Nigeria and Zaire,[5] continue to drift toward anarchy and lawlessness spearheaded by the state, while the international advocates of democracy and multi-party politics passively look on. Nigeria, Togo, and Zaire are some of the examples of democratic transitions in which the international community has failed to support domestic democratic forces in challenging the status quo, thus reinforcing impoverishment and the marginalization of millions of people by the state. There are, however, promising cases of democratic transition. Countries such as Benin, Ghana, Kenya, Madagascar, Malawi, Mali, Tanzania, and Zambia have implemented major political reform measures without paralyzing the state machinery and capacity to govern.[6] Even countries in transition from devastating conflicts to tranquility, such as Angola, Ethiopia, and Mozambique have held free elections based on multi-party democracy.

The introduction of multi-party politics has, however, brought with it additional pressures that might derail the current economic reforms being implemented by a large number of African countries. According to Skålnes, "several authors are highly skeptical of democratisation in the context of clientelist politics, and predict that competitive party systems will exacerbate the tendency to disperse the resources of the state rather than mobilise a country's capital for productive purposes" (1993:404). Donald Emmerson further points out that:

> . . . .between economic and political liberalization lie two related kinds of contradiction: ones of inception and ones of consequence. If IMF-style economic reforms are to be implemented in the first place, the government must be able to override the interests of key threatened groups. And when implementation occurs, the government must have the power to prevent these groups from reversing the reform. (1991:12)

What is implicit in Emmerson's analysis is the inherent incompatibility of simultaneously implementing economic and political reforms. Once this incompatibility is recognized and acknowledged, the concern then should be on how to sequence the two reforms. The sequencing would depend on the prevailing objective conditions in each country, though in the case of Africa the order of events seems to have already been predetermined, that is, political reform is following economic adjustment, which began in the early 1980s. But, according to Hettne, "Sound economic policy is inconsistent with consolidating political legitimacy, particularly of countries in the process of transforming disintegrating dictatorships into some kind of pluralist democracies" (1990:22). This implies that political change is a precondition for economic reform. Evidence from Ghana lends support to Hettne's view, in that Rawling's government had to reverse some structural adjustment measures just before the multi-party democracy elections in 1990. This reversal has had a negative impact on the economic performance of the Ghanaian economy over the last few years. In the case of Kenya, however, multi-party democracy has revitalized the

Kenyan economy, through more accountability, transparency, and better governance.

As was the case with economic adjustment, there is an urgent need for sequencing the various measures of political reform. One should, however, first know the main elements of a political reform package before embarking on any meaningful sequencing. Achieving democratic development and sustaining it over the long term, according to Schmitz and Gillies (1992), "requires a complex sequence of many contingent and interdependent factors." They caution us that "there is no guarantee of success in political transitions or permanence as to their consolidation. But it is possible to identify at least some of the major elements that support stable democratic development." In this regard, the following six key elements should form the basis for a sustainable democratic development in Africa:

a)   National democratic movements/forces with conviction and knowledge of indigenous traditions and modern democratic values in which human rights are central;

b)   A relatively strong bureaucracy that is founded on the principles of good governance and, cultural and political pluralism;

c)   A judicial system that is independent, neutral politicaly, and with high moral values and professional ethics;

d)   Law enforcement agencies, such as professional military, police, and security forces that are conscious of their role in a democratic society, including respect for civilian authority and control in the interest of the country as a whole;

e)   An independent, reliable, and responsible press; and

f)   A constitutional and legal order which is based on the twin principles of secularism and pluralism, as the underlying mechanisms for ensuring the other five key elements.

Protecting The Environment

Africa's natural resource endowment includes land, forests, and water. These resources are the principal assets of Africa and of the mainstay of a large majority of the African people, a point well-articulated by the African Common Position on Environment and Development, which was adopted in Abidjan, Cote d'Ivoire in November 1991 with emphasis on 24 priority areas, as part of Africa's preparation for the Earth Summit. Moreover, Africa's natural resources provide a life-support system for a variety of living species, such as livestock, fisheries, wildlife, plants, birds, and other living organisms, which in turn ensure the richness of African biodiversity. The United Nations Environment Program (UNEP) has also identified the following six elements as "peculiar to Africa: (i) relatively higher fragility and variability of ecosystems; (ii) dependence on the resource-base for creation of national wealth; (iii) high direct dependence rate on the resource-base by the majority; (iv) the active role of traditional values, institutions, and knowledge systems in sustaining the resource-base; (v) the imperative of popular participation; and (vi) insufficient mobilization of the available human resource-base" (UNEP, 1994:1). Hence, the quest for ecological harmony -- a delicate balance between ecology and economy -- is one of the leading issues in African development in the 1990s and beyond.

In the distant past, African economic 'man' was in a symbiotic relationship with his surrounding environment. This ensured ecological harmony, as ecosystems reciprocated within and reached harmonious co-existence among themselves (Riddell, 1981). According to Clement Tisdell, "All traditional societies are imbued with a strong conservation ethic and engage in desirable conservation practices, given their dependence on local ecosystems" (1990:41). African policy-makers have been, at least on paper, conscious about the importance of environmental issues in the development process. For instance, Nyerere advised very early on that "when building new houses in a town it is necessary to plan for public spaces and leave room for community buildings even if you cannot build them immediately;. . . .and it is essential to spend that minimum amount of money which is necessary to prevent the destruction of that natural beauty or wildlife which could never be replaced if it was once allowed to disappear" (1968:11). Moreover, the Lagos Plan of Action (LPA), issued in 1980 with a long-term perspective (1983 -2008) by African heads of state and government, has a chapter on environment and development, which identifies the following as priority areas of concern:

a) Environmental sanitation, health, and safe drinking water supply;

b) Deforestation and soil degradation;

c) Desertification and drought;

d) Marine pollution and conservation of marine resources;

e) Human settlements;

f) Mining (rehabilitation of mined-out sites);

g) Air pollution control; and

h) Environmental education and training, legislation, and information.

It is interesting to note that even the World Bank was not really concerned, at the time, with environmental issues in Africa. This is evidenced by the briefest reference, which seems to me to be accidental, to conservation in the most acclaimed publication of the World Bank (1984): *Toward Sustained Development in Sub-Saharan Africa, A Joint Program of Action*. This publication referred correctly to conservation as a long-term constraint, but on less than half a page containing only four paragraphs. One therefore wonders as to how development could be sustained in Africa without a clear and comprehensive strategy for natural resource management. In retrospect, then, Africa was ahead of the World Bank and IMF as far as environmental protection is concerned. But, these were the decades (1970s & 1980s) of the "trickle down" hypothesis -- economic growth first, then redistribute income and clean up the environment later. In this regard, it is obvious that structural adjustment programs in the 1980s were not concerned with the eight priority areas with respect to the environment as stated in the Lagos Plan of Action. Hence, I agree with Tisdell that most of the African environmental problems are of external origin, especially in light of her dependence on primary commodities for exports. A fascinating explanation in support of this point is given by Tisdell as follows:

> Demand from developed countries for exports of natural resources from LDCs to support their economic growth and their high living standards is seen as a further contributor to the natural resource depletion in LDCs. While these factors are not unimportant, attention should be given in addition to other developments that increase the difficulties of conserving resources in LDCs, including the growth of markets and the market system, the rapidity of technological change, and the development of institutions that have undermined local authority, responsibility, and concern. (1990:42-43)

There is now an emerging body of empirical work on the impact of structural adjustment programs on African natural resources and the physical environment in general. Preliminary results tend to show an increase in the rate of deforestation in countries that were implementing adjustment programs in the 1980s (Lufumpa, 1995), especially those emphasizing policies that raise agricultural output and prices (Angelsen, Shitindi and Aarrestad, 1996). This has led a recent workshop organized by the United Nations Environment Program (UNEP) and the World Bank to conclude that: "The main message of the workshop for (a) international financial institutions is to incorporate social and environmental objectives in the design of SAPs explicitly; (b) governments implementing SAPs to enforce and implement economic, social and environmental measures fully and effectively; (c) donors to coordinate policies and aid programmes and make them consistent with the economic, social and environmental objectives of the country; (d) NGOs and other stakeholders to work closely with governments to take into account environmental, social and cultural considerations; and finally, (e) academicians and researchers to adopt methodologies to help design better SAPs and ensure convincing evaluations" (UNEP, 1996:3).

Furthermore, environmental indicators are being developed which should in turn enhance our ability to assess the impact of various policies on the physical environment. Of particular interest are the four general or composite indicators developed by the World Resources Institute (WRI, 1995). These are:

(i) pollution index
(ii) resource depletion index
(iii) ecosystem risk index
(iv) environmental impact on human welfare index.

Moreover, Robert Riddell (1981) provides a useful classification of worldly resources into four main categories, which can be of great help in appreciating the current debate on environmentally sustainable development in Africa. They should also provide a framework for designing various scenarios for sustainable utilization of natural resources. The first category consists of continuing resources (e.g., solar energy and gravity, see table 3.1). The second group covers renewable resources (e.g., water, soil, air, fauna and flora), which are essentially life-supporting. The third category consists of two sub-groups: recyclable non-renewable (example, gold, copper, lead, and so forth) and non-recyclable non-renewable resources (fossil fuels, coal, minerals, for example). The fourth category is composed of extrinsic resources (e.g., human institutions and man-made artifacts).

Table 3.1: The Four Worldly Resources

Class	Form	Character	Functional uses	Future
Continuing resources	Solar Gravitation Air & Wave motion Magnetic	In regular continuing supply	Energy input to life support	Continuing
Renewable resources	Clean Water Clean air Natural flora Natural Fauna Living Soils	Flowing but relative fixed supply varying in quality according to the purity of the ecosystem	Pollutant dispersal, enviromental, cleasing, life support	Impaired Purity
Non renewable resources	Non living minerlas & Fossil Fuel	Fixed quantity	Energy synthesis, structure, protection & ornamentation	Depletion
Extrinsic resources	Human institutions & man made arifacts	Both incorporeal(inst.) & corporeal(artifacts)	In nature-none.accessories to human existence	Some conservation

Source: Robert Riddell, 1981

In light of the above four categories of worldly resources and given their characteristics and functional uses as shown in table 3.1, environmental protection should no longer be seen as a subject of green-peace activism, but rather as a matter that concerns the very survival of Africa as a continent. Hence, issues of ecological balance are paramount in the African development agenda in the 1990s and beyond, as envisioned in the Lagos Plan of Action. Being in the tropics, Africa can for instance, make use of continuing resources (e.g., solar energy) to embark on what Riddell calls ecodevelopment "leading to economic 'equity', social 'harmony' and environmental `balance' " (1981:viii). However, development of solar energy will require initial massive investment, bearing in mind that Africa does not have requisite resources for such an endeavor. Yet, solar energy has great potential to enable Africa to combat diseases and reduce poverty by providing rural households with cheaper sources of energy for cooking, heating water, etc..

Renewable resources pose a special challenge, since they constitute the basis for African development. They are different from continuing resources in that their quality can be impaired by human activities, either temporarily or permanently, which in turn would have serious consequences on the whole life-sustaining systems of many living organisms. In this regard, three issues are increasingly becoming of great concern in the new search for a sustained balance between African ecology and economy. The first of these is the hazardous and toxic wastes of the industrialized countries being illegally transported from Europe and dumped in Africa. In the 1980s and early 1990s, stories coming out of Nigeria, Somalia, and Sudan were telling.[7] The most shocking one was Somalia, where Italian firms were busy dumping toxic chemicals and industrial wastes at the time (1992) when the whole world was engaged in a massive relief effort aim at saving the lives of millions of Somalis from a devastating man-made famine. The second issue of concern is the threat of an encroaching desert compounded by deforestation. It is estimated that the annual average rate of deforestation in Africa is 0.52 percent (African Development Bank, 1994). This rate varies across countries. It is on the high side in Cote d'Ivoire (5.2%) and Nigeria (6.9%); and low for Central African Republic (0.2%) and Congo (0.1%). The third issue is urban environmental degradation -- mainly air and water pollution -- in most of the highly populated African cities, such as Abidjan, Cairo, Dakar, Ibadan, and Lagos.

Although many countries are now putting in place environmental policies, institutions, and legal frameworks, most of Africa is still far away from the day when it will effectively tackle the issue of hazardous and toxic wastes being illegally dumped on the continent. Besides their likely negative effects on human health, hazardous and toxic wastes can also reduce the quality of renewable resources, especially through land degradation and water pollution. Land

and water are critical elements in the development process, especially in Africa, where agriculture is still the engine of economic growth and mainstay of a majority of the population. However, Africa does not have the financial resources to speed up her environmental management and monitoring capabilities in the foreseeable future, to implement environmentally sustainable development. In fact, the six leading issues that are the focus of discussion in this chapter are competing for scarce resources, which are also dwindling.

The threat of encroaching desert is becoming real. This is due mainly to deforestation and other types of land degradation. According to Badiane and Delgado (1995), "80 to 85 percent of land in Africa is threatened by degradation, and some 4 million hectares of forest are lost every year" (1995:7). Africa is the only region in the world where poverty (especially in the rural areas) is on the rise (Deng, 1995; World Bank, 1994b) and population is growing faster than the economy (African Development Bank, 1994). This implies that trees are cut down out of necessity to survive. Conservation of natural resources under such circumstances becomes a secondary concern. However, this conventional view of the perceived relationship between rapid population growth and land degradation is being challenged by new empirical findings. For instance, Arild Angelsen (1996) has recently found that in an open access regime of land tenure system, forest clearing does not necessarily originate from rapid population growth, but more from farming activities, which use deforestation as a "title establishment strategy." He further points out that: "In a situation where rights to forest land are obtained through forest clearance, then facilitating more secure land rights, for example by offering cheaper land titles and more legal protection by the state, would increase the net present value of the deforestation investment" (1996:24). John English, Mary Tiffen, and Michael Mortimore of the World Bank have also recently refuted the conventional view using the Machakos experience from Kenya. One of their main findings runs as follows:

> The Machakos experience deviates from the conventional experience. Increased population leading to increased cultivation did not lead to environmental damage, but rather to improvements in environmental quality. This experience has potential for replication. On the other hand, the Machakos experience provides some validation for the hypothesis advanced by the agricultural economist Ester Boserup that increases in population density induce technological change and increase in farming intensity. (1995:1)[8]

The most important lesson from a sustainable development perspective that could be drawn from the Machakos experience is the empowerment of the local people -- envisaged beneficiaries of development projects/programs -- to fully participate in the design, implementation, and management of these projects/programs. In addition, it should be stated that it is not rapid population growth per se that causes land degradation, but rather poverty, which compels poor households to use environmentally unfriendly production techniques. The poverty-population-environment nexus is articulated by Ismail Serageldin, in declaring that "Sub-Saharan Africa is suffering from the intertwined nexus of problems relating to poverty, rapid population growth and environmental degradation" (1995:38). Moreover, it is now generally acknowledged that poor households tend to have larger families for economic and old-age social security reasons (Ainsworth, 1994; Dasgupta, 1994; Deng, 1995; Deng and Fadayomi, 1994). According to Ainsworth (1994), "low quality of life, high child mortality, and economic uncertainty predispose couples to want large families. This means that slowing population growth must involve policies to reduce high fertility and child mortality while raising population quality."

Raising the quality of life of a population is the main objective of any public policy in any given society -- developed or developing. However, the key to raising the quality of life of the African peoples is through rational utilization of renewable resources in the development of African agriculture. As shown by Serageldin, the failure of African agriculture to achieve a reasonable growth rate has essentially compounded the intertwined nexus of problems relating to poverty, rapid population growth, and environmental degradation. The following passage illuminates the point being made here:

> Rapid population growth, environmental degradation, and slow agricultural growth in Sub-Saharan Africa are closely linked. Shifting cultivation and transhuman-pastoralism, adapted to low population density situations that were common in the Africa of the past, are environmentally damaging when population densities become high. With population density, traditional farming and livestock practices cause soil and forest degradation. Soil degradation causes crop and livestock yields to decline, curtailing agricultural growth. Slow agricultural growth contributes to slow economic growth and inhibits the demographic transition to lower population fertility rates. A rapidly increasing population of poor rural people preys on the rural environment, wildlife, forests, and land for survival. (Serageldin, 1995:39, Box 3-4)

The surest way, then, to protect the African environment is through agricultural structural transformation. I have argued elsewhere (Deng et al, 1995) that the current debate on agricultural transformation in Africa has rightly been triggered by the failure of African agriculture to "i) help people feed themselves either directly or through income generation; and ii) stimulate broader economic growth" (Staatz, 1994). The discourse has, however, unduly focused on African agricultural research problems (Ogbu, 1993) and policy reform (World Bank, 1989, 1994a; Cleaver, 1993; Cleaver and Donovan, 1995; Spencer, 1995). Two important missing links in this debate -- African farmers and regional economic integration -- will have to be included if African agriculture is to perform its historical role of being the engine of growth at the initial stages of development. Moreover, the linkage between farmers and markets is an important factor in the process of agricultural transformation. Such a linkage is, in my view, represented by traders and processors[9].

The role of the African farmer is critical in the protection of the environment. The adoption of yield-enhancing production techniques would enable African agriculture to lay a solid foundation for sustainable development by, first, helping the poor to feed themselves and, secondly, by generating an investable surplus that can be reinvested economy-wide and/or in agriculture itself. In order for African agriculture to enable people to feed themselves, due attention and resources should be given to the African farmer. It should be pointed out that African farming includes livestock, which plays an important role in the transformation process. In fact, livestock has three multiple roles -- as output, input (i.e., technology, animal traction and manure, for example), and means of transport. Three key questions arise with respect to the African farmer: Who is this African farmer, anyway? Is there a typical African farmer? What is the shape of her/his demand curve for technology? These three questions constitute one of the basic challenges in African development in general, and African agriculture in particular.

A typical African farmer is a woman. Although women produce over 70 percent of Africa's total food output, their access to renumerative activities and resources is very limited. In many instances, cultural barriers stand in the way of their progress. While it is generally recognized that women play a significant role in economic activities, especially in the agriculture sector, limited measures have been taken to remove the constraints faced by them. It is not uncommon for women in some African cultures to be barred from owning land even though they are responsible for most of the production activities. Women in many instances gain access to land through a man. This situation limits their access to credit as they lack the necessary collateral in most cases. Lack of credit in turn limits their ability to improve their production capacity through appropriate technologies. Extension services, when they are available, are usually geared toward serving male farmers. Very few women farmers are targeted. This is especially the case for female head of households. Since extension work is dominantly carried out by men, cultural constraints usually limit their contacts with women, especially female heads of households. Since women produce over 70 percent of Africa's total food output, the creation of a favorable environment for women through the removal of constraints would help to improve food production, reduce poverty, and eventually enhance the quality of the environment.

By correctly identifying who is the African farmer, the issues of agricultural research (e.g., technology), policy environment (e.g., getting prices right) and regional integration (e.g., more specialization and markets) would then be meaningfully addressed. For instance, agricultural research should also be able to respond to demand for technology by various groups of African farmers, by providing them with technologies that are ready for use on the farm. The tendency has been for researchers to produce technologies that remain "on the shelf" forever. By focusing on the farmer and her demand for technology, the debate on intensification versus extensification would essentially become a function of resource endowment for each category of farmers, which is largely determined by physical, political, social factors, and institutions. The practice so far has been to select both, technology and crop for the African farmers, without any consultation with them as to what kind of technology and crop they would have preferred, if they were given the opportunity to choose. Hence, productivity growth in African agriculture will only occur once those who work on the farm are sufficiently empowered to use production techniques of their choice in growing what is profitable from their perspectives. Of course, such production techniques will have to be environmentally sound, economically viable, and culturally acceptable. In fact, environmental screening and impact assessment are now an integral part of the traditional project cycle of development projects and programs.

It should be acknowledged, however, that the emphasis on identifying the different technological needs of different types of farmers has been a major effort of farming systems research (FSR) over the last fifteen years. For instance, FSR practitioners often define different "recommendation domains," which are groups of farmers facing different physical and socioeconomic circumstances, and try to tailor technologies for each group. Considerable effort has been made in some countries through FSR to address the technological needs of different types of farmers. It has not always been successful, and it often has only looked at farm-level constraints without considering market opportunities and constraints. Nevertheless, I would like to acknowledge these efforts of FSR.

Furthermore, creating an enabling environment through policy reforms would only have significant impacts if African farmers were empowered to make choices with respect to technology and crop. And for African farmers to be able to make informed choices, there must be adequate investment in physical, economic, and social infrastructure (for example, roads, storage facilities, credit, extension services, education, water sanitation, and so forth).[10] These would, in turn, facilitate transmission of market signals between the various economic agents -- including farmers, traders, processors, and researchers. It should be recalled that laissez-faire is the underlying principle of the current economic policy reforms in Africa, and denying African farmers the freedom of choice of production techniques would be contradictory. Moreover, it should be emphasized that the behavior of the African farmer, in light of the prevailing conditions surrounding her, is rational and consistent with economic fundamentals. There is now a strong body of literature indicating that African farmers will not, in the absence of good roads and other support systems, adopt production technologies that are dependent on the markets (Spencer, 1995; Cleaver and Donovan, 1995). This point is well articulated by Cleaver and Donovan:

> When marketing and input supply systems do not work, and producer prices are artificially low relative to input costs, the risks to farmers who are dependent on these systems increase. Risk-averting farmers will not use these market-dependent methods in this situation. The extensive African farming and livestock systems which use much land, little capital and labor, and which are less dependent on markets, are rational farmer responses to these various natural and government-made constraints. (1995:5)

The challenges facing African traders and processors should also be considered since they are essentially the glue between farmers and markets. Their role is also important with respect to the African environment, as they are among the economic agents that are likely to influence the African farmer in her choice of environmentally friendly production techniques. In addition, traders and processors often face technical and institutional constraints that reduce efficiency and raise costs throughout the food system. Examples of constraints that can be easily cited are the numerous roadblocks that one finds in Cote d'Ivoire, Nigeria, and other West African countries. Hence, the same set of questions can also be asked: Who is the African trader? Who is the African processor? Like African farmers, there are many different types of traders and processors, each group facing their own opportunities and constraints, which in turn implies that different technical and institutional solutions will have to be designed for each category.

Regional economic integration is also critical for African agriculture to produce what John Staatz (1994) calls "a surplus above the current consumption needs." The lack of regional integration encourages African countries to seek misguided food self-sufficiency policies and strategies that perpetuate food shortages on the continent, and hence threats of environmental degradation. In this regard, a recent World Bank projection of a food shortage of 250 million tons for Africa by the year 2020 (MSU, 1994) should act as a last "wake-up call" for African leaders to take concrete and serious actions toward regional economic integration. The issue, however, is not self-sufficiency but rather food security for the millions of Africans who now derive their livelihood from agricultural activities. The drive for self-sufficiency in food production by each and every African country is not only undesirable but unattainable. It does not allow for greater specialization in agricultural production; hence, countries are unable to produce according to their comparative advantages and then trade among themselves.

I would think that the emphasis on food security will create awareness among countries that they do not need to produce all the food they want to consume, at all costs. They can exchange goods and services through regional economic integration. President Nelson Mandela, in his opening statement to the first Southern Africa Development Community

(SADC) Summit hosted by South Africa in August 1995, saw regional integration as an important vehicle for planting "seeds for Africa's rebirth." And with regional integration in place, greater specialization would be achieved as goods and services move freely between and within countries. In this regard, the role of traders and processors is critical in this movement of goods and services both within and between countries. In fact, regional integration would resolve many institutional constraints with respect to the environment at both national and regional levels. It would allow each agro-ecological zone to specialize in what is physically feasible within each region, and thereby resolving any institutional bottleneck constraining adoption of appropriate production techniques. The following passage from Badiane and Delgado helps illustrate this point:

> A key institutional problem that hinders the adoption of appropriate strategies toward the management of natural resources is the lack of consistent and coordinated national efforts, with actions too often dispersed within several ministries. Strategies for resource conservation should include, among others, the development of and diffusion of environmentally friendly production techniques that are acceptable to farmers. However, conservation policies that are successful in one type of setting can be doomed to failure under another. What works in the arid, Sahelian countries may not work at all in the humid or subhumid parts of the continent. (1995:7)

The above citation lends support to our conviction about the importance of regional economic integration as one of the key pillars for Africa to achieve a balanced combination of economic growth with effective poverty reduction without degrading the potential of her conditionally renewable natural resources. In this regard, Africa can be divided into the following six main agro-ecological zones[11]:

a)   Mediterranean and arid north Africa;
b)   Sudano-Sahelian Africa;
c)   Humid and sub-humid west Africa;
d)   Humid central Africa;
e)   Sub-humid and mountain east Africa; and
f)   Sub-humid and semi-arid southern Africa.

A meaningful discussion could, therefore, be made about environmental concerns within the overall framework of agricultural structural transformation in each agro-ecological zone. Moreover, the four central points -- technology, enabling policy environment, empowerment of farmers, and regional integration -- should guide our search for the technical feasibilities of agricultural production techniques in each of the agro-ecological zones. Stated differently, the process of agricultural transformation must emphasize sustained harmony between ecology and economy in each zone, so as to ensure that while deriving economic benefits, natural resources are preserved and not degraded. Agro-ecological zones are, according to Spencer (1995), "a very useful basis for discussing agricultural development issues, since the natural resource base, including biodiversity, is a key determinant of agricultural production possibilities." This is due to the fact that depletion of the natural resource base will constrain efforts at economic growth and poverty reduction, which would in turn reinforce the vicious cycle of degradation, stagnation, and hunger. In chapter four, an agriculture-led economic growth is conceived as one of the key elements of African model of sustainable development. Attempts are, therefore, made in chapter four to provide a general picture of agricultural production in each zone, that is arable land, percentage of resource (land) utilization, main products, and so forth. It is my hope that this should in turn provide a useful framework for economic integration strategies, projects and/or programs by development institutions, such as the African Development Bank, and sub-regional organizations (examples, SADC, ECOWAS, Megharib Union, COMESA, and so forth).[12]

The World Bank's projections of food shortages notwithstanding, we strongly believe that African agriculture will be able to feed the population and generate a surplus for the world economy twenty-five odd years from now. This optimism -- yes, it is time for Afro-optimism -- emanates from our view that African agricultural transformation is predicated on four key considerations (or factors) - empowerment of farmers to select environmentally sustainable production techniques for the crops of their choice; technological breakthrough; enabling policy environment (including public investment in infrastructure); and regional economic integration. In addition to these, our conviction is strengthened through recent findings by Rosegrant (1994) and Peter Veit et al (1995). There is now an emerging consensus among researchers and policy analysts that "future food production growth must be driven [sic] primarily from yield growth on rain-fed soils." But, "prospects for growth in cultivated area are bleak, with the possible exception of rain-fed production in Sub-Saharan Africa."(Rosegrant1).[13] There is therefore hope that African agriculture will be able to lay a solid foundation for sustainable development. But, this will require a true partnership between farmers, researchers, policy makers, and donors.

A true partnership would, in turn, enable African agriculture to help people feed themselves and thereby ensure protection of the environment. As farmers produce more than they can consume, a surplus is generated, which can be sold in the domestic, regional, and international markets. Farmers can then use this additional income from sales of their surplus in the purchase of non-farm products (e.g, durable consumer goods such as household appliances, and so forth). They will also be in a better financial situation to send their children to schools with anticipated positive effects -- high rates of return to investment in schooling -- on productivity growth not only in agriculture, but also economy-wide. Moreover, this productivity growth in agriculture would further raise the purchasing power of the rural population, to the extent that the agricultural sector can now begin to fulfil its historical mandate -- generating an investable surplus for the other sectors of the economy. Thus, Serageldin's intertwined nexus of problems relating to poverty, rapid population growth, and environmental degradation would have been broken.

Reducing Poverty

A recent report on The Many Faces of Poverty in Sub-Saharan Africa, by the World Bank (1994b), is a useful point of departure for examining poverty reduction as a leading issue in African development in the 1990s and beyond. The recognition that poverty in Africa has multiple faces has encouraged me to identify two main types of this malaise, which are also interrelated as well as negatively reinforcing. The first one, which I must admit will be controversial, is what I would call 'intellectual poverty'[14]. The second is the conventional type of poverty that arises as a result of lack of and/or inability to access basic human needs.

'Intellectual poverty' has allowed inappropriate development policies and strategies that are inconsistent with African thought and culture to be applied with impunity. And when these policies and strategies do not work, African social institutions and culture(s) are seen as impediments to modernizing process and to economic development (Lloyd, 1967; Arnold, 1990; Etounga-Manguelle, 1994; Soyinka, 1994). I agree with Wole Soyinka that: "Culture must be constantly recalled as an expression of a total way of productive life, one which encompasses more than the physical precipitations that are marketed or displayed as proofs of a cultural reality, the distinctive marks that separate a supposedly brutish existence from a 'cultured[15] one' (from Serageldin and Taboroff, 1994:202). This perception of African systems of thought or culture as obstacles to development perpetuates the general state of underdevelopment and subsequently marginalization and the emergence of the other face of poverty -- the inability to have access to basic human needs. The combined effect of the two faces of African poverty is vividly illustrated by Wole Soyinka:

> . . . .for us in the Third World especially, we become the consumed. By succumbing to hunger for the latest novelty, we paradoxically consume ourselves, and what is left of us is consumed in turn by the industrial machine which churns out the latest novelty, one which, to complete the cycle of illusion, is held up as the signpost of modernism, and therefore of a dynamic, contemporary world culture. Is this perhaps what is meant by development? (From Serageldin and Taboroff, 1994:208-209)

The 'intellectual poverty' in Africa manifests itself mainly in the absence of a serious African scholarship that can systematically guide development policy formulation and ensure its consistency with African thought and culture[16.] Such a poverty has been widely acknowledged, but only few dare to mention it explicitly out of fear, perhaps of being branded as polemical and radical. The approach so far has been to mask this type of poverty with coded phrases, such as lack of analytical capacity, institutional weakness, and so forth. Hence, attempts to alleviate this type of poverty have mainly (and rightly so) focused on capacity-building and institutional strengthening. While such efforts are necessary and commendable, they are insufficient to produce a viable African development school of thought, which is urgently needed to provide alternative analysis of African problems and appropriate strategies for their solution.

I would therefore argue that capacity-building and institutional-strengthening initiatives undertaken in isolation of African social systems of thought would normally lead to what Hettne calls 'imitative' development. This 'imitative' development has essentially landed Africa to where she is today -- with slow growing, if not stagnant, economies with rising poverty, indebtedness, faster population growth, civil strife, and threats of natural resources degradation.

Turning now to the other face of African poverty, it should be stated at the beginning of this section that there are definitional and methodological problems with respect to the measurement of this type of poverty[17]. In search of an appropriate generic definition, the point of departure should begin at normalcy. That is, to define poverty as a deviation from a normal situation for, say, an individual in an African society. Edward O'Boyle (1991) has articulated this point by asking: What does it mean to be a person? I would argue that it means to have dignity and self-respect, which presupposes having the basic needs of a normal human being met. These basic needs consist of primary and secondary needs. The former is comprised of food (including water and clothing) and shelter; and the latter consists of economic, social, cultural, and political services. Examples of secondary needs are health, education, security, liberty, freedom of expression and religion, individual rights to own property, to have access to productive employment, credit, and so forth. Primary and secondary basic needs could be met through one's own resources, family, community, and/or through a combination of these sources.

The lack of these resources leads to a state of powerlessness, helplessness, and despair, which in turn forces a person to perform undignified and disrespectful actions. In addition, the inability to protect oneself against economic, social, cultural, and political discrimination, deprivation, and marginalization can also lead to this type of poverty. For instance, to be a person in a Dinka society of the Sudan is to have dignity and self-respect, two concepts that are not possible to quantify and yet are central to the very existence of the Dinka social fabric. A Dinka family must have requisite resources to support the primary needs of its members if it is to achieve its stated goal. This situation seems to be common to all traditional societies in the Third World as shown by James Scott: "In order to be a fully functioning member of village society, a household needs a certain level of resources to discharge its necessary ceremonial and social obligations as well as to feed itself adequately and continue to cultivate. To fall below this level is not only to risk starvation, it is to suffer a profound loss of standing within the community and perhaps to fall into a permanent situation of dependence" (1976:9).

A conducive environment should also prevail for individuals to undertake economic and social activities that would enable them to improve their well–being within the framework of community prosperity and progress. Moreover, the community should be able to provide resources, such as land, security, and so forth, for the household to meet its secondary basic needs, which would in turn ensure that dignity and self–respect are protected. In this regard, social disintegration happens only through an external force, such as natural calamities or man-made disasters. For instance, the current civil war in the Sudan has destroyed many families and has caused social disarray for a large number of southern Sudanese communities. Yet, stories by foreign relief workers talk of how the internally displaced people as well as those in the refugee camps in the neighboring countries are keeping their dignity and self-respect despite of all the odds against them. This is because cultural values and social norms are still predominant in southern Sudan, though they have their negative side sometimes - especially when they are evoked by the elite for their own personal ambitions for power.

The quest for human dignity and self–respect requires dual functions, that is, individual and communal (societal) duties, if they are to be achieved simultaneously. The concept of 'person-in-community' used by Herman Daly and John Cobb (1987) is of importance to our analysis here. At the individual level, a person aims not to bring shame to himself/herself and/or her/his family. As Nyerere has put it: "There is, in fact, no substitute for the individual moral courage of men" (1968:20). Theft, rape and murder in a Dinka world, for example, are incompatible with the prescribed social norms of the community, and must therefore be guarded against. This implies that a household (family) should be able to meet primary basic needs which enable an individual member to observe the family goal of dignity and self–respect. Similarly, for a person to fully participate in the defense and maintenance of the community goal of dignity and social well–being, s/he should be in a position to meet some of or all his/her basic needs as a member of the society. In this particular case of the Dinka society, acquiring a farming plot from the communal land is one of several methods a person is supported by the society. There are also traditional structures and social safety–nets that provide support to those who may be in need (Deng, 1984). With the current global acceptance of human rights and pluralism, these concepts are becoming central in the development agenda of many countries. They are therefore important building-blocks for rethinking African development policy formulation as presented in chapter four.

The inability to meet basic needs is, therefore, considered as constituting a state of poverty. This predicament can lead to desperation and hopelessness if the community/society is indifferent to the plight of its poor, which could in turn produce violence, theft, thuggery, and other forms of family and value-system breakdown and decay of social institutions. Hence, the way poverty is viewed here is somewhat different from the conventional approach, which measures poverty in terms of income and nutritional requirements. The World Bank (1990a, 1993a) uses a global poverty line of US$370 per annum to determine the number of poor in the world. This figure is based on an income that can purchase a basket of goods and services necessary to meet the minimum nutritional requirement. According to this global poverty line, "about 1.1 billion people in the developing world live in poverty — struggling to survive on less than $370 a year." However, this poverty line is based only on primary basic needs, and to this extent it is a partial measurement of poverty. Others (Greer and Thorbecke, 1986) have used food deprivation as a basic dimension of poverty. Greer and Thorbecke state that "food poverty is defined as a condition of lacking the measures necessary to acquire a nutritionally adequate diet. . . .Individuals who have the ability to meet their minimum needs should not be considered poor even if they do not do so." Moreover, the Human Development Index (HDI), used by the UNDP to estimate the quality of life in ranking countries according to the level of human development, is also a partial measurement of poverty as it only focuses on three indices -- per capita GNP, life expectancy at birth, and educational attainment index -- without including measures of political and cultural deprivation.

A full measure of poverty should take into account both its quantitative and qualitative aspects. The qualitative dimension of poverty can be described as social, cultural, and political deprivation. The two dimensions of poverty are best seen if policy objective function is formulated along the lines of human dignity and self-respect. This would in turn ensure that development is a multi-dimensional dynamic process. Using the various measurements of poverty -— quantitative and qualitative -— it is possible to identify the main groups of Africa's poor. In addition, it is not unusual to find poor households intermingled with rich ones in most African cities (e.g., Abidjan and Addis Ababa). However, the incidence of poverty is very prevalent in the unplanned settlements and most peripheral areas of the urban centers and remote rural locations. For the purposes of our analysis here, Africa's poor are considered to fall into one or more of the following seven general categories of poverty:[18]

a)   those households or individuals below the poverty level and whose incomes are insufficient to provide for basic needs, as defined by the World Bank (1993a), UNDP (1995), Lufumpa (1994), Ahn (1990), and so forth;

b)   households or individuals lacking access to basic services, political contacts, and other forms of support. This category include the urban squatters and "street" children;

c)   people in isolated rural areas who lack essential infrastructure such as basic services;

d)   female–headed households (especially pregnant and lactating mothers and infants) whose nutritional needs are not being met adequately (see Ndisale, 1995);

e)   persons who have lost their jobs and those who are unable to find employment (such as school leavers and college graduates) as a result of economic reforms introduced under the adjustment programs, that is, those who are in danger of becoming the "new poor;"

f)   refugees and internally displaced populations due to civil strife; and

g)   ethnic minorities who are marginalized, deprived, and persecuted economically, socially, culturally, and politically.

The number of poor people in Africa, using the World Bank's poverty line of less than US$1.0 per person a day, can be estimated at 300 million, which reflects only the first group out of the above identified categories. The World Bank (1994b) estimates that Sub-Saharan Africa (excluding North Africa and South Africa) may now have more than 210 million poor people. It is obvious that the number of people in poverty in Africa would be higher than 300 million if the other categories are included, especially refugees, oppressed ethnic minorities (or even majorities as in the case of Burundi and Rwanda), and internally displaced populations. In addition, recent studies by the African Development Bank (see, for instance, Lufumpa 1994, 1995; Ndisale 1995) and the World Bank (1990a, 1993b, 1993c) indicate that poverty in Sub-Saharan Africa is essentially a rural phenomenon. This is a consequence of decades of neglect and marginalization of the rural areas through economic policies that favored the urban elite. Rural areas were made to (i) supply urban groups with food and labor at very low returns; (ii) produce export crops and receive less than 10 percent of the international prices.[19] (for example, cotton and gum Arabic in Sudan); and (iii) pay taxes and receive no services in return. Moreover, the consumption pattern of the urban elite shifted with the passage of time away from domestic products to imported goods and services in keeping up with the "Joneses" in the international economy. This further led to the marginalization of rural Africa, as the urban areas were now made to adjust to alien economic conditions.

The Human Development Index (HDI) of the UNDP, which is used to estimate the quality of life in a country, is useful since it brings out other dimensions of poverty, such as life expectancy and education indices, that are glossed over by the World Bank's global poverty line (GPL). The 1995 Human Development Report gives HDI for the world to be 0.888, which ranges between the highest HDI of 0.95 for Canada and the lowest HDI of 0.207 for Niger. That is, Niger is at the bottom of the list of 174 countries in the world covered by the report. The same report ranks all African countries, except 6 countries, in the bottom 50 percent of all the 174 countries in the world covered by the report. The six African countries that were in the upper 50 percent were Mauritius (ranked as 60 with HDI of 0.821), Seychelles (rank: 62, HDI: 0.81), Libya (rank: 73, HDI: 0768), Botswana (rank: 74, HDI: 0.763), Tunisia (rank: 75, HDI: 0.763), and Algeria (rank: 85, HDI: 0.732). Moreover, out of a total of 22 least developed countries in the world with a low level of the quality of life (i.e., with HDI less than 0.337), only three countries (Afghanistan, Bhutan, and Cambodia) were non-African. Since the HDI is a consolidated index of life expectancy, education, and income levels, the poor ranking of African countries is a manifestation of the nature and magnitude of underdevelopment in Africa. These three indicators depict a rather gloomy and alarming picture of poverty in Africa. A further analysis of each of the HDI components is necessary in order to appreciate the state as well as the underlying causes of poverty in Africa.

Factors that influence life expectancy could generally be stated as consisting of (i) access to safe drinking water; (ii) sanitation; and (iii) access to health services. Poor sanitation and limited access to safe drinking water also exacerbates the situation by making a large portion of the African population vulnerable to diseases, especially water-borne ones. The prevalence of hunger, malnutrition, and other diseases in Africa affects productivity and therefore reduces the ability of poor people to earn a meaningful income. Such situations have inevitably contributed to perpetuating poverty. Civil conflicts in some parts of the continent have further compounded poverty by displacing over five million people, and therefore condemning them to life under conditions of absolute poverty.

Only about 35 percent of Africa's rural population has access to safe drinking water, compared to 60 percent for other developing countries. This is much lower in some countries, for instance, it is reported to be only 2 percent for Congo (UNDP, 1995:167) compared to 92 percent for her urban population. In this particular example of Congo, the problem seems to be more of a misallocation of resources in favor of the urban population. The state of sanitation is equally pathetic. A very small proportion (36%) of the African population has access to safe sanitation. And about 56 percent of the population have access to health services. These three factors combined do impact on the overall life expectancy in Africa. In addition, the maternal mortality rate for Africa is about 600 per 100,000 live births, which is double that of the other developing regions of the world. Infant mortality in Sub-Saharan Africa is about 97 deaths per 1,000 live births compared to 70 in the other developing regions of the world. Hence, the overall life expectancy in Africa is estimated around 51.3 years, which is much lower than 63.1 years life expectancy level in the other low-income countries of the world. This situation is compounded by shrinking expenditure levels in many African countries on health services, which is a mere 2.5 percent for Sub-Saharan Africa (UNDP, 1995:179).

With regard to education, the indicators are not any better. About 69 percent of Africa's school age children are enrolled in primary schools. The corresponding enrollment rate for the other low-income countries is 99 percent. With regard to female enrollment, only about 60 percent of females in the school-age group are enrolled in primary schools compare to 99 percent in the other low income countries of the world. Similarly, about 62 percent of Africa's female population aged 15 and above is illiterate. Overall, about 46 percent of Africa's total population aged 15 and above is illiterate.

Economic problems in many African countries have worsened poverty situations. The current state of low-production agriculture is exacerbated in most cases by a lack of policy initiatives to ameliorate the situation. Farm gate prices in many instances have not been high enough to provide the necessary incentives for increased farm production. Poorly coordinated and supported research and extension institutions in many African countries have done little to significantly improve the situation of farmers. The poor state of rural infrastructure has severely limited people's access to markets, especially urban markets. This in turn has limited small farmers' ability to earn meaningful incomes. The lack of income has further limited farmers' access to improved methods of farming since they are unable to afford essential farm inputs like improved seeds and fertilizers. This situation is compounded because rural credit in many African countries is not well streamlined, and therefore limited in coverage. The circumstances surrounding small farmers have continued to make it hard for these farmers to break out of their cycle of low-production farming and low incomes, and eventually out of poverty.

The persistent semi-subsistence nature of African agriculture has caused many African countries to constantly have food shortages in the face of increasing populations. The fact that Africa's population is increasing at a faster rate than food production constantly threatens its food security position. The index of agricultural production indicates that while Africa's total production is increasing, per capita production is declining. Similarly per capita food production in Africa has fallen from an index of 101 in the 1978-80 period to 96 in the 1988-90 period.[20] Hence, the occurrence of a natural disaster such as a drought often results in serious threats of hunger for the majority of the affected people. This was the case during the long drought of four years ago which affected the whole southern Africa region. The frequent occurrence of droughts during the 1980s not only affected agricultural production and national economies in general, it also undermined the food security situation of a large majority of Africans, especially in the rural areas. According to the World Resources Institute (1991), the average annual donations of receipts of food aid increased from 3.36 million metric tons during 1977-79 to 5.72 million metric tons in the 1987-89 period. In per capita terms, food aid increased from seven kilograms per person in 1977-79 to nine kilograms per person in the 1987-89 period.

The majority of the poor live in rural areas where their main source of livelihood is from agriculture and such related activities as hunting, animal husbandry, and fishing.

Almost 80 percent of the population of Africa is rural-based, where agriculture is the main source of employment. Moreover, agriculture accounts for between 20 to 33 percent of Africa's GDP, 40 percent of its exports, and employs 60 percent of its labor force (see chapter four). In addition, a majority of African farmers are semi-subsistence farmers who engage in low- production agriculture. Small-scale farmers in Africa account for well over 70 percent of farm households and of total food production. African small-scale farmers typically use hand tools for cultivation and very few capital inputs. Agricultural production in these instances is geared more toward meeting basic needs, supplemented by little income from other sources.

In the urban areas, the poor performance of many African economies has resulted in the shrinking of productive activities and employment opportunities in the formal sector. As a result of this phenomenon, informal sector activities have proliferated and flourished. It is estimated that by the year 2020, more than 60% of urban employment in Africa will be in micro-enterprises (World Bank, 1992c). The poor in the urban areas include the unemployed, the self-employed, the meagerly paid public servants, and most of the people employed in the informal sector businesses. Many of the informal sector establishments include such activities as shoe shining, tailoring, metal work, auto repair, arts and crafts, knitting and weaving, plumbing, carpentry, food processing, textiles, leather works, and retail.

Corrective actions such as macroeconomic adjustment measures seem to have contributed, at least in the short run, to a rise in the level of absolute poverty. Laid off workers from the public sector do not normally find employment in the private sector, since they have limited skills. Hence, these laid off employees join the poverty group of an adjusting economy. This is confirmed by a recent finding of the Cornell/USAID study, which has concluded that adjustment has not hurt the poor, but has only hurt the urban non-poor in sub-Saharan Africa in the 1980s. Among the group of the so-called urban "non-poor" are the retrenched public sector workers. According to the principal authors of the Cornell/USAID study (Dorosh and Sahn, 1993), retrenched public sector workers are not poor, though vulnerable. And if one agrees with this view, then one can interpret it as follows: yes, adjustment has not hurt the poor, but it has contributed to the current increase in poverty, since it hurts vulnerable urban groups, such as unskilled and semi-skilled workers in the public sector -- who were marginally above the national poverty line before the introduction of SAPs. This interpretation is consistent with the contemporary development literature on economic reform (see for instance the work of the World Bank, UNDP, UNICEF, and so forth), which found the number of poor to be increasing in Africa during the period 1985-1992. It should be recalled that this was when many countries adopted far reaching reform measures. According to the World Bank, "Sub-Saharan Africa has a large -- and growing -- proportion of the population living in poverty. Between 1985 and 1992, the number rose by almost 1.5 percent, such that there may now be over 210 million people in Sub-Saharan Africa surviving on less than $1 per person per day."[21]

The challenge, then, facing African researchers, policy analysts, and institutions is not to debate whether or not adjustment hurts the poor, but rather to rethink the process of macroeconomic policy formulation itself. This would also reorient the African research agenda for the 21st century. A number of African countries have began, over the last few years, to design and implement macroeconomic policies that contain complementary micro-projects/programs for mitigating the likely negative effects of the recommended economic reform measures. This approach has ensured two things. The first one is that macroeconomic fundamentals are paramount and must be respected, if conducive environments for private initiative and productive investment are to prevail. Secondly, both economic and social policies are essentially two arms of a public policy, which implies that economic reform can be sustained only if its social aspects are integrated into various measures of macroeconomic adjustment, which in turn guarantees political acceptance of the reform program by the major stakeholders in the status quo.

I would agree with Cornell's findings, that adjustment has not hurt the poor, since the Computable General Equilibrium (CGE) model does not capture this group of people. This is because the CGE and the Social Accounting Matrix (SAM) models used in the Cornell/USAID study exclusively focus on the formal sector (public and private) of the economy. It is a common knowledge that the poor are in the informal sector. Moreover, the findings of the Cornell/USAID study are based on results from a simulation exercise, which uses historical and/or imported data. Besides, the CGE does not capture the dynamic aspects of the adjustment process. For example, changes in relative prices normally produce a chain of instantaneous reactions as well as coping mechanisms by various socio-economic groups in an adjusting economy. In this regard, it would be empirical fantasy to measure the effect of macroeconomic reform on the poor after they have had already adjusted to the new situation so as to ensure their survival. But, poor groups are in all likelihood not captured by the CGE/SAM models. The most appropriate approach would be to observe over the adjustment period how individuals and/or households in poverty cope on a daily basis with changes brought about by the economic reform measures. Such an approach would enable policy analysts to determine some of the mechanisms the poor use to survive the negative effects of the adjustment process.

A comprehensive understanding of the coping mechanisms adopted by the poor for their survival is a prerequisite to a meaningful analysis of adjustment by the poor. I would, therefore, argue that it is inappropriate to pose questions such as; Has structural adjustment hurt the poor in sub-Saharan Africa during the 1980s? An appropriate inquiry should be; How did the poor cope with structural adjustment programs in sub-Saharan Africa during the 1980s? Here, the missing link in the research on adjustment and the poor is our comprehension of the coping mechanisms that individuals and/or households in poverty usually adopt to survive during upheavals -- be they man-made or natural disasters. Knowledge of these coping mechanisms would enable public policy formulators to initiate policies that tend to empower the poor to design and manage their own productive activities within the overall framework of a national economy.

Controlling Indebtedness

The origin of the debt problem in Africa could be traced to the first oil shock of 1973 and subsequent petrodollars that lured many governments to borrowing at very favorable terms, and to invest the borrowed funds uneconomically. The main effect of the petrodollar, however, was, to delay the adjustment process, which would have naturally taken place. Balance of payments difficulties that culminated from the oil crisis of the 1970s were seen as temporary -- to the extent that there was no effort made to adjust both consumption and production habits. Africa later paid a heavy price for borrowing unwisely and for not adjusting to the changing economic realities. Moreover, it was not only the African states that borrowed unwisely. The money lenders also were not prudent enough in their financial and economic analysis of the projects/programs in which they invested. It was also an investment on the part of the money lenders, and they should have anticipated the kinds of risk involved.

A careful examination of the debt service ratio and of total external debt as a percentage of GDP shows that the magnitude of these two indicators differ greatly among the highly indebted countries (see table 3.2). For instance, the debt service ratio ranges between a high rate of 72.9% for Algeria to a low rate of 6.5% for Sudan. The total debt as a percentage of the GDP ranges between a high of about 300% for Côte d'Ivoire to a low of 28.5% for Nigeria. One additional point with respect to total external debt concerns its magnitude in terms of local currencies, which has often been overlooked in the adjustment literature. The devaluation of the local currency makes the debt larger when measured in the national currency of the borrower. This implies that the debt-service payments will now take more resources in terms of local currency, which further increases the domestic indebtedness of the government. A rising domestic indebtedness has recently led Philip English and Harris Mule to observe that: "A new associated problem is the creation of huge domestic debt arising from governments' heavy borrowing in domestic money markets and their capacity to raise tax revenues to service it. High domestic debt makes it difficult for governments to service external debt even when a country has adequate foreign exchange reserves" (1996:142).

The failure by both borrowers and creditors to give greater attention to the productivity of borrowed funds has made Africa to accumulate a total external debt of about US$300 billion by 1994 compared to only US$31 billion in 1975. A real investment project should be able to repay its own debt. The debt has now become one of the obstacles hindering economic development and social progress in Africa. This has caused the African Development Bank to conclude that "despite many attempts to reduce the debt of regional member countries, the debt situation remained a real impediment to economic growth, investment and development; and weighed heavily on African countries" (African Development Bank, 1995:29). The debt service ratio[22] was also on the rise -- exceeding 35 percent in 1994 compared to 28 percent in 1993, though this could be a good sign of African countries' improved capacity to generate more foreign exchange. It is, however, a troubling sign in light of the current low levels of investment and GDP growth. And if Africa continues to pay 35 cents of every dollar of her export earnings to service the debt, a reasonable rate of economic growth high enough to support a rapidly growing African population, on the one hand, and to repay the debt, on the other, is unlikely to be achieved in the near future. This is because such an economic rate of growth would undoubtedly originate from the agricultural sector, but this would require massive investment. Dunstan Spencer (1995) has recently argued, for instance, that US$38 billion will be required annually just for investment in the rural road network to enable Africa to reach, by the year 2010, that of India in the 1950s. Furthermore, and in agreement with Philip English and Harris Mule, I believe that "the reduced imports of real goods and services that are the inevitable consequences of debt service payments have meant multiple setbacks: reduced capacity utilization in both the private and public sectors, hence reduced levels of income and fiscal revenues; increased inflationary pressures arising from budget deficits; reduced capacity to save and invest; and weakened prospects for future growth and employment" (1996:142). This vicious circle of debt service payments should hopefully highlight the gravity of the debt problem, which I have identified as one of the key leading issues in African development in the 1990s and beyond.

Various attempts to tackle the problem of Africa's debt have not yielded the desired results (for a review of debt relief initiatives, see English and Mule, 1996). Initiatives designed by the donor community (mainly the G-7 countries) without input from the debtors themselves are not likely to produce mutually satisfactory solutions. This situation will continue as long as Africa refuses to think strategically, by maintaining the status quo of paying 35 cents or more of every dollar of her export earnings to the debt. But can Africa do otherwise?

Africa has two options to consider. First, she can put a moratorium on her debt service payments for a period of ten years and/or until a sustained real rate of economic growth of 4 percent is achieved. Alternatively, Africa can call for the 'privatization' of her outstanding public and publicly guaranteed external debt. Let us briefly examine each of these two options.

The first option would bring into play the international dimension of Africa's debt crisis, which has been missing so far. This would be through a 'contamination effect' that could trigger a series of crises within the multilateral financial institutions (e.g., IMF, World Bank, and ADB) and subsequently the international financial markets. However, this option will require a fundamental change in African thinking and strategic behavior in her relation with the donor community, especially with the IMF, the World Bank, as well as the African Bank.[23] The difficulty with this option is the hostages' dilemma (Dixit and Nalebuff, 1991) African countries find themselves in. There are many indebted countries (see table 3.2 below), each pursuing her own 'national' interest, so that it is almost impossible to agree on a common strategy and stick to it as stipulated by the first option -- not servicing the debt for an agreed-upon period of time. Each debtor country will be afraid that the creditors will punish her while rewarding other debtors who might be induced and/or intimidated not to follow the group action. In fact, it is the superiority of punishment over reward that makes the countries not entertain such an idea. Avinash Dixit and Barry Nalebuff illustrate the principle of superiority of punishment over reward as follows: "The dictator might keep the populace peaceful by providing it material and even spiritual comforts, but this can be a very costly proposition. Oppression and terror relying on the Hostages' Dilemma can be a much cheaper alternative" (1991:17). This should explain the net outflow of resources from Africa to the IMF and World Bank that I have referred to earlier in this chapter. Jeremy Bulow et al (1991) also confirmed that the order of preference of debt service payments is as follows: the IMF; private creditors; USA and/or G-7 creditor; and other international financial institutions. Yet, a possible show of unity (among the hostages) could send some signal to the capital markets that Africa was seriously considering defaulting on both the bilateral and multilateral outstanding debt. This line of reasoning might become clear if we examine the nature of Africa's debt. In addition, a small number of countries account for a relatively high share of Africa total external debt, which would make it easier to agree on a common strategy.

It is estimated that about three-quarters of the total external debt is owed to official public creditors (African Development Bank, 1995; English and Mule, 1996) and not commercial banks, as was the case in Latin America. This should provide a basis for some strong arguments for a political resolution to Africa's indebtedness, instead of wasting scarce resources in search (e.g., rescheduling) of economic solutions. As argued by English and Mule, "Repeated rescheduling negotiations preoccupy the few senior economic officials who should be devoting their time to improving the policy environment and implementing a coherent long-term development strategy" (1996:142). Some of these searches and negotiations may, however, produce fruitful results. For instance, the African Development Bank has shown that "the Paris Club has now, in principle, agreed to apply 67 per cent reduction of debt and debt service for heavily indebted poor countries that have remained in compliance with IMF and Paris Club agreements for at least three years. It is hoped that an effective resolution to the region's debt problem will shortly be at hand" (African Development Bank, 1995:10). Moreover, it is interesting to note that about 50 percent of the total external debt of Africa has been accumulated by only five countries (see table 3.2 below). These are Egypt

($43.9 b.), Nigeria ($33.44 b.), Algeria ($27.1 b.), Morocco ($22.1 b.), and Côte d'Ivoire ($20.2 b.). These are the countries that can provide the leadership for the highly indebted African states to take the first option. But three of these countries -- Egypt, Morocco and Côte d'Ivoire -- are the darlings of the West, the IMF, and the World Bank. They would not have any economic and political incentives to join the 'strike' in solidarity with the rest. Algeria, on the other hand, is having internal political problems and needs all the external support, such that it would be suicidal for her to join the march. These four countries have about 40 percent (38.3%) of Africa's total external outstanding debt in 1994. Hence, it is only Nigeria that has the potential of providing leadership to those having the remaining 60 percent of Africa's debt, though she also has enormous internal problems of political nature.

By including those countries with $10 billion or more of external debt, four additional countries join the 'big five'. These are Sudan ($16.9 b.), Zaire ($11.8 b.), Angola ($10.1), and Tunisia ($9.5 b). This implies that the 'big nine' accounts for about two-thirds of Africa's total external debt. And if we include countries with $4 billion or more, then we find that 19 African countries have about 84 percent of Africa's total external debt in 1994 (see table 3.2). There are fifteen countries that are likely to follow option one. I will from here on refer to them as the G-15.

A second look at the debt as a percentage of real GDP and debt service ratio for the G-15 highly indebted African countries further shows that some of them would feel better off by not going with the call for a moratorium on their debt. In fact, even Nigeria (see table 3.2) does not have a debt problem per se, as reflected by these ratios. But, it will have political incentives to take the lead. I would therefore think that the G-15, which account for about 44 percent of Africa's debt, can as a group go for the first option. If they do, the reaction of the creditors would be to restrict access to the financial markets for the G-15 countries; write off 16 percent of Africa's total outstanding debt owed by the other smaller economies; and to reduce substantially the remaining 40 percent owed by Egypt, Algeria, Morocco and Côte d'Ivoire.

Table 3.2: Highly Indebted African Countries With More Than US $4.0

COUNTRY	TOTAL EXTERNAL DEBT IN $ MILLION	AS % OF AFRICA	AS % OF REAL GDP	DEBT SERVICE RATION[24]
ALGERIA	27,094	9.0	43.7	72.9
ANGOLA	10,085	3.4	145.2	7.4
CAMEROON	7,080	2.4	110.7	213
CONGO	5,288	1.8	248.5	18.1
COTE	20,156	6.7	295.9	7.8
EGYPT	43,883	14.6	103.1	91.3
ETHIOPIA	4,977	1.7	59.7	33.7
GABON	4,150	1.4	103.9	7.6
GHANA	4,817	1.6	70.9	12.6
KENYA	7,369	2.5	86.7	26.9
MADGASCAR	4,792	1.6	147.2	24.8
MOROCCO	22,092	7.4	123.5	59.9
MOZAMBIQUE	5,585	1.9	96.8	53.7
NIGERIA	33,436	11.2	28.5	20.5
SUDAN	16,847	5.6	170.3	6.5
TUNISIA	9,486	3.2	83.0	34.0
ZAIRE	11,790	3.9	258.5	16.9
ZAMBIA	6,992	2.3	281.0	31.2
ZIMBABWE	4,368	1.5	80.0	31.2
TOTAL	250,287	83.7	49.8	23.9

SOURCE: CONSTRUCTED USING DATA FROM 1995 AFRICAN DEVELOPMENT REPORT, THE AFRICAN DEVELOPMENT BANK.

However, this course of action would cost the creditors more than the G-15. For instance, 44 percent of Africa's debt owed by the G-15 would be a complete loss. Add to this any amount of debt forgiveness and/or grants for the rest of the debtors as a reward for not joining the call for a moratorium. A quick look would indicate that creditors would lose at least 60 percent of the loans owed to them if they try to punish the G-15 while rewarding others. And if they only punish the defaulters without rewarding the compliants, then more debtors would join the line of defaulters. Moreover, this would in turn increase the political milage and image of the G-15 countries in the eyes of the ordinary people in Africa as being patriotic in forcing a resolution to the problem. They would also attract support from the NGO community in the West and the private sector from both the West and Asia, especially the emerging markets in China. These will enable the G-15 to easily regain access to international capital markets. The cost associated with this course of action would in turn induce the official creditors to rethink their strategy and begin to cooperate in finding a mutually satisfactory resolution to Africa's debt problem. In fact, the creditors know that the market value of some of their loans to countries such as Zaire is less than 10 percent (see table 3.3 below), and would therefore be careful in dealing with the debtors under the first scenario.

In fact, it is Africa that needs to be awakened to appreciate her strengths in dealing with the creditors. Even people like President Mobutu would know how to deal with them. I admire the way Mobutu has been doing business with some of Zaire creditors, including the IMF and the World Bank. For instance, it is reported that a crisis erupted in 1988 between Zaire and Belgium, when the Belgian prime minister proposed some debt forgiveness and the rescheduling of commercial loans owed by the Zairian state. The rest of this story is vividly told by William Coplin and Michael O'Leary as follows:

> Mobutu complained that the scheme was not generous enough, and this set off a wave of negative commentary on Mobutu and Zaire in the Belgian press and among opposition politicians. Asserting that funds to relieve Zaire's debt could be better spent at home, the critics contrasted Mobutu's opulent life style at Gbadolite and at his many homes in Europe with the poverty and misery of the majority of

> Zairians. Mobutu retaliated by suspending all re-
> payment on Belgian debts, calling home all Zairian
> students in Belgium and ordering Zairian state com
> panies in Brussels to relocate. Belgium, in turn, sus-
> pended its aid to Zaire. (1991:Zaire, B-3)

The stalemate between Zaire and Belgium was not to last
for long. There was a mutually satisfactory outcome and
this is what I think would happen if the G-15 indebted African countries were to suspend repayments on their debts.
As shown by Coplin and O'Leary in the case of the Zaire-
Belgium confrontation:

> Mutual self interest, however, is a potent force in
> this relationship, and the two sides made progress
> toward healing the breach in July 1989. Mobutu and
> Martens reconciled at the French bicentennial celebra-
> tions, and Belgium announced a debt forgiveness
> program a few days later. Zaire pledged that the
> Zairian companies would return to Belgium and that
> any discrimination against Belgian businessmen in
> Zaire would cease. (1991:B-3)

The second option is to 'privatize' the outstanding debt that
is owed to the bilateral and multilateral creditors, which accounts for about three-fourths of Africa's total external debt.
That is, to trade this portion of the debt in the secondary
capital market. One-fourth, which is owed to private creditors, is already being traded in the international secondary
markets where privately owned developing country debt is
sold. Normally, the portion owed to the multilateral development institutions, such as the African Development Bank,
the World Bank, and IMF, cannot be rescheduled or be written off. This arrangement does not provide sufficient incentives for rational behavior by these institutions. One could,
for instance, argue, from the perspective of a civil society in

Africa, that some of the money was irresponsibly lent by these institutions to governments that were notoriously violating the basic human rights of their citizens, lacked legitimacy, and were certainly not credit worthy at all (for example: Barre's Somalia, Doe's Liberia, El-Bashir's Sudan, Mobutu's Zaire, Numeiri's Sudan, and so forth). In addition, these institutions supported African governments and financed their programs of literally 'crowding out' farmers, and implicated themselves in the growing and marketing of export crops, instead of building roads, schools, health centers, extension services, and so forth. They should therefore share the responsibility and cost of irresponsible lending to countries that were governed by politically risky regimes and for financing shaky investment projects/programs. The only neutral judge in this is the free market.

The new development paradigm (Ndulu, 1996) being practiced in Africa for more than a decade now, through the good guidance of the IMF and World Bank, provides an important point of departure for African policy analysts dealing with the debt problem. I fully support the principle of privatization embedded in the new paradigm. African policy analysts should now be able to apply this principle in dealing with the debt. As shown in table 3.3 below, the risk-based market value of every dollar of the African debt in 1994 ranges between about 80 cents for Tunisia and 8 cents for Zaire. These values are determined by the forces of the free market, which are reflecting the economic and political realities in these countries. The market is saying that the cost of holding, say, a debt owed by Zaire to the creditors is about 80 percent of its face value compared to 20 percent for holding a Tunisian debt. Stated differently, if I were a creditor that had loaned say, one hundred dollars (US$100) to the government of Zaire, and would now like to trade it in the secondary market -- I would only get twenty (US$20) dollars! In the case of Zaire, with a total external outstanding debt of US$11.79 billion in 1994, the market value then was only US$0.9 billion or US$961.0 million. The value of Africa's debt will continue to depreciate in the international secondary market with the passage of time and as long as the vicious circle of indebtedness is not broken. The figures in table 3.3 will eventually be utilized by Africa and her allies in the civil society of the West to find lasting solutions to the problem. They would also reinforce the negotiation position of the G-15 countries when pursuing the first option, which I have presented in the preceding paragraphs.

In fact, one is tempted to draw an analogy between the *apartheid* system in South Africa and Africa's debt. *Apartheid* prevented South Africa from joining the community of civilized nations for a long time, in spite of a fierce struggle against it from both the ANC and the African Front-line states. It was only brought down when the civil society in America and Europe forced both the business community and governments there to divest and disassociate themselves from *apartheid* South Africa.[25] Now the debt problem, as shown earlier, is hindering economic development and social progress in Africa, to the extent that it is preventing African states and people from joining the community of developed nations and free societies. Africa should therefore take her case to the civil society in America and Western Europe. Africa is not asking for debt forgiveness, but for debt 'privatization' -- allow Africa's debt owed to the bilateral and multilateral institutions to be traded in the secondary market. This is because the publicly owned multilateral institutions (IMF, World Bank, ADB, and so on) have no comparative strength (or advantage) in lending money to anybody including governments -- the private sector has a clear comparative advantage. As table 3.3 illustrates, those 19 countries that now have US$250 billion in debt, would repay, according to the market's opinion, only US$109.5 billion.

The difference between the total loans outstanding and the risk-based loan value shown in table 3.3 is about US$141 billion. This amount will be borne by the creditors as a penalty for lending to the above 19 countries -- it is the cost of imprudent investment. Those countries will now have to pay US$109.4 billion instead of US$250.3 billion, but this time to new private owners who bought it from the secondary market. This is the verdict of the free market, which must be respected by both sides -- 19 African states on the one hand, and their public creditors on the other. The market has spoken!

The new owners of the African debt can now begin a more serious business with these countries. It will be to the new creditors interest for African economies to restore sustained growth soonest than later, as this would expand business opportunities. They are also likely to receive enhanced packages of investment incentives, ranging from tax-holidays to other preferential treatment. The role of the multilateral institutions, such as the IMF, the World Bank, and the African Development Bank, would now be confined to policy advice only. Money lending would be left entirely to the private sector. In addition, these institutions will have to compete for policy advice to countries with other private 'think-tanks' and business firms. In fact, the world does not need a 'publicly owned' development bank, nor does Africa need one. The role of the IMF, as a 'central bank' of the world, would be more relevant in this new era of global village and its economy.

Table 3.3: Market Value of Debt of 19 African Countries With More Than US$4.0 Billion in 1994

COUNTRY	TOTAL EXTERNAL DEBT IN $ MILLION	RISKBASED MARKET VALUE[26]	RISK-BASED LOAN VALUE $MILLION
ALGERIA	27,094	46.03	12,471
ANGOLA	10,085	19.9	1,925
CAMEROON	7,080	37.24	2,649
CONGO	5,288	30.44	1,610
COTE	20,156	37.69	7,597
EGYPT	43,883	57.95	25,430
ETHIOPIA	4,977	29.24	1,455
GABON	4,150	46.49	1,929
GHANA	4,817	56.94	2,742
KENYA	7,369	50.45	3,718
MADGASCAR	4,792	39.69	1,902
MOROCCO	22,092	72.06	15,920
MOZAMBIQUE	5,585	20.88	1,166
NIGERIA	33,436	40.78	13,635
SUDAN	16,847	14.6	2,460
TUNISIA	9,486	80.32	7,619
ZAIRE	11,790	8.15	961
ZAMBIA	6,992	25.08	1,754
ZIMBABWE	4,368	56.46	2,466
TOTAL	250,287	na	109,409

na: Not Applicable

However, the IMF would not be allowed to involve itself in the business of money lending, so as to avoid the apparent conflict of interest between policy oversight and rent-seeking. Others may well be privatized or go out of business in fulfillment of the gospel they have been preaching to Africa during the last decade and a half. In fact, these institutions could begin to sell their recipes on macroeconomic formulation, which could be bought by countries if they so wish. Countries would in turn begin to utilize their national experts fully, and hire the services of foreign experts from the market when need arises. There are, for instance, private firms in America that supply temporary personnel to a number of agencies in government and/or the private sector.[27]

I will be the first to admit that those two options are basically unrealistic and naive, given the current weakness of political movements in Africa. They are, however, not ingenuous if the intention, as is the case here, is to provoke critical thinking within the African development policy community, so that lasting solutions to Africa's debt problem are found. I am particularly intrigued by President Mobutu's retaliation referred to earlier. It seems to indicate that Africa's strong men or is it dictators -- General Abacha, Col. Ghadafi, Marshal Mobutu, and so forth -- could force a lasting resolution to Africa's debt problem. But only if they could see some gains, be they political or otherwise, as illustrated by the Zaire-Belgium drama of 1988/89. If these three soldiers do it, they would definitely go down on the bright side of African history.

On a more serious note, President Nelson Mandela has the vision, moral courage, and integrity to convene in South Africa a special session of the OAU to build a consensus among the African leaders on an appropriate course of action that they should take with respect to the debt problem. The African intellectuals should provide various debt relief strategies with a clear cost-benefit analysis for each of them. These will be the policy position briefs on which Africa's consensus would be forged, using the traditional African methods. Once political will and determination is arrived at through consensus, there will be a way for a lasting solution to Africa's debt, a solution that meets the mutual self interest of both the debtor and the creditor.

Resolving Internal Conflicts

Africa's internal conflicts are among the major obstacles toward achieving social harmony, ecological stability, and economic growth in the continent. Although internal conflicts are presently taking place in less than half a dozen countries, their 'contamination effect' within the sub-regions in which they are occurring make their quick resolution one of the leading issues in African development. For countries that are at war with themselves, it is difficult to see how the four other leading issues -- economic reform, democratization, environmental protection, and poverty reduction -- could effectively be addressed without first resolving the conflict. Besides loss of innocent life, scarce resources (human and material) are being diverted from productive activities and channeled into more military expenditure. This has led Nadir Mohammed to conclude that "military spending is generated mainly by its internal logic, unconfined by the calculus of marginal loses and gains implied by the rational optimization of the State of some well-defined social welfare function, as might be the case in developed countries" (1993:96). Richard Joseph (1995) has recently reminded us of Thomas Hobbes' point that "conflict is intrinsic to the human condition," a factor which "underlies the necessity of organized society endowed with an accepted political authority. Otherwise, life degenerates into a war of all against all"(1995:11). It is the lack of accepted political authority that is the root cause of Africa's economic, social, and politi--cal problems. The intrinsic nature of conflict to the African condition will become clearer if we look at its primary roots.

There are, according to Richard Joseph, three fundamental sources of conflict in Africa. These are: "struggles to consolidate political power, boundary disputes and interstate hegemonic rivalries" (1995:10). Furthermore, Margaret Vogt (1995) has identified four major factors characterizing the new generation of African conflicts. They are: (a) struggle for the reform and democratization of the political and economic systems; (b) ethnic competition, steaming from the collapse of the old patterns of relationships that provided the framework for collaboration among the many ethnic groups of which most African countries are composed; (c) issues relating to religious and ethnic differences and religious fundamentalism; and (d) disputes over traditional land boundaries, resource sharing, and equitable distribution of political and economic power within the state system. The first two factors (a & b) identified by Vogt are essentially covered by the first point in Joseph Richard's three sources of Africa's conflict.

I believe that it is the first source -- the struggle to consolidate power -- which often triggers the conflict. It is the failure of the state to guarantee an equitable sharing of resources (economic, social, and political) which leads to the eruption of conflicts in most cases. As shown by Mohammed, civil wars "usually develop out of domestic conflict over the distribution of wealth or political power, or as a result of internal repression" (1993:103). A seminal work of Crawford Young, which has culminated in his 1994 book, The African Colonial State In Comparative Perspective, provides a valuable guide to how the post-independence nationalist state took on the functional structures of its predecessor. Instead of being a liberator and equalizer for all, the nationalist state used cultural pluralism and ethnicity to galvanize the civil society, to divide it and rule it along ethnic cleavages in the name of consolidating national unity. The imperative of nation building was thus missed, a point which led Hettne some years ago to ponder:

> If the development of nation states really was a necessary path to progress, the African people in particular will have to pay a heavy price. According to South (January 1985) 25 states of the 51 members of the OAU are under military rule, 90 coups have taken place since 1960, the armed forces comprise 6.2 per 1,000 (to be compared with a Third World average of 3.4), the import of arms 1976-80 amounted to 55.5 billion dollars (26.5 billion in the rest of the Third World) and more than 3.5 million people have been killed in uprisings, civil wars and massacres. In spite of all this suffering, the nation states do not seem to be on firmer ground today than when they emerged after decolonization. (Hettne, 1990:31)

African people have paid a heavy price because a national state was constructed through "the application of overwhelming military force" (Joseph, 1995:12). Such a nation state would undoubtedly be unstable and/or unsustainable as evidenced by the case of the former Soviet Union and/or Ethiopia prior to May 1991. Traditional African methods of mediation, conciliation, and consensus building could have been used in forging a multi-ethnic nation state. And the current global consensus on basic human rights embedded in freedom and liberty should enable Africa to apply new methods -- free democratic elections/referendum -- to ascertain the free will of the people to live, or not to live, together in a nation state constructed through a military force. In agreement with Mamadou Dia, it is important that in "ethnically divided societies - which means most countries of Sub-Saharan Africa - finding a workable medium between national reconciliation and the preservation of institutional and ethnic pluralism (as was done in South Africa) may be one promising way of achieving peace and stability" (1996:250).

The other two sources of conflict in Africa --boundary disputes and interstate hegemonic rivalries -- are, in my view, induced by the 'contamination effect' referred to earlier. African states quite often blame their neighbor(s) for their own internal problems (e.g., Sudan), which in turn reopens old disputes over traditional land boundaries. This also created, in some instances, the interstate hegemonic rivalries, which were largely influenced by the ideological flickering of the competitive politics of the Cold War era. This ideological glimmering is vividly dramatized by one of the first African leaders of independence -- Kwame Nkrumah. In the introduction of his book on neo-colonialism, he stated:

In the first place, the rulers of neo-colonial States derive their authority to govern, not from the will of

the people, but from the support which they obtain
from their neo-colonialist masters. They have therefore little interest in developing education, strengthening the bargaining power of their workers employed by expatriate firms, or indeed of taking any
step which would challenge the colonial pattern of
commerce and industry, which it is the object of neo-
colonialism to preserve. (1965:XV)

As illustrated by the above citation, I would argue that
boundary disputes and ideological/hegemonic rivalries were
used as scapegoats for internal repression, which inevitably
fuelled civil wars. It will be recalled that Africa was an important battleground of the Cold War, evidenced by the
Congo crisis in the 1960s and by Angola and Ethiopia in the
1970s and 1980s. But according to Richard Joseph: "All three
vectors of actual and potential conflict in Africa have been
contained by the combined action of certain forces and phe-
nomena: Cold War geopolitics; the Africa policy of particular European and Middle East states; the commitment to
preserving African boundaries and respecting non-interfer-
ence in the internal affairs of the OAU and other continental
bodies; the `apolitical'[28] postures of multilateral and bilat-
eral providers of aid and loans, who persisted in making
external financial resources available regardless of the nature of the regimes in power; and the inability of African
political and civil society to halt or reverse the entrenchment
of authoritarian regimes, whether civilian or military (or
amalgams of the two)" (1995:10). In spite of this contain-
ment, Africa witnessed during the last three decades conflicts at several fronts.

The horn of Africa has been at war with itself and with
nature for most of the 1980s, and internal conflicts are continuing in Somalia and Sudan. The Somali state has collapsed,
but the conflict has not spread beyond her boundaries. The
conflict in Sudan is, on the other hand, threatening regional

stability. Chad, Eritrea, Ethiopia, and Uganda are likely to be drawn into the conflict generated by the hegemonic behavior of Sudanese Islamic fundamentalism. Uganda achieved peace and tranquility after the National Resistance Army (NRA) came to power in 1986. There are still, however, pockets of resistance in the northern part of Uganda, which can affect long-term economic development and social progress in the area. The NRM, which I have referred to earlier as a broadly based political movement, provides the kind of accepted political authority that is necessary to guarantee tranquility and happiness in the country.

In Southern Africa, the conflicts in Angola and Mozambique have been resolved at last. *Apartheid* has been finally dismantled in the Republic of South Africa, with the victory of the African National Congress (ANC) and with Nelson Mandela becoming the first black president. In Central and West Africa, tensions and/or civil wars are continuing in Burundi, Rwanda, Liberia, and Sierra Leone[29], despite the efforts of the Organization of African Unity (OAU) and the Economic Community of West African States (ECOWAS) peace-keeping force.

The final front is what Margaret Vogt has identified earlier as the "struggle for the reform and democratization of the political and economic systems" (1995:2). For instance, attempts at multi-party politics have rekindled religious, ethnic, and regional tensions in Burundi, Cameroon, Kenya, Nigeria, and Zaire. In addition, the threat of Islamic fundamentalism is jeopardizing stability and development in North Africa, especially in Algeria and Egypt.

But the end of the Cold War should provide an important opportunity for Africa to rapidly and peacefully resolve all the current internal conflicts. However, if the current wave of Islamic fundamentalism continues, Africa may once again find herself as a battleground between Islamic-capitalist fundamentalism on the one hand, and neoliberal capitalism on the other. Africa is quite vulnerable to the two opposing capitalist systems, due to the fact that it shares common features with each of them. It shares with Islamic-capitalist fundamentalism the importance of social solidarity, Islamic, and traditional cultural values over the free market mechanism and its institutions. On the other hand, Africa and neoliberal capitalism have a common view on the need to respect basic human rights and civil liberties, emphasizing the separation between the state and the church. It would seem to me that the rise of Islamic-capitalist fundamentalism, at least in the case of Algeria, Egypt, and Sudan, results from the perceived subordination of the Islamic culture -- religious and traditional social values -- to those of the market. This has been compounded by what Robert Klitgaard (1994) calls "the failure of dependent development in Africa." The challenge, then, is for African scholarship to critically examine the two contentious points that are likely to turn the continent into a battleground over them, and to come up with appropriate strategies. I would argue, however, that the `contamination effect' of Islamic fundamentalism will go beyond the African boundaries -- it will creep to the rest of the world, if it is not contained and eliminated now!

A recent workshop on the international response to conflict in Africa, organized by the Christian Michelsen Institute, concluded that: "In the post-Cold War world, armed conflicts such as civil wars are no longer simply the internal affairs of states, as envisaged by the United Nations Charter when it was framed 50 years ago. Today, they affect all of us, whether we live in their proximity or far afield" (1995:5). The resolution of Africa's civil wars will, however, require political courage and resources, which seem to be in short supply both in Africa and the rest of the world, as epitomized by the U.N.'s premature disengagement in Somalia and Rwanda. African political courage and vision are needed to resolve these conflicts. This is because the "political authority remained in a state of war with its own people" (Joseph, 1995:12). Once this political authority realizes --

as was the case with F.W. de Klerk's *apartheid* South Africa -- that such a war is not sustainable, the solution becomes within reach. One may disagree with the policies of F.W. de Klerk, but one should admire his courage and vision to see the non-viability of the apartheid system and therefore to dismantle it. This should provide exit models for those who are still maintaining a political authority that is at war with its own people. Mandela's South Africa has proven de Klerk right in peacefully dismantling the *apartheid* system. President Mandela provided what Mamadou Dia rightly calls "a leadership commitment to a more inclusive institutional formula behind which entire nations can rally" (1996:250). These are the kind of political leaders that Africa needs in resolving her internal conflicts, so as to ensure prosperity and human dignity for all the African people in the 21st century.

Conclusion

We have thus far examined the nature and magnitude of the six leading issues in African development. These issues will undoubtedly continue, in my view, to dominate the development agenda of Africa at the turn of the century. There are several recipes -- policy prescriptions for the treatment of Africa's multi-faceted malaise -- currently on the shelves and many more are being produced year-round. From them Africa can choose suitable ones for each of the leading issues. What seems to be lacking, though, is the kind of broad-based political movement that is urgently needed to provide the necessary and sufficient conditions for the implementation of these recipes. That is, an acceptable political authority which is in a constant state of dialogue with its people would have by definition tackled the intertwined issues of democratization and conflict resolution. The challenge, then, for such a political authority would be to simultaneously address the other four issues -

- economic reform; poverty reduction; environmental protection; and debt relief -- in African development.

By way of achieving an acceptable political authority, Africa will have to revisit her past in search of models that could be modified and adapted to the present global environment. The geopolitics of the post-Cold War era seem to be, in my view, favorable for Africa to experiment with various systems of government. What, for instance, can be learned from Nyerere's Tanzania? Was it not at peace with her self and in a state of dialogue with her people? Tanzania has now fully completed a smooth transition to multi-party democracy, a transition made smooth because of the spirit of a person-in-community rooted in *ujamaa*. Nevertheless, I would argue that economic *ujamaa* was a failure, and this is what the new political leadership in Tanzania will have to address now.

Africa now has, more than any other time in her post-independent history, an array of models of political systems to choose from without being harassed. Two of these models stand a good chance for rescuing Africa from her present complex problems. These are the South Africa model of inclusion and the Ugandan multi-ethnic broad-based political movement. In fact, Nelson Mandela has shown that in Africa politics and/or governing should not be a zero-sum game. It is a point that has been romanticized by Jeune Afrique Economie as follows:

> What simplicity, what modesty by the victorious. In fact, except for the extremists to whom Nelson Mandela continues to extend a reconciliatory hand, there are no losers. Everyone is victorious. What a lesson in tolerance from this South African experience. The major philosophy behind this is the strong and unanimous desire of all political actors not to marginalize anyone during this transition phase. And this is the essential lesson that the rest of Africa

should retain from the wisdom coming from the south of our continent. How much time would have been gained, how many tears and how much suffering our people would have avoided, if at the ends of the national conferences and other democratic experiments, the emphasis had been on building transitions that are foundations for national reconciliation instead of arenas for the sterile struggle to get even.[30]

I share the sentiment forcefully expressed in the above passage, that the South African model of inclusion and tolerance is a contribution of which Africa should be proud. The quest for prosperity, social harmony, and human dignity in the 21st century should be the preoccupation of all the African political movements and their leaders. For this would in turn guarantee that economic policies and strategies which undermine the social fabric of African societies, reduce the quality of natural resources, lead to political polarization, and alienate national expertise are not applied. It is therefore the duty and moral obligation of African intellectuals to begin the search for integrative models that will facilitate the reconstruction of an African development paradigm.

NOTES

1. Quoted from the Financial Times of May 6, 1996, page 14.
2. Siegfried Pausewang of the Christian Michelsen Institute (CMI) has pointed out to me, while reading one of the manuscripts of this book, that the concept of civil society in its historical context refers only to urban intellectuals and the business sector. It is, however, used in this book in a much wider context of an African community, which includes all segments of the society including urban elites and the business sector.
3. Brackets in the original text.
4. Uganda is the first country in Africa to have a woman Vice President of the Republic.
5. The situation in Zaire has now been resolved by Laurent Kabila's Alliance Forces which overthrew Mobutu in May 1997 and renamed the country as Democratic Republic of Congo.
6. I have left out South Africa from this list, since it is a special case.
7. Numeiri, then president of the Sudan, in his last days of desperation to stay in office, is reported to have signed an agreement with a European firm to dump toxic chemicals and industrial wastes in Sudan. As for Nigeria, I came across a confidential correspondence in 1992, between a Nigerian company and a Norwegian firm, in which the former was trying to convince the latter to look for business of exporting industrial toxic wastes to Africa. This was published in Eco-Afrique newsletter of the Environment and Social Policy of the African Development Bank (ADB). In addition, the ADB alerted the Nigerian authorities to the scam.
8. Quoted from Findings. Number 31, January 1995, published by Africa Technical Department, Africa Region, The World Bank, Washington, D.C. (USA).

9.   The importance of traders and processors was pointed out to me by John Staatz of Michigan State University (MSU), while commenting on a draft of a paper for a workshop on Agricultural Transformation in Africa. See Deng et al (1995).

10.   Dunstan Spencer (1995) has estimated that a total investment of US$38 billion will be required "in order to bring the rural road network to a level equivalent to that of India in the early 1950s, by the year 2010, in high potential South and East Zones" of Africa. This is a substantial amount of money that will be difficult to come by if the present trends continue.

11.   Spencer (1995) gives a different classification for sub-Saharan Africa. But a group of African researchers and development practitioners recently agreed in Abidjan, Cote d'Ivoire, on six categories: arid/semi-arid; moist savanna/sub-humid; humid; medium/high altitude; mediterranean; and high veld (temperate). This group of experts made a statement with respect to the categorization as follows: "The above classification is useful not only for guiding technology generation, but also for defining resource management programs, examining issues related to comparative advantage and specialization, as well as for general policy formulation. In using this stratification for policy formulation, one would need to take into consideration other factors such as: the prevailing political, institutional, administrative and economic systems; the existence of regional economic organizations, as well as factors relating to demography and infrastructure."

12.   ECOWAS stands for Economic Community of West Africa States, and COMESA is Common Market of East and Southern Africa.

13.   Quoted from a paper produced by MSU entitled "Confronting the Silent Challenge of Hunger: A Conference Synthesis." This conference was held on 28-29 June 1994.

14.   Claude Ake (1995) has recently referred to it as "poverty of ideas," while Mahmood Mamdani (1993) has earlier called as "ideological poverty." I would think that we are all saying the same thing -- 'intellectual poverty.'

15.   Inverted commas in the original text.

16.   A lot has been written by African scholars, as evidenced by the above quotation from the first African Nobel lau reate in literature, Wole Soyinka. However, it has not been incorporated in a systematic way into the formulation of an African development paradigm by those responsible for Africa's development, i.e., policy-makers (of course, with the exception of Nyerere) and development practi tioners. In addition, most of this writing is published and disseminated outside Africa, thus making it inaccessible to policy analysts, though not to institutions such as the African Development Bank.

17.   Most of this section of the chapter has been published else where. See Lual A. Deng. (1995). Poverty Reduction: Les- sons and Experiences from Sub-Saharan Africa, Environ- ment and Social Policy (ESP) Working paper number 6. African Development Bank: Abidjan, Cote d'Ivoire.

18.   These categories are not necessarily mutually exclusive.

19.   Until recently, cocoa farmers in Ghana were getting about 36 cents out of every US$1.0 of cocoa export earnings.

20.   The statistics are obtained from tables in WRI, World Re- sources 1992-93. 1992, p.272.

21.   From "Findings," number 35, March 1995, Africa Region. The World Bank: Washington, D.C.

22.   These are actual payments. The ratio is low for some coun- tries such as Sudan (see table 3.2) that are not fully servic- ing their debt because of sympathy from creditors (Côte d'Ivoire) or just because of unwillingness to pay (Sudan). But it could be due to high domestic debts, as pointed out by English and Mule (1996), which make the countries unable to meet fully scheduled external debt service payments.

23.	Mr. Babacar Ndiaye, former President of the African development Bank (ADB), and Dr. Ismail Serageldin, Vice President for Environmentally Sustainable Development of the World Bank, frequently refer to the ADB as the African Bank. I agree with their sentiment, for it gives me a sense of pride to say "the African Bank." I used to admire the motto of the bank then: "ADB in the service of Africa!" I think I included this aphorism in some of the major statements of President Ndiaye that I was asked sometimes to draft, especially with respect to the new areas of environment, poverty, population, social policy, and women in development.

24.	This is calculated on the basis of debt service payments actually paid. It is not on the basis of scheduled debt service payments due, which have made the ratio much higher for all the countries. I thank Philip English for asking me to make this important distinction.

25.	Of course with courageous and visionary leaders on both sides of the divided country -- Mandela's democratic South Africa on the one hand, and de Klerk's *apartheid* South Africa on the other.

26.	These rates are from a table on "AfDB Loan Portfolio at Market Value as of 30 September 1994," given to the author on 27 February 1995 by a USA Treasury Official.

27.	I believe even the World Bank uses such services for its support staff!

28.	Inverted commas in the original text.

29.	Elections for a multi-party democracy have been held recently and a civilian president has taken office, but was overthrown by a new military coup in May, 1997.

30.	Quoted from Mamadou Dia (1996:250).

CHAPTER FOUR

IN SEARCH OF AN AFRICAN MODEL OF DEVELOPMENT

◆

There is, however, another lesson which we can learn from the Chinese revolution. It is that courage, enthusiasm, and endurance are not enough. There must also be discipline, and the intelligent application of policies to the needs and circumstances of the country and the time. There is no single answer which is applicable in all times and at all places. Each country and each generation has to deal with its own problems in its own way, exploiting to the greatest possible advantage such opportunities as are available to it. This means that the different countries of the world will use different methods, and different systems, of economic, social and political organization. It is only by doing so that each of them will achieve the common aim of human progress and betterment.

-Julius Nyerere (1968:33)

The needs and circumstances of Africa have evolved over the last thirty years. However, the objective of public policy —human progress and betterment —has not changed. As shown in the preceding chapters, the failure of the African development project was due mainly to lack of discipline (witnessed by corruption and nepotism) and the unintelligent application of uncritically examined development paradigms drawn from entirely different circumstances to the objective conditions of Africa during the last thirty years (1965-94). Yet, we must not lose sight of the fact that Nyerere's generation of African leaders brought political independence to Africa and should therefore be commended for it. The challenge now is for the contemporary generation of African researchers and policy analysts to provide appropriate frameworks for solving Africa's problems of persistent underdevelopment. This is essentially a call for the second independence, which will have to be fought for and brought about by the African intellectuals[1]. The first independence was a political one, while the second would be economic[2]. The two are interdependent, and no one is complete without the other. Some may argue, however, that it was the failure of the political authority in the post-independence period which aborted an economic sovereignty. But the nature of the competitive security geopolitics of the Cold War era could not have made it otherwise. Whatever is the case, Africa is now beset with problems that are multivariate and which urgently need attention and concerted efforts toward their solution.

Africa is currently being advised by some policy analysts with, good intentions, to try the 'Asian miracle' model. I would, however, argue that the time has come for Africa to look at her own history; a history which is full of both glory and humiliation — but so is the history of mankind as well as of nations. This is because development models that are based on entirely different histories would not, in my view, be legitimized by African history. For instance, the analysis in the preceding chapters, especially with respect to the various attempts at African development during the period 1965-1994, has shown how and why these efforts have not generally been successful in improving the well-being of a majority of African people and in producing an African model of development. What we have seen instead was a systematic attempt at 'imitative' development—from both capitalist and Marxist-Leninist models—with inherent contradictions and incompatibility with African system(s) of thought. In an overview, more than a decade ago, of the African economic crisis, Deng and Mou concluded that "both capitalism and communism have failed to answer problems of underdevelopment in Africa, in that they failed to meet the needs of the vast majority of the African populations as manifested by the present crisis" (1985:36).

Claude Ake has also recently reminded us that "in the past, Africa tended to proceed ad hoc, responding to apparent opportunities but mostly driven by pressures in the domestic and international environment, in what has proved to be a journey without maps to an uncertain destination" (1995:17). As elucidated by the above epigraph from the writings of Julius Nyerere, it is the duty of our generation to provide these `maps' for a journey toward Africa's destiny, by tackling the six leading issues in African development, identified and presented earlier in chapter three. This is to be done through frameworks that integrate African social values and institutions with the economic fundamentals contained in contemporary development theories. Microeconomic theory, for instance, provides useful frameworks for the analysis of the behavior of various economic agents—consumers, producers, households, and firms. Of particular interest are the principles of welfare economics and household production models. This is because the individual is, in my view, the fundamental unit of the family, community/society, and the state. And the quest for development is about the well-being and dignity of each and every individual person in any African community, and not about macroeconomic indicators aggregated in the GNP, inflation rate, money supply, and so forth. In agreement

with Herman Daly and John Cobb, I "believe that economics can rethink its theories from the viewpoint of person-in-
community and still include the truth and insight it gained
when it thought in individualistic terms. . . and the willingness to subordinate the market to purposes that it is not
geared to determine" (1989:8). This useful concept of a "person-in-community" can be elucidated further through the
following words by Francis Deng: "Since permanent identity and influence is both communal and individual, rights
over property are also communal and individual. Even the
mythicals, who are often referred to as a collectivity, have
claims as individuals. It is important to expose the true balance between individual and social interests in wealth and
the factors conditioning their expression" (1971:245). This
balancing between individual and social interests in wealth
should, in my view, constitute the basis for a sustainable
development that one would like to see in Africa.

Furthermore, Abdelwahab El-Affendi urges us to "start
thinking about Africans," as "the living, flesh and blood
individuals who populate the continent, each of whom is a
distinct human being with his own history, life, concerns
and individual personality" (1991:37). The challenge, then,
is for a development policy formulator to make use of some
of these principles in the concerted search for an integrative
African model of development. It should be mentioned here
that we are not looking *per se* for a theory of development to
explain Africa's inability to develop. Our main preoccupation is to find an African model of sustainable development
that would restore human dignity and decent living to ordinary people in Africa. In the words of Michael Prowse, "On
the eve of the 21st century, people ought to be accorded equal
dignity and an equal shot at the attractive jobs and positions in society.[3]" Stated differently, the new model should
essentially be an 'africanization' of economic principles
and/or knowledge in its application to the needs and circumstances of Africa in the 1990s and beyond. And as ar-

gued byW.P.Preston (1987), "all knowledge is culturally context-dependent." In this regard, the consistency between development theory and practice would be inherent in the model, for it would be based on African culture which, according to Wole Soyinka, is to be seen "as an expression of a total way of productive life." With an integrative model as a `road-map', Africa would then be able to join the community of developed nations in their long quest for sustainable development that is characterized by stability, prosperity, happiness, human dignity, and self-respect.

A common understanding of what is meant by sustainable development is needed at this juncture before we examine the basic elements of an integrative African model. I define sustainable development as a development that combines economic growth with poverty reduction, protection of the environment, and enhancement of social capital[4], within the overall framework of a stable political system of government. Sustainable development, conceived in this way, should ensure that attention and resources are objectively allocated among its four main components. But this presupposes a broad-base political authority which can ensure the active participation of all the stakeholders in the management of their development. As shown by Mamadou Dia, there are now emerging examples of this political authority in Africa. I fully agree with Dia's assessment that "The South African model also conjures up interesting possibilities of decentralization involving genuine empowerment of local or regional entities in an ethnically and culturally divided society without sacrificing national unity" (1996:250). Moreover, such a broad-based political authority would enable Africa to implement strategies for achieving the four components of sustainable development. As stated earlier, the problem in Africa is not the lack of policy packages (many are on the shelves), but rather the inability to translate policies into effective actions. Our focus, then, should be on those frameworks that would enable Africa to manage her development—the political authority for implementing prescribed policy packages as an integral part of the African model of development. This will be the day on which Africa would have achieved both political and economic independence.

There are many definitions of sustainable development, but only four will suffice. The first one is provided by the Brundtland Commission, which in fact brought the concept of sustainable development to the contemporary literature on development. The Commission defines sustainable development as "meeting" the needs of the present generation without compromising the needs of future generations" (1987:8). It qualifies this concept by stating that "In the end, sustainable development is not a fixed state of harmony, but rather a process of change in which the exploitation of resources, the direction of investments, the orientation of technological development, and institutional change are made consistent with future as well as present needs" (1987:9). The second definition is a relatively comprehensive one, by David Pearce, Edward Barbier, and Anil Markandya (1990). They first define development as "a vector of desirable social objectives; that is, it is a list of attributes which society seeks to achieve or maximize" (1990:2). In this regard, they identify six elements of this vector as: (i) increases in real income per capita; (ii) improvements in health and nutritional status; (iii) educational achievement; (iv) access to resources; (v) a fairer distribution of income; and (vi) increases in basic freedoms. Then they define sustainability as "the general requirement that a vector of development characteristics be non-decreasing over time, where the elements to be included in the vector are open to ethical debate and where the relevant time horizon for practical decision-making is similarly indeterminate outside of agreement on intergenerational objectives" (1990:3). Third, Jan Pronk and Mahbub ul Haq view sustainable development as "a process in which economic, fiscal, trade, energy, agricultural,

The challenge is therefore upon us, in the case of Africa, to add indices of cultural and social values; liberty and/or political participation; and natural resource conservation. In fact, the UNDP (cf. the 1995 Human Development Report) is aware of these needs, and attempts are under way to create methodologies that would make it possible to include additional components in the HDI. A recent study by two economists — Oladeji Ojo and Temitope Oshikoya — of the African Development Bank has found that "civil liberty appears to be the only proxy for political instability with a significant negative effect on growth" (1994:17). Moreover, life expectancy and educational attainment indices should normally reflect the social values and cultural heritage of the country being considered. They also reflect the nature and magnitude of poverty (Deng and Tjønneland, 1996). Hence, the development problem can be restated as: *The development objective in Africa is to achieve an HDI of 0.95 by the year 2020,* subject to the following general constraints:

a) economic reform;
b) democratization;
c) environmental protection;
d) poverty reduction;
e) controlling indebtedness, and
f) resolving internal conflicts.

As stated earlier, I have taken the HDI as an approximation of a public policy objective, which each African state should aim to acheive at a given point of time by stating its value and the time-frame. This formulation of the social welfare function in terms of HDI is practical since its value is known. Moreover, it is a more convenient way to analytically express the social welfare function. As given in chapter three, the global HDI average is 0.88, while the highest is 0.95 for Canada. For African countries to achieve the present Canada's HDI of 0.95[5] by the year 2020, they will have to simultaneously tackle the leading issues in African development — that is, the above six constraints[6]. However, there industrial and all other policies are so designed as to bring about development that is economically, socially and ecologically sustainable" (1992:1). And finally, the UNDP calls it sustainable human development if it is "pro-people, pro-jobs and pro-nature" (1994:4).

The objective of a sustainable development is human progress and betterment. The most important aspect of the objective as stated here is that it elucidates what Preston (1987) calls "the centrality of human life" in the development process. In fact, human progress and betterment is essentially a total life of the community/society and not of an individual, for that of individual comes to an end with death. A real society does not die. But, if we add the spiritual dimension, then we can also include eternal life for an individual. There is no end to human progress and betterment, it is "being-in-the-world" (Preston, 1987:45) and in paradise. Moreover, it is articulated in Francis Deng's concept of the permanent identity and influence conviction of the Dinka people of southern Sudan. It will be recalled from the preceding chapter that for a normal person to have dignity and self-respect, s/he must have basic needs met. The basic needs of a normal human being consist of primary and secondary needs. The role of public policy, then, is to safeguard the overall well-being of each and every individual in a community. This is possible only in a broadly based political system of government in which ordinary people are sufficiently empowered to fully participate in managing the development of their respective communities. In this regard, it will be assumed that there exists a community/society social welfare function, which is synonymous with that of each and every individual of the community. I consider this approach to be superior to the conventional microeconomic technique of assuming a two-person economy and then generalizing from there. It also facilitates a broad conceptualization that goes beyond economics, but without excluding it.

One important lesson from the failed efforts at African development over the last thirty years is that we can no longer focus only on growth while ignoring the other three components with the hope that they will automatically be tackled when economic growth "trickles down" to them. The four main parts (there could be others depending on the situation at hand) have to be consolidated into a single objective of public policy. I have stated earlier that human progress and betterment were the main objective of public policy, but I believe that the concept of sustainable development is more consistent with the current global thinking, as articulated by Pearce, Barbier and Markandya (1990). It is also conceptually consistent with our approach to the six leading issues in African development, which are constraining this objective of public policy in Africa. Hence, we can conceptually state that the development problem facing a policy formulator in Africa is how to achieve sustainable development—maximize the society's well-being or a vector of desirable social objectives—subject to the following constraints:

a)   economic reform;
b)   democratization;
c)   environmental protection;
d)   poverty reduction;
e)   controlling indebtedness, and
f)   resolving internal conflicts.

Another way of stating the above development policy problem facing a policy analyst is to express it in terms of the UNDP Human Development Index (HDI) that I referred to in chapter three. That is, making the HDI as a proxy for public policy objective. This will make it possible to measure progress toward the objective of sustainable development. The HDI, as mentioned in the previous chapter, consists of three main indices—life expectancy at birth, educational attainment, and adjusted real GDP per capita. Three

additional indices on cultural values, environment, and ci
liberty could be added, to create an enhanced HDI. It w
be recalled that there are two aspects of the developme
objective - quantitative as reflected in progress and quali
tive captured by betterment. In this regard, I would thi
that a useful quantitative measurement of human progre
is the HDI, especially its life expectancy and education i
dices sub-components. The gross national product and GN
per capita are not good measures of human progress, f
they tend to gloss over the humane aspect of developme
by focusing only on the quantitative growth of physic
objects (for example, increase in the number of cars pr
duced), rather than on human beings. As regards to hu
man betterment, one is forced to be subjective to a grea
extent and use some moral judgements such as rates of crim
increase, rate of family unit breakdown, social disintegra
tion, and so forth. These rates, from the perspective of so
cial harmony, are negatively correlated with human be
terment; that is, the higher they are, the lower the qualit
of human betterment and vice versa. However, a real mea
sure of human betterment with respect to social harmony
and stability is tranquility in all its dimensions. A state o
tranquility ensures dignity and self-respect for all the indi
viduals in a given community/society/state. In describing
the concept of *cieng* among the Dinka people of southern
Sudan, Francis Deng states that "good human relations are
expressed in the demand for unity and harmony among
men and the attuning of individual interests to the interests of others. This goal is more than avoidance of conflict
and violation of other people's rights; it imposes a positive
obligation to foster a solidarity in which people cooperate
in the shaping and sharing of values. Coercion is contrary
to *cieng*, for solidarity, harmony, and mutual indulgence
are more meaningful if achieved voluntarily or by persuasion" (1971:26).

are inherent contradictions within the constraints, on the one hand, and between them and the development policy objective itself, on the other. But, in agreement with Hettne, "it is the totality of and inherent contradictions in this situation that constitutes the development problem to be addressed by development theorists, not the relationship between inflationary rate, balance of payment and budget deficits, which is a purely economic problem" (1990:22). Furthermore, Hettne warns us that "a society cannot be reduced to its economic sector and the economic sector cannot be reduced to impersonal market forces" (1990:22). This is the underlying assumption of our project.

The role of a policy analyst/formulator, then, is to recommend economic strategies that seek the greatest good for all the African people. For it is now well documented that African traditional economic system(s) sought the greatest good for all its members, since this is embedded in their cultures and social institutions. Moreover, the individual is envisaged to maximize her/his own utility within the economic and institutional constraints of the community. The utility function constrains development policy formulators not to formulate policies and strategies that would impinge on the individual utility, for it could negatively affect overall human progress and betterment in the society. Again, Platteau observes this important feature in stating: "We have seen above that in agricultural tribal societies guaranteed access to land plots with varying risk and fertility characteristics together with self-insurance strategies normally allow all member households to obtain a minimum income and to avert starvation over a full weather cycle" (1991:125). This would, in my view, ascertain the humaneness and justness of development policy.

In light of the preceding paragraph, policy analysts and development policy formulators should be able to design appropriate policies and strategies that enable persons-in-community to have a decent living and human dignity. What they need first, as Platteau (1991:155) articulates, is "more scientific humility, owing to the bewildering variety of the organizational forms encountered" in traditional societies. And secondly, they need a correct understanding of the economic, social, and political institutions and processes underlying the structures of African societies or nation-states. In addition, they should carefully listen to Rudiger Dornbusch's (1988) valuable advice on some of the mistakes to be avoided with respect to economic policy formulation: "The list of mistakes to be avoided is endless. The problem is that no clear set of rules can easily be applied to any policy situation. . . . Resource allocation that is a little bit worse but provides a more equal distribution of consumption and opportunities does not have to be condemned. Economics does not require that efficient resource allocation take precedence over social considerations. In economics, as in other fields, there is often more than one way to skin a cat. Other things being equal, we should pick the one that raises consumption for some without lowering that of others" (1988:51). In the context of African development policy formulation, such an understanding is further illustrated by the following citation from Platteau:

> In the first place, there are all the collective rules and mechanisms that govern the distribution of available productive assets or work opportunities in such a way that every household in the community has a reliable guarantee of survival over the full weather cycle. At one extreme, one finds kin-based societies (for example, descent groups of a corporate kind such as the many African patrilineage systems)[7] in which a relatively egalitarian access to natural resources is guaranteed to each member. (1991:156)

The dilemma of an African development policy formulator — adherence to economic fundamentals in the formulation of development policies, on the one hand, and of respecting the African social fabric (institutions and value systems), on the other — should now be resolved in light of the above well articulated passages from Dornbusch and Platteau. An enhanced HDI would be able to appreciate the need for such a balance. By way of establishing mechanisms for the assessment and monitoring of progress toward the stated public policy objective of achieving 0.95 HDI value by the year 2020, the HDI is to be conceived as a function of the following six indices:

a) Adjusted real GDP per capita index;
b) Life expectancy index;
c) Educational attainment index;
d) Cultural values (or social capital) index;
e) Environmental index; and
f) Civil liberty or political pluralism index

The index of cultural values[8] (social capital) can be approximated by violence and crime indices given in the 1995 UNDP Human Development Report. There is an inverse relationship between social capital, that is cultural values and social norms, on the one hand, and violence and crime, on the other. A higher index of violence and crime, for example, would imply a deterioration in the value systems of the society, which would subsequently impact negatively (reduces HDI) on human progress and betterment. That is, violence and crime deplete and depreciate the social capital (trust, norms, horizontal networks, and so forth) of the society. The volume of human and material resources being used in combating violence and crime is increasing in a number of countries. These are resources which could have been utilized in enhancing the quality of life of the society, and in this respect, crime is not only a moral problem, but also an economic one. Similarly, the environmental index is a composite of indices on CO_2 (carbon dioxide) emission, air and water pollution, soil erosion, deforestation, toxic chemicals and industrial wastes, and so forth. These also have negative effect on the level of HDI, since they are being approximated by factors that would reduce its value through any marginal change (increase) — lower the quality of life instead of enhancing it. Most of these indices are reported in the UNDP Report. Moreover, the index of civil liberties and/or political pluralism can be approximated by indices on the number of privately owned daily newspapers, radio, and TV stations, number of community based organizations (CBOs), non-governmental organizations (NGOs), and political tolerance and freedom of expression, including freedom of religion. Some of these indices will undoubtedly contain elements of subjectivity and value judgement, but should improve over time and become more objective.

We have shown in the preceding paragraphs how to formulate a development policy in such a way that it reflects the values of person-in-community, not of 'person-in-market.' The well-being of a person-in-community is identical to the communal social welfare. This objective is to be maximized by the political authority subject to a simultaneous solution of the six key leading issues (problems) in African development. As articulated by Abram Bergson, "among the elements affecting the welfare of the community during any given period of time are the amounts of each of the factors of production, other than labor, employed in the different production units, the amounts of the various commodities consumed, the amounts of the different kinds of work done, and the production unit for which this work is performed by each individual in the community during that period of time" (1938:311). Bergson's emphasis on the welfare of the community is consistent with the way the objective of development is stated here. This is because consumption and production decisions are interdependent in Africa, since more than 70 percent live in rural areas, where farm households exhibit this feature. In addition, African traditional economies tended to display characteristics of James Scott's (1976) "moral economy," in which "social rights of minimum subsistence are secured to all members" (Platteau, 1991:113). This in turn tends to guarantee social responsibility in the community. Moreover, I am inclined to think that African traditional economies tended to operate so that there is a Pareto-optimal allocation of goods and services, because "another person's happiness is an influence on one's own utility" (Silberberg, 1978:480). Similarly, another person's misery in the world of person-in-community is also an influence on one's own utility.

The behavior of the African household "as a unit of consumption and a unit of production," in the view of the World Bank, "creates special problems for predicting the consequences of policies "because "within the majority of African households there is an interdependence between consumption and production decisions, so that decisions on output also directly affect consumption and labor supply, and vice versa" (1990b:40). But, this interdependence, which is causing "special problems" for the World Bank in predicting the likely impact of macroeconomic policies, is precisely the strength of our argument for reformulating development policies in such a way that will allow them to take into account or, put more strongly, integrate these unique characteristics of the African household. This should also resolve, in the context of the African model of development, the difficulty in the concept of group preferences (Silberberg, 1978; Arrow, 1950), in that the well-being of each and every individual is identical to that of the whole community. The policy implication of this is to design and implement economic policies that guarantee minimum social rights for the preservation of human dignity without making anybody worse off.

With the specification of the development policy objective — human progress and betterment — in terms of HDI, the identification of the key elements of what I call an integrative African model of sustainable development becomes more conceivable. The elements of the model when put together should enable us to effectively address the constraints on the development policy objective. In this regard, I have identified the following as the main components:

a) A "consensual" democratic system or state;
b) agriculture-led economic growth;
c) social integration; and
d) ecological harmony.

A Consensual Democratic System of Government

The nature and magnitude of the leading issues in African development necessitate that any concerted search for their sustained resolution must take the state as a point of departure. In conventional economic policy formulation, the state is often taken as given — an exogenous factor that a development policy formulator does not take into account or worry about when formulating strategies and programs of action. This tradition is not followed here. The state is conceived as an integral part of the African model of development. Furthermore, neoclassical economics conceives the state as a rational entity — just like any economic agent, though assumed to be class neutral to the extent that it maximizes the social welfare function of its citizens, subject to the resource constraints of the national economy. The postcolonial African state would appear to have defied the neoclassical assumption of its rationality. This assumption of rationality is, however, followed here for a new type of African state. The role of community/civil society is now widely acknowledged and is becoming more prominent. This global consensus should enable a new type of African state to command broadly based political support in achieving the objective of public policy as stated in the preceding section. In this regard, two types of African political systems of government are likely to emerge as fitting the characteristics of the kind of state that could pursue the noble objective of sustainable development, exhibited in human progress and betterment. These are Mandela's South African model of inclusiveness, symbolized by the Government of National Unity (GNU), and Museveni's Ugandan model of a broadly based political movement, reflected by the NRM competitive participatory democracy.

The Sudan Socialist Union (SSU) under Numeiri almost achieved this feature in southern Sudan during the period 1978-1983. Everybody in the south then was considered to be a member of the SSU. There were territorial constituencies based on the size of population, and candidates contested elections for the people's assemblies on the merits of their individual programs (similar to the American system of primaries). Then there were seats at the provincial level allocated to women, youths, professionals, workers, military, police, business, farmers, and so on, with each group electing (with the exception of regular forces) its own representative through competitive democratic elections as in the territorial constituencies. In this way, all segments of the society were represented in both regional and national people's assemblies. This is, in my view, one of the strategies for ensuring a consensus-seeking system of governance in Africa as she approaches the 21st century.

Museveni's model is essentially an extension of, and a modification of, African socialism, with some elements from the pro-Western social democracy model found in the Scandinavian countries. I refer to these two models — South Africa and Uganda — as "Consensual Democratic Political Systems." They can also be described as consensus-based or consensus-reinforcing competitive politics, which also means political pluralism, thus constituting what could best be called an African model of democracy. The multi-party democracy in the Unites States and United Kingdom is in reality a two-party democracy. What is important, however, is not the number of parties, but the rules governing the entry and exit from the game of politics — liberty and freedom of speech and association, and the role of community/civil society in the system of government. These two African models have devised, in the words of Mamdani, "an agenda that will appeal to both civil society and peasant communities, that will incorporate both the electoral choice that civil society movements seek and the quest for community rights that has been the consistent objective of peasant-based movements" (1993:47). Nyerere has advised that "elections are not the beginning and end of democracy" (1968:5). Democracy in an African context is embedded in the normal daily strategic behavior of a community and its individual members therein. I must admit that I am venturing into "foreign territory," for this belongs to the political science domain, and not the development economics realm that I am familiar with.

One has to understand, however, the political economy of African traditional societies in order to appreciate the nature and behavior of state that is envisaged to operate under the consensual democratic political system. One of the main features of the political economy of an African traditional society is consensus-seeking focusing on unifying rather than dividing the community. It can be time consuming, to be sure, but once decisions are arrived at through this process, they become an integral part of the social fabric and are therefore respected, and defended. This in turn ensures loyalty and a sense of belonging to one's community/society and/ or state, and consequently contributes to social harmony and stability. The state, thus, becomes a true rational actor, which is capable of maximizing the social welfare function of all its stakeholders. This loyalty and sense of belonging to one's community is seen as an insurance against future uncertainties and hazards. Platteau has articulated this point as follows: "traditional methods for controlling the risk of falling into distress have usually enabled the people to counter natural and other hazards in a rather effective way," this is because "people were very keen to avoid being expelled from their social group and that expulsion was viewed as the gravest possible sanction in any traditional village society suggests that the social protection it afforded its members was of utmost significance" (1991:156). Hence, individual behavior — economic, social, and/or political — in a typical African traditional society is within the context of communal value systems, that have been collectively accumulated over the life of the community, and in this sense it can be viewed as a 'social capital.' Moreover, this constitutes what many African scholars refer to as culture, encompassing all aspects of economic, social and political life: value systems, institutions, organizations, methods, pattern of behavior and social norms (see for instance, an excellent collection of essays on culture and development in Africa by Serageldin and Taboroff, 1994).

In a "consensual democratic political system," the objective of public policy — human progress and betterment (or sustainable development) — is consistent with societal/communal and/or national values, institutions and structures. This is because the system itself, is a genuine outcome of a consensus process among all the stakeholders — community/civil society and its various structures and institutions; women and youth; peasant farmers; the business community; workers; bureaucrats; the military and law enforcement agencies; politicians; and so forth. In this regard, the role of a development policy analyst and/or formulator should be conceptually simpler. For instance, a development economist, in her/his capacity as a policy formulator, should now be able to formulate the objective of development as if it were a utility function for a person-in-community. This is because such a person-in-community is a typical representative of all the stakeholders, given the knowledge and better understanding of economic, social, and political processes and institutions of an African consensual democratic state. I am in total agreement with Francis Deng that: "The personal aspect of the system must be emphasized. Even in the case of the chief, benefits are given to individuals conceiving of him as the father of all. The relations of man to man and man to community are such that the individual is naturally conscious and responsive to the needs of others. In confronting individuals conditioned by these values, the decision-maker, whether tribal, subtribal, or familial, puts emphasis on persuasion rather than on coercion" (1971:251). In fact, persuasion is a key element in consensus-building and is inherent in the strategic behavior of any individual member — men, women, old and/or young — of a community at any level of decision-making. I take all activities to require making a decision of some kind; even sleeping or playing a game is an act of decision-making on the part of the actor irrespective of gender or age. Coercion and/or violence can, of course, erupt when persuasion fails to produce a consensus.

The state, it will be argued, is a product of the consensual democratic political system in which all the members or stakeholders (I prefer to use the term stakeholder, since it conveys a strong sense of participation) fully take part in the affairs of their community and/or country. Decisions in a "consensual democratic political system" are arrived at through consensus and not imposed or dictated through the so-called majority vote. Any critical observer of multi-party democracy as it has been in Africa during the last four years in, for example, Cameroon, Cote d'Ivoire, Kenya, Togo, Zaire, and even Zambia, would come to the conclusion that the cardinal principles, structures, and institutions of multi-party politics are not yet rooted in most of these countries. This does not, however, imply that there are no principles of political pluralism in a typical African traditional society. The problem lies in the exclusive nature of multi-party politics with respect to the executive branch of government. That is, the party which gets a clear majority normally forms a government by itself, while the other parties are excluded. I would argue that this essentially reduces multi-party politics to "ministerial positions competitive-politics," instead of focusing on visions and programs in the service of the population. Africa would need a transitional period of, say, ten years, during which a proportionate-representative system of government that would allocate ministerial positions to political parties according to their number of seats in the legislature assemblies is practiced.

In contrasting the Western system of law with the African traditional one, Francis Deng, quoting T. Olawale Elias, states: "The traditional method aims at adjusting disturbances of the social equilibrium and restoring peace and good will while the European method tends to widen the gulf between the parties by concerning itself with facts and application of legal principles, granting all rights to one of them and excluding the other without consideration of the social implications" (1971:26, footnote 5). This description fits very well with multi-party politics in Africa. It may therefore be more appropriate to encourage the formation of governments of national unity, following multi-party elections. All parties that get a reasonable number of seats in parliaments (legislative bodies) should be included in governments, as this is likely to give incentives to the opposition to respect the rule of law and participate in the elections and subsequently in the executive branches of new governments. In this regard, multi-party democracy will have to be nurtured carefully, and investment has to be made in strengthening and/or integrating its basic elements with that of the African traditional system of consensus-building.

In most African societies, all stakeholders' views do matter, and to this extent the emphasis should normally be on the integration and harmonization of various positions into a single stance, which would in turn permit everybody to associate herself/himself with it. I will not dwell further on this particular point, but would hope that other researchers and scholars with strong backgrounds and interest in political science and state will, pursue this as one of the challenges in African development. Crawford Young seems to be calling policy science scholars to arms when he ponders the current waves of democratization in Africa: "Can they be rewoven to permit the emergence of a new kind of polity, one that employs the discourse of democracy but connects itself to the deeper African cultural heritage?" (1994:292). I would say that they can be rewoven, since, in the words of President Julius Nyerere, "it is generally claimed and believed that slave-owning and women-ignoring ancient Greece invented democracy; in that spirit it might also be claimed that African tribes had developed their own ways of democratic governance. The Elders sit under a tree and talk until they agree" (1993:16).

Anybody who has been to Crawford Young's Bula Matari state would very much hesitate to entertain the idea of including the state as one of the key elements of an African model of sustainable development. But students of this distinguished scholar of African development will not shy away from this often-neglected factor in the analysis of Africa's economic problems and prospects. There is a strong reason, however, for this courage. As stated earlier, a masterpiece by Crawford Young (1994) has recently appeared, *The African Colonial State in Comparative Perspective.* Young provides eight important attributes of the state and six determinants of its behavior which I find to be extremely useful to our analysis here. The attributes are: territory, population, sovereignty, power, law, nationhood, international actor, and the state as an idea. Furthermore, the set of determinants that guide state behavior or action are stated as six imperatives: hegemony, autonomy, security, legitimacy, revenue, and accumulation. Young, quoting Dyson, defines the state as follows:

> Besides referring to an entity or actor in the arena of international politics, the state is a highly generalizing, integrating and legitimating concept that identifies the leading values of the political community

with reference to which authority is to be exercised;
emphasizes the distinctive character and unity of
the "public power" compared with civil society; focuses on the need for depersonalization of that
power; finds its embodiment in one or more institutions and one or more public purposes which thereby
acquire a special ethos and prestige and an association with the public interest or general welfare; and
produce a socio-cultural awareness of (and sometimes dissociation from) the unique and superior
nature of the state itself. . . .The idea of the state is
dedicated to the value of reason, placed at the service of a set of public norms that are to be guaranteed against violation by individuals who are attempting to satisfy egoistic wants. Its grandeur as
an institution lies in its authority, but equally power
(though not a good in itself) is a necessary basis of
its action.[9] (1994:25-26)

For the idea of state to be "dedicated to the value of reason,
placed at the service of a set of public norms that are to be
guaranteed against violation by individuals," as articulated
by the above definition, there needs to be a transparent partnership among all the stakeholders in an African state, a
partnership in which the comparative strength of each stakeholder or groups of stakeholders is effectively utilized in the
quest for achieving and sustaining human progress and betterment. In short, all the stakeholders must be involved in
all aspects of the development process. Such involvement
presupposes an empowerment of all the stakeholders, without sacrificing national unity (Dia, 1996). This empowerment
would in turn enhance the political authority of the state in
tackling the leading issues in national development, which
has not been the practice in Africa until recently. It would
also ensure depersonalization of the state and a tendency
toward a 'policed-economy,' which has no genuine public

policy other than generalized repression as a way of guaranteeing the survival of the ruling elite. I will therefore focus on how attributes and imperative variables of the state simultaneously interact and impact on the general well-being of the community/society.

A policy matrix is constructed (see appendix I at the end of the book) from Crawford Young's attributes and action determinants (variables) of the state. I will take liberty to drop two attributes — territory and population — from the matrix, since I consider them to be the overall defining features of the state. There are 36 possible outcomes from the simultaneous interaction of the state attributes and determinants (or imperative variables). How can a development policy formulator/analyst utilize these interactions in designing a program of action that the political authority would be able to implement? One can justify, for instance, that the political authority uses sovereignty in legitimizing the state hegemony on revenue and commonwealth, which are used to guarantee security and the other basic human rights (freedom and liberty) of its citizens, individually and/or collectively. But this sovereignty must come from the people themselves, otherwise it is not sustainable. Similarly, we can take each of the other attributes (power, law, nationhood, international actor, and idea) of the state in interaction with its variables (hegemony, revenue, accumulation or commonwealth, security, autonomy, and legitimacy) in designing appropriate policy options in pursuit of the objective of sustainable development.

It should now be obvious why the nature of the state is one of the limiting (constraint) factors to the realization of the objective of development in Africa. Neoclassical assumptions about the rationality of state notwithstanding, our attempt to assign quantitative values, which are subjective, to the attributes and imperatives of the state is essentially intended to encourage economists, especially development economists, to fully integrate the nature of state into their economic analysis. This should also enable economists to participate in the quest for the invention of a new African state, in response to Crawford Young's query: "Can a new state be invented that sheds the debilitating traditions of the past?" (1994:292). Hence, the usefulness of the policy matrix is essentially to enhance our analytical capacity in integrating the state into the development model.

Moreover, the nature of the state should now be central in the analysis of multilateral institutions, such as the African Development Bank, the International Monetary Fund, and the World Bank, which have in the past continued to lend money and provide development aid to some of the countries that had lost their imperatives and were slowly drifting to chaos, anarchy, and disintegration.[10] A state which is at war with itself or, in the words of Richard Joseph, a political authority in a state of war with its people, uses power in an attempt to legitimize its hegemony to collect revenue and commonwealth for its own well-being. It believes in the hostages' dilemma and oppresses and terrorizes its people as a much cheaper alternative (Dixit and Nalebuff, 1991) to improving their well-being. This is a Bula Matari state, which has de-legitimized the state in the eyes of ordinary people in Africa. Yet, development experts and international development agencies have been prescribing 'development policies' and lending money to such a state. Although Crawford Young uses Bula Matari, which means a crusher of rocks, to describe an African colonial state, it is employed here to characterize Abacha's Nigeria, Acheampong's Ghana, Amin's Uganda, *apartheid* South Africa, Barre's Somalia, Bokassa's Central African Republic, Doe's Liberia, El-Bashir's Sudan, Mobutu's Zaire, Mangistu's Ethiopia, Numeiri's Sudan, and so forth. When a state persistently exhibits negative values for its imperatives — and in turn fails to guarantee social well-being, development policy enforcement and implementation, a sense of citizenship, basic human rights, liberty, freedom of speech and association, and international recognition through the flow of financial resources — then the governing elite is either replaced or the state withers away. In the case of state disappearance, the values of the imperatives (hegemony, revenue, commonwealth, security, autonomy, and legitimacy) are all zero as demonstrated by Somalia after Barre, Liberia after Doe, Ethiopia after Mangistu, and Zaire (Democratic Republic of Congo) after Mobutu. Our memory of history sometimes seems to be very short in Africa, but Crawford Young reminds us of Amin's shocking atrocities: "not only of killing an estimated 300,000 Ugandans, but of having cost Uganda a decade during which not a single school, hospital, or road was constructed. Coffee production, extorted from farmers to supply the terror apparatus of the regime with the bulk of its resources, fell by one-third, while cotton output dropped from 450,000 bales just before Amin to 60,000 by 1978" (1982:5). The Ugandan economy is now growing, in real terms, at an impressive 10 percent for more than two years in a row and under a new style of consensus-based political pluralism. Yet, it is being threatened by the disciples of multiparty democracy.

With the type of a consensus-based African state in place, the two leading issues in African development — political reform and conflict resolution — would have been resolved by deduction. The basic assumption here is that the social values reflected in the views/convictions of all the major stakeholders (ethnic groups, class, or gender, and so forth) are integrated into public policy in the process of consensus-building. It becomes a "political agenda that can energize and draw together various social forces in the highly fragmented social reality that is contemporary Africa" (Mamdani, 1993:47). Once a public policy program of action is agreed upon, then all segments of the society/community identify themselves with it at various levels. This in turn enhances social cohesion and stability. A stable environment characterized by tranquility would further provide legitimacy for the state to implement the key elements of public policy, such as restoring economic growth through reform; protecting the environment through effective natural resource management; reducing poverty; and controlling indebtedness. The quality of the state reflected by its attributes of sovereignty, power, law, nationhood, international actor, and idea (conviction), is a function, in my view, of mass participation in its affairs (Mamdani, 1993). Hence, the importance as well as the centrality of broad-based as well as consensus-seeking political movements in an African model of development.

Agriculture-Led Economic Growth

The second key element of an African model of sustainable development is an agricultural-led economic growth. We have seen the magnitude of crisis in the first half of the last decade, when macroeconomic conditions were unstable for a large number of African countries. This instability is characterized by internal and external imbalances. I will not examine here the causes of the macroeconomic imbalances of the 1980s, as they have been much debated in the preceding chapters. However, I would think that the underlying or root cause of the crisis was the inability of African agriculture to produce a sustained surplus, due to the fact that it was being over-taxed, combined with a risky production environment and limited access to yield-enhancing inputs, including credit. This was recognized by the Organization of African Unity (OAU) in its summit in Monorovia, Liberia (1979), as observed by Crawford Young: "the difficulties that beset many countries could no longer be over-looked . . . .The swelling urban centers could no longer be supplied with food from domestic production, and scarce foreign exchange had to be committed to grain imports. The rural sector had quite generally been a disappointment; only a few countries could point to real achievements for smallholder populations" (1982:7). In fact, the scarce foreign exchange committed to grain imports was earned, in most cases, through primary commodity exports from the agricultural sector.

Growth has to be restored to African economies for human progress and betterment to be attained and sustained. But, economic growth is not an end in itself; it is an instrument (or means) for achieving the noble objective of human happiness and prosperity. This is further articulated by Badiane and Delgado: "The future prosperity of Africa depends on political stability, sustainable growth in agricultural production, reduction of the rate of population growth, and the protection of its natural resources" (1995:5). In this regard, economic growth is further constrained, at least in the short-run, by other factors — the Pareto-optimality condition embedded in social integration and consonance; the green sustainability requirement underlying ecological harmony and balance; political stability; external debt repayment; and the need for enhanced institutional capacity. In agreement with Badiane and Delgado, "Success in these matters will require specific attention paid by policy-makers to fostering the right institutional, infrastructural, and financial environment for growth" (1995:5).

Much of the discourse in African development has, since the beginning of the 1980s, focused mainly on constraints to economic growth, which are often stated as inappropriate macroeconomic policies, rapid population growth, human resource development, and infrastructure (OAU, 1980; World Bank, 1984a; African Development Bank, 1995). These are legitimate concerns in their own right and therefore should be examined. However, an important area — sources of growth — has not been given the kind of intellectual attention and analysis that it deserves. I am not referring to the conventional sources of economic growth, which are normally attributed to factor productivity. They are fully discussed in famous models such as the Harrod-Domar model and other work (see, for instance, Kaldor, 1955; Solow, 1956, 1957, 1970; Taylor, 1979; and so forth), but my reference is more to the broader concept of sectoral sources of growth. It is perhaps more appropriate to identify the sectors of growth, and then within them point out the conventional sources of growth.

A recent paper by Stanley Engerman and Kenneth Sokoloff (1994) on Factor Endowments, Institutions, and Differential Paths of Growth Among New World Economies: A View from Economic Historians of the United States, is quite interesting, at least from an African perspective, as the continent has literally been robbed of its initial factor endowments (for example, African human capital that ended up as slave labor in the economies of the new world). It is also of importance in light of our emphasis on the need for a broad-based political authority to implement appropriate strategies for achieving sustainable development by the year 2020 as envisioned by IFPRI. Engerman and Sokoloff identify initial factor endowments, institutions, and political power as important sources of growth differentials:

> This paper highlights the relevance of substantial differences in the degree of inequality in wealth, human capital and political power in accounting for the variation in the records of growth. Moreover, we suggest that the roots of these disparities in inequality lay in differences in the initial factor endowments of the respective colonies. Of particular significance were the suitability of the country for the cultivation of sugar and other crops, in which there were economies of production in the use of slaves, and the presence of large concentrations of Native Americans. Both of these conditions encouraged the evolution of societies in which relatively small elites of European descent could hold highly disproportionate shares of the wealth, human capital, and political

power — and establish economic and political dominance over the mass of the population.[11]

Sources of growth in Africa are logically rooted in the agricultural sector. In this regard, agriculture should be the leading sector for the revitalization of economic growth in Africa. This is because African agriculture is still the mainstay
of a majority of people as well as one of the leading sectors
for foreign exchange earnings for a large number of countries (Ogbu, 1993; Platteau, 1993; Cleaver and Donovan, 1995;
Spencer, 1995; African Development Bank, 1995). In addition, it is common knowledge that agriculture is the engine
of growth at the early stages of economic development. This
implies that there must be a net inflow of resources into agriculture before there is any net transfer of resources from it
to the other sectors of the economy. Yet, African agriculture
has not received, in the recent past, the type of attention and
support that is commensurate with its contribution to the
economy at this critical stage of development in Africa.
Hence, the inability of African agriculture to feed the population. And population is, paradoxically, a viable source of
growth as elucidated by the above passage: Instead of being
seen as a long-term constraint to development, people are
the means and end of development itself. They are a means
of development through developed human capital, and are
an end, in that the objective — in fact, the goal of development — is to enhance human dignity through sustained
social harmony, progress, betterment, happiness, and prosperity.

We have argued earlier in chapter two that the focus of
the modernization school of thought on industrialization,
with a corresponding neglect of agricultural development,
is one of the root causes of present African economic problems. The way out, then, and as stated in chapter three, is
through agricultural structural transformation, but without
corresponding neglect of industry and other sectors of the

economy. I favour an agricultural-led sustainable development, with emphasis on sectoral linkages that are likely to enhance this process. The importance of agriculture at this stage of development becomes more obvious if we look at three fundamentals given by John Staatz (1994). These are:

a)   In order for growth to occur, the economy must produce a surplus above current consumption needs;

b)   In most low-income countries, most of the initial investable surplus has to be generated out of agriculture and related rural activities because these sectors play such a preponderant role in the economy; and

c)   In the early stages of economic growth, the non-agricultural sectors are so small that even if they generate high profit rates, the total amount of surplus produced is small relative to the investment needs of the economy.

In light of the above three fundamentals, the main objectives, in our view, of agricultural transformation in Africa should be to (i) enable people to feed themselves and allow the economy to produce a surplus above current consumptions; and (ii) lay the foundation for sustainable economic growth as well as sustainability of development itself. According to Seckler, agricultural transformation is "the process by which agriculture shifts from being dominated by highly diversified, subsistence-oriented farms towards more specialized production oriented towards, and dependent on, markets."[12] Moreover, the process of agricultural transformation, according to Staatz (1994), "involves a greater reliance on input and output markets and increased integration of agriculture with other sectors of the domestic and international economies." These two interpretations of the process of agricultural transformation are retained here. I would add that agricultural transformation is a dynamic process and not a static one. For African agriculture to meet these two objectives, four conditions must prevail, as mentioned in chapter three: a) empowerment of African farmers; b) regional economic integration; c) agricultural research, infrastructure, and institutions; and d) a conducive macro-policy environment. Moreover, these objectives are consistent with the recent IFPRI 2020 vision with respect to Africa, where a 4 percent growth rate has been set as the minimum target to be achieved by the year 2020. Badiane and Delgado elucidate this as follows:

Achieve a rate of agricultural growth of at least 4 percent. This is a controversial issue in African and donor policy debates. Yet there is a need to step back to consider that there is no other choice if Africa is to progress. It is simply not realistic to believe that African incomes will go up enough outside agriculture by 2020 to permit the import and distribution to all who need it of sufficient food to support a population growth rate of 2.8 percent per year. (1995:6)

The IFPRI's 4 percent growth rate for African agriculture is a reasonable one, especially given the fact "that this growth rate is well within the technical and economic capacity of most African nations, provided that reaching this goal is made top priority in public investment for research, producer support systems, and infrastructure, in a way that effectively mobilizes private production activity" (Badiane and Delgado, 1995:6). It should be recalled that both the invisible-hand of capitalism (symbolized by Lewis model of economic growth) and the "visible-hand" of communism (articulated by Stalinist model of collective farms) were crudely applied in Africa, with very disappointing results. For instance, the uncouth application of the "visible-hand" of Stalinism in Nyerere's Tanzania and Mangistu's Ethiopia led the first African Nobel Laureate for literature, Wole Soyinka, conclude:

Even more disastrous, and on a horrendous scale, was the same relocation policy as executed by Ethiopia. Supposedly an answer to perennial, drought-induced nomadic routine of the far-flung sections of Ethiopia, it proved to be nothing but a copycat variant on the Russian model. It was a far less humane exercise than Tanzania's, lacking even the educative preparations undertaken by Tanzania, lacking even the compensatory amenities in the new settlements which Tanzania at least attempted to provide. Let us simply sum it up as a crime against humanity, undertaken in the name of ill-designed centralist notions of a scientific development process. (from Serageldin and Taboroff, 1994:205)

To avoid a repeat of the past failed policies with respect to agricultural development, African farmers — subsistence, smallholder, medium, and/or commercial — will have to be empowered. It is my conviction that Africa's agriculture will not be able to produce a surplus above current consumption levels, nor will it lay the foundation for sustainable development, if African farmers are not sufficiently empowered to use productive techniques of their choice in producing what they think is profitable. The Empowerment of African farmers would in turn enable them to fully participate in the search for truly appropriate technologies from their own perspective. Here, the farmer is the "king" and not the researcher - the former is a "consumer" of technologies produced by the latter. In this regard, farmers should not be expected to follow blindly the strict recommendations made by researchers in their research stations and passed down to farmers via extension service agents. Farmers must be convinced — for they are rational economic agents — that it is advantageous and profitable to adhere to strict recommendations passed on to them by researchers.

The role of researchers would then be to provide a broad array of technical options from which farmers can choose from. For, as shown by Platteau, "While agricultural research expands the set of technologies from which farmers may choose, their ability to actually use them crucially depends on the country's stock of infrastructure capital and the resulting costs of infrastructural services" (1993:17). In fact, researchers will have to compete among themselves in the production of technologies that meet farmers' dem and.[13] As illustrated by Badiane and Delgado (1995), "Much has changed in Africa over the past 15 years, and the region has achieved many if not all the preconditions for sustained growth in agricultural production." The consensual democratic system is the most appropriate political framework, in our view, for achieving an agricultural-led industrialization, and hence generalized growth in the African economies, since such a system would enable farmers and researchers to interact with each other and with other major stakeholders. The views of rural farm households would be reflected in the national development strategies, which would be formulated by a broadly based political authority of the new African model of state discussed in the preceding section of this chapter.

The remaining three conditions for achieving agriculture-led growth — regional economic integration; agricultural research and infrastructure; and macro-policy environment — will be appreciated better if they are analyzed within the framework of agro-ecological zones given earlier in chapter three. In particular, development policy formulators within each zone should be able to identify countries that are likely to achieve the 4 percent target and in what agricultural products. This would in turn lead to the development of and general recommendations on, the type of technologies that are being demanded by farmers, their environmental sustainability, regional comparative advantages, and steps needed toward harmonization of regional macroeconomic and sectoral and trade policies and strategies. It should be emphasized, however, that regional economic integration and empowerment of African farmers are the keys to a dynamic process of agricultural structural transformation in Africa. This is because issues of infrastructure and research would be properly addressed within the context of regional economic integration and with the full participation of African farmers — all categories of farmers — through their various organizations. In addition, macropolicies will have to be harmonized at the regional level, so as to avoid countries being encouraged to produce the same export crop, as happened with SAP policies. The six agro-ecological zones are:[14]

a) Mediterranean and arid north Africa;
b) Sudano-Sahelian Africa;
c) Humid and sub-humid west Africa;
d) Humid central Africa;
e) Sub-humid and mountain east Africa; and
f) Sub-humid and semi-arid southern Africa.

There is one problem, however, with the above classification — countries inhabit more than one agro-ecological zone. For the sake of analysis we proceed with this caveat in mind and with the hope that it will trigger applied research that would in turn assist in the generation of environmentally, economically, socially, and institutionally sound production techniques; in the formulation of resource management methods; and in the design of regional economic integration strategies. Before discussing the agricultural growth possibilities in each agro-ecological zone, some basic steps that need to be followed by African countries in their quest for regional economic integration should be stated first. Moreover, Africa is often compared to Asia, a comparison that often glosses over the basic realities and uniqueness of problems facing each continent (see table 4.1).

Table 4.1: Some Selected Indicators for Africa and Asia, 1994

Region	Total Pop.(000)	Harvested Land as % of arable land	Total Cereal product kg/ha	Total No. Tractors
Africa	708,285	25.0	1,200	508,026
Asia	3,333,188	64.6	2,900	5,667,217
World	5,630,240	na	2,800	25,703,904

Source : Compiled from FAO 1994 Production Yearbook, Vol. 48 and WRI (1995)

NA: Not applicable for our analysis here.

From table 4.1, we can state the following general facts: (i) the population (3.3 billion) of Asia is 4.7 times that of Africa (0.7 billion); (ii) land under cultivation as a percentage of arable land is 65% in Asia compared to only 25% for Africa; (iii) number of agricultural tractors in Asia is 11.2 times that of Africa; (iv) the population of Asia is 59.2% of the world total population compared to 12.6% for Africa; and (v) total cereals production yield (kg/ha) is about 2,900 in Asia compared to about 1,200 in Africa (the world average is about 2,800). This fact-sheet should provide the basis for our optimism that Africa can regain her image and dignity in the world through regional economic integration, which takes agriculture as its point of departure. In fact, there are many images of Africa and the one that seems to have stuck in the minds of many TV viewers the world over is the one portrayed by the victims of both man-made and natural disasters emanating from the Horn of Africa since 1984 and recently from Rwanda and Liberia. This negative perception of Africa is vividly captured by Jean-Marie Cour and David Naudet in their recent observation: "When people look at Africa these days, they see crisis. The main signs of current trends on the continent all involve disorder and violence: ethnic conflict, widespread poverty, anarchic city growth, desertification, extinction of traditional societies, and more. In every area — political, social, economic, financial, food, education, health — crises are multiplying and seem to be gradually taking over the whole of African societies. The future of Africa is thus generally perceived to be unpredictable chaos or at best a process of regressio" (1996:20).

But why did Africa allow her image to be tarnished by less than half a dozen countries that are being misgoverned by leaders who are insensitive to the general welfare of their people? One of the main reasons, in my view, for Africa's inability to present her real image is due to recent technological advances in transportation and communication (CNN and the Internet or the electronic super-highway, for example). These have essentially brought down walls of 'ignorance', thereby creating a global psychological interdependence (Cooper, 1986). What comes out of Africa in the form of graphic CNN pictures from Liberia, Somalia, Sudan, and Rwanda strengthens old stereotypes about the inability of Africans to govern and/or feed themselves. What comes into Africa through this new medium encourages adoption of alien norms, which in turn tends to undermine the social fabric of many African societies. For instance, this psychological interdependence lures African elites to adopt alien life-styles and consumption habits that are not consistent with the economic realities of Africa, and in turn reinforces reliance on imports with negative consequences for the local production of goods and services. There is, therefore, a need for a new framework that would foster positive thinking by enabling researchers and policy analysts to develop new modes of analysis in their studies as well as the formulation of policies that are relevant to the objective conditions of Africa. This view is further articulated by Cour and Naudet in the following passage:

The evidence of failure revealed by official statistics shows mainly that development of the expected sort did not occur, but hardly reflects the reality of the African economy. The same could probably be said of many economic, political and social analyses of Africa. They are unknowingly based on a vision of chaos, violence and widespread poverty. Anything that confirms that picture is accurately perceived and regarded as important. Any evidence that might directly refute it − social and political stability, sustained economic growth − could also be detected, but how can that be expected in a period of upheaval? And whatever lies outside the field of vision does not show up. Anything hidden in the disorder is disregarded. No one looks for the overall movement and so it is not seen. If Africa is to be looked upon with different eyes, one must first change this unwitting image of its future. (1996:24-25)

The organization for Peace and Appropriate Development in the Horn of Africa (PADA) eloquently states: "Africa will have a political role in international affairs and a space within the international trading system only when Africa becomes economically independent, politically strong, and proud of its own culture. . . .Africans must be willing and prepared to put their collective efforts into their own well being, while maintaining healthy relationships with the rest of the international community."[15] This is essentially saying that Africa lives in an interdependent world and must, therefore, know the rules of behavior or the norms of conduct to be a member in the new global village with full rights and obligations of membership. It also recognizes, in my view, the urgent need for African countries to identify their strengths as well as their weaknesses and to integrate their economies to ensure sustained economic growth led by the agricultural sector, thus ascertaining the well being of ordinary

African people within the framework of international trade. Moreover, Africa must acknowledge and accept the fact that she is solely responsible for her own destiny. It is a destiny which lies in regional economic integration with the initial focus on agriculture as the engine of growth, on the one hand, and the vehicle for poverty reduction and environmental protection, on the other. With a balanced combination of economic growth with effective poverty reduction and protection of the environment, Africa would be able to take her place in the global assembly with dignity, self-respect, and a shared vision of humanity in an interdependent world. It should be emphasized here that Africa must participate in this global assembly as a policy-maker and not as a policy-taker, which for decades now has contributed to the marginalization and humiliation of the continent.

From the preceding analysis, it is obvious that individual African countries will not be able to get maximum gains from the new international trading arrangements without a collective approach as well as strategic alliances among themselves and/or with non-African regional trading/economic blocs. The path, then, to Africa's real image recovery, sustained growth, competitiveness, and prosperity is through regional economic integration. There are currently, at least on paper, more than half a dozen sub-regional groupings in Africa. We have, for example, the Common Market for Eastern and Southern Africa (COMESA), East Africa Community (EAC), Economic Community of Central African States (ECCAS), Economic Community of West African States (ECOWAS), Inter-Governmental Authority on Development (IGAD), Southern Africa Development Community (SADC), Union Monetaire de l'Ouest Africaine (UMOA), and so forth. These sub-regional groupings could, if strengthened, provide important road-maps toward a prosperous Africa in the 21st century, one which would be based on consensus-seeking, sharing, and mutual trust. An excellent review of

various attempts at regional economic integration is provided by Ralph Onwuka and Amadu Sesay (1985),
Anyang'Nyong'o (1990), and Wilfred Ndongko (1985). A
quick look at these sub-regional groupings suggests that
Africa so far has been concerned mainly with what I call
institutional integration, with an emphasis on symbolism of
political unity rather than on concrete steps toward economic
cooperation. Institutional integration is used here to mean
creation of institutions of political solidarity and symbolism
rather than institutions of economic cooperation and development. I would argue that this is necessary for a political
integration, but it is insufficient to generate economic development and social progress in the integrating economies.

This line of reasoning is supported by Timothy Shaw who
argues that attempts at regional integration in Africa have
been "part of a diplomatic strategy to improve the balance
of forces between the continent and the rest of the global
system. This approach conceives of regionalism not so much
as a development strategy or an attempt to restructure the
international division of labour, so much as a diplomatic tactic
designed to enhance Africa's visibility and autonomy — a
collective form of decolonisation. Its focus has been on regional constitutions and institutions — the form rather than
the relationship — and on mediation and liberation rather
than structural transformation" (1985:14). But what Africa
needs at this point is structural integration — harmonizing
basic social and economic structures (for example, markets)
across national geographical boundaries. A complete model
of regional economic grouping is viewed here to consist of
both institutional and structural integration. The European
Union (EU) is, for example, a full (or complete) regional economic integration, while the North American Free Trade
Agreement (NAFTA) is a case of structural integration. I
consider structural integration such as NAFTA to be sufficient for the purpose of generating economic growth for
members of the grouping, which is, in any case, the main

objective of regional integration. Both types of integration require a strong leadership capable of charting the course toward the common objective — political solidarity and/or economic cooperation. The relatively industrialized and politically stable countries within each sub-regional grouping (for example, COMESA, EAC, SADC, UMOA, and so on) will have to provide this leadership for economic integration to be viable in Africa.

In light of the preceding, the path to Africa's economic integration would consist, in my view, of four general and long steps. These will have to be taken at the level of sub-regional groupings or agro-ecological zones so as to ensure the viability of a continent-wide economic cooperation that could eventually evolve into an African common market.[16] For the sake of analysis, Africa — especially continental Sub-Saharan Africa — is assumed to be homogeneous in taste and outlook (Cooper, 1996). This assumption is intended to underscore the importance of the current quest for regional economic integration in Africa. It would also faiciltate the design of appropriate and operational strategies toward regionalism, which as shown by Sally Washington, is becoming a strategic instrument for collective bargaining in the post-Cold War world:

> Governments are also organising regionally to achieve global influence. The development of groupings — such as the European Union, NAFTA and APEC — and international or multilateral agreements, particularly those related to trade, such as the World Trade Organisation, has obvious implications for national governance. On the surface, regionalism and multilateralism appear contracdictory, but may in practice be complementary trends. Regional groupings may be one way for countries — particularly small, peripheral economies — to maximise their influence in global or multilateral fora. During the

> Uruguay Round, for instance, the European Union showed how the bargaining power of individual member states could be enhanced by collective action. (1996:25)

It should be pointed out here that the proposed steps toward economic integration in this chapter do not necessarily follow a particular sequence, and can therefore be taken in any order. I would argue, however, that the first step — the esatblishment and/or restoration of the institutions of good governance within each memeber state — should be the point of departure for African economic integration. Stated differently, a minimum requirement for a member state to join a regional "economic cooperative" or club is to have in place institutions of good governance. This is a necessary, though insufficient condition for the realization of the other three steps. Institutions of good governance basically presuppose a democratic environment, on the one hand, and a broadly based political authority, on the other. The lack of accepted political authority with a broad-based support from all segments of the civil society is, in my view, one of the root causes of economic, social, and political problems in those countries that are now at war with themsleves (for instance, Liberia, Somalia, Sudan, and so forth). This lack of a broadly based political authority delegitimizes the state in the eyes of the civil society, and in turn perpetuates armed conflict in the country and threatens to destabilize the entire region.

A broadly based political authority would facilitate the process of regional economic integration, since it derives its legitimacy from mass participation by the major stakeholders at various levels of governance. This point has consistently been ignored by various attempts at regional economic integration in Africa, to the extent that the situation has been analogous to trying to "mix apples with oranges" — attempting to integrate politically incompatible nation-states. There is no mention, for instance, of any minimum requirement for membership in the African common market. As shown by Onwuka, subregional and regional economic activities toward integration were to be introduced in six distinct stages as follows:

"(a) the fostering of sectoral integration at all levels in many fields including food and agriculture, industry, transport, science and technology;
(b) the abolition of obstacles to free movement of persons, ideas, services and capital between the member states;
(c) the harmonisation of development strategies, policies and plans and the promotion of joint projects particularly in the economic fields;
(d) the harmonisation of financial policies and monetary integration among the member states with the ultimate objective of adopting a single unit of currency by the member states;
(e) the establishment of a Common Development Fund for cooperation, compensation, guarantee, and development; and
(f) such other activities that would promote the grand objectives of the Community as may be decided upon" (1985:60-61).

The missing link — the glue of regional economic integration — in the above six stages is a broadly based political authority in each member state. By way of achieving an acceptable political authority, Africa will have to revisit her past in search of models that could be modified and adapted to the present global environment. The geopolitics of the post-Cold War era seem to be, in my view, favorable for Africa to experiment with various systems of governance. Africa now has, more than any other time in her post-independence history, an array of models of political systems to choose from without being harassed. Two of these models, as statd earlier, are providing hopeful signs — indicating that Africa may at last be able to tackle her present complex problems. These are the South African model of inclusion and the Ugandan multi-ethnic and gender-equalizing broad-based political movement.

The second step toward African economic integration is for the regional groupings (ECOWAS, IGAD, SADC, and so on) to abolish trade barriers (including tariffs) between member states in the respective sub-regional groupings and harmonize/unify their tariffs on international trade. This will be feasible when we have political authorities with mass participation in their affairs within each African state. However, some governments that derive a significant portion of their revenues from tariffs are likely to lose in the short-run. This would be more than compensated for through gains to consumers in the form of lower prices, on the one hand, and reduced cost of production to producers, on the other. As shown by Martin and Winters, a sub-regional economic grouping whose trade liberalization leads to larger reductions in the domestic prices of imports would, generally speaking, enable its member states to enjoy enormous gains in real income: "Consumers can buy what they need from the most efficient source. Producers can scale back on the production of goods made more efficiently in other countries and increase the output of goods produced at home. . . .Further gains can be achieved by greater exploitation of scale economies in production — and from improvements in the range and quality of specialized products available to producers and consumers" (1995:6-7). In addition, integration would allow free movements of people, goods, and services across borders, thereby augmenting political stability and social harmony within the sub-region and laying the basis for other key steps that need to be taken toward regional economic integration. More importantly, it would lead to a correct portrayal of Africa's face on CNN the world over.

184

The third step is the harmonization of macroeconomic policy frameworks within each sub-regional grouping. For instance, national fiscal, monetary, and exchange-rate policies should be consistent with the free movements of goods and services within the sub-region. And this calls for the coordination of these policies at the sub-regional level so as to ensure consistency between national economic objectives and those of the sub-regional grouping. The main purpose behind harmonization of macroeconomic policies is to safeguard the envisaged benefits of collective action. If individual countries insist in pursuing what each perceives to be its legitimate economic objectives, the gains from regional economic integration would not be fully realized. Moreover, it is increasingly becoming clear that national autonomy in monetary policy, fixed exchange rates, and the free movement of capital are incompatible in an interdependent world (Cooper, 1986). A regionally coordinated monetary policy combined with flexible exchange rates and free movement of capital would attract foreign invetment into the economies of the region, which could further lead to the expansion of their combined gross domestic product (GDP). But the most important aspect of harmonized macroeconomic policies, in my view, is that they would enable member states of a sub-regional grouping to ensure optimal provision of public or collective goods (roads, research & development, telecommunications, and so forth), which would in turn foster cooperation, economic development, and social progress within the region. Furthermore, harmonization of macroeconomic policies would allow policy-makers to reduce economic disturbances and risks associated with policy failure.

The fourth and final step toward regional economic integration is the harmonization of sectoral policies. This step is the key to Africa's competitiveness in interantional markets. Member states should encourage and allow specialization within the sub-region. Countries that have comparative advantages producing, say, food crops, should be allowed to specialize in their production for the entire sub-region, with the surplus being exported to other African sub-regional groupings and/or to the rest of the world. Similarly, countries with comparative advantages in the production of manufactured goods should specialize in them. The interlinkages (both backward and forward) between the leading sectors of the region would be greatly strengthened through the harmonization of sectoral strategies that emphasize comparative advantage-based specialization. By way of illustration, income growth in the rural sector would create effective demand of rural households for goods and services produced in the urban sector, which further raises, *ceteris paribus*, the purchasing power of urban households and their demand for agricultural products. The problem in Africa has been that African demand for almost anything has, in most cases, been running ahead of its output leaving the gap to be filled by the rest of the world and thereby creating a negative perception in the minds of many people that the continent is not capable of meeting the basic needs of her population. Yet, Africa has natural resources, such as land and water, that could contribute to a marketable surplus even if only 50 percent was made use of in the production of food and other cash crops. With integrated markets and favorable sectoral strategies, Africa would be able to scale back the production of goods in which she has no comparative advantage and to focus on those she can produce efficiently.

Let us now turn to the agro-ecological zones that could act as the basis for regional economic integration with agriculture as the main engine of sustained growth.

a)   Mediterranean and Arid North Africa

This agro-ecological zone is predominant in the following five countries: Algeria, Egypt, Libya, Morocco, and Tunisia, where about one-fifth (18.3%) of Africa's population lives on also about one-fifth (19.4%) of total land area of Africa. In addition, some selected agricultural indicators show that the region has respectively 14.8%, 8.0% and 2.0% of Africa's total arable land, pasture land, and forest and woodland (see table 4.2). It should be noted that the region's arable land is relatively underutilized, since only 37% is harvested. This, however, ranges between a higher percentage of utilization of about 86% in Egypt to only 15% in Tunisia. Moreover, the contribution of agriculture to GDP is about 13% of the region's GDP, but about one-fifth of agricultural value-added (or 4.2% of GDP) for Africa in 1994.

The process of agricultural structural transformation is relatively advanced in this zone. This is reflected by two indicators of structural transformation — share of agriculture in GDP (13.4%) and in labor force (25.4%) — given in table 4.2 below. There are, of course, variations between countries. In Libya, for instance, agriculture contributed only about 5% to GDP in 1994. Similarly, the percentage of labor force absorbed in agriculture and the contribution of agriculture to GDP are very low in Libya and Algeria compared with other countries in the zone.[17] The access to advanced production techniques (for example fertilizers) reflected in high yields for most agricultural products in the region — which are higher than average yields in the whole continent — also supports the state of structural transformation of the zone's agriculture. For example, the average yield of 6,382 kg/ha for maize in Egypt is more than three times the average yield for Africa; while millet's yield in Morocco is higher than the world average, and about twice the African average yield. Egypt's yield in rice is twice the world average yield and more than three times Africa's average yield. North African's sorghum yield is more than twice the world average, six times Africa's average yield, and more than nine times the average yield of sorghum in the Sudano-Sahelian zone; and Egypt's groundnut yield is twice the world average yield, three times Africa's average yield, and more than four times of the groundnut average yield in the Sudano-Sahelian region.

The use of advanced agricultural production techniques (e.g., fertilizers) and the productive utilization of natural resources seems to have led to substantial increases in agricultural yield and total agricultural production. For instance, the river Nile is the major source of water for Egypt and the country seems, in my view, to be productively making use of its water for irrigated agriculture. However, yields tend to be influenced by a number of factors — among them are relative factor prices (labor, land, and other inputs), relative factor endowments, and levels of subsidies. One may ask, for example, do the high yields in Egypt result from subsidies on the cost of water for irrigation and/or fertilizer? If so, then, there is the important question of economic and environmental sustainability.

Table 4.2: Some Selected Agricultural Indicators In The Mediterranean Zone, 1994

Country	Total arable land (mm ha)	Pasture Land (mn ha)	Forest & Woodland (mn ha)	Harvested Land as % of arable land	Agri. Value as % of GDP	Agri lab as % of labor force
Algeria	7.9	30.7	4.0	36.7	10.9	22.3
Egypt	2.8	n.a	0.031	85.7	19.1	38.6
Libya	2.2	13.3	0.84	19.5	4.9	12.6
Morocco	9.9	20.9	9.0	61.6	18.4	33.1
Tunisia	5.0	3.1	0.7	14.8	13.7	20.6
Region Total	27.8	68.0	14.6	37.2	13.4	25.4
Africa Total	187.9	852.6	760.8	42.52	21.1	60.7

Source : Compiled from FAO 1994 Production Yearbook, Vol. 48 and 1995 African Development Report of ADB.

(a):   mn ha stands for million hectares.

In terms of yield, it would seem to me that the Mediterranean and arid North Africa (mainly Egypt and Morocco) has reached maximum sustainable yields in four major food crops. These are maize, rice, sorghum and millet. These maximum sustainable yields have been achieved through intensive agriculture, which depends mainly on agricultural production techniques (e.g., fertilizers) and farmers' access to them. The region can expand its production of these four crops through more focus on regional economic integration within the zone and subsequently within Africa. For instance, skilled agricultural labor from Egypt, Morocco, and Tunisia can be combined with oil resources from Algeria and Libya in the utilization of, at least, 50% of the region's unused arable land. In addition, the region can expand its present industrial-base by expanding trade and economic ties with the rest of Africa. Morocco seems to be the only country in the region that is pursuing vigorous and strong trade ties with the rest of Africa and EU. In particular, the region has a potential for growth of agro-based industrialization as well as labor-intensive light industries that led the way to development for the newly industrialized countries in East Asia. In fact, the distance between Europe and Asia is longer than that of Europe and North Africa, and to this extent labor-intensive light industries can begin to migrate to this region in search of inexpensive factors of production.

There are three main problems that are likely to hinder sustained economic growth in this region. The first concerns regional political stability, especially in Algeria and Egypt. The threat of Islamic fundamentalism is real and can spread like a bush fire if appropriate measures are not taken. There could be a regional approach toward assimilation of Islamic political parties in both the legislative and executive branches of governments in the region. The second problem facing the region is external debt. It will be recalled from chapter three (cf table 3.2) that out of 19 highly-indebted African countries, four are from this region, with a total external debt of about $103 billion or 35 percent of Africa's total external debt. And the third issue is environmental, especially with respect to water, fossil fuel, and desertification.

b)   Sudano-Sahelian Africa

This region includes the following eight countries: Burkina Faso, Chad, Gambia, Mali, Mauritania, Niger, Senegal, and Sudan, with a total population of 74.4 million, which is about one-tenth (10 %) of total African population. In 1994, the agricultural share of the region's GDP was only 31%, while labor force engaged in agriculture was about 76% of the region's total labor force (see table 4.3 below). The total arable land of the region is 28.8 million hectares (mn ha) or about 15% of Africa's total arable land, with about 75% under cultivation. However, the region has 242 mn ha and 115 mn ha of permanent pasture and forest land respectively. The data also show that, in the Sudano-Sahelian zone, agricultural production per capita and yield are all lower than African averages. A number of issues come to mind when reviewing data on agricultural productivity given in this section. One issue concerns interpretation of yield per hectare as a measure of productivity. Since inter-cropping is practiced in the Sudano-Sahelian zone, it is most likely that there are multi-products per harvested hectare, which in turn tends to underestimate yields per hectare. In this sense, the yield on a particular crop may not necessarily reflect the farming system's productivity. A second issue concerns the subsidy of inputs in the North Africa region in comparison to the Sudano-Sahelian zone. However, some of the North African per hectare yields are higher than the world averages.

In Search of An African Model of Development

Table 4.3: Some Selected Agricultural Indicators in The Sudan-Sahelian Zone, 1994.

Country	Total arable land (mm ha)	Pasture Land (mn ha)	Forest & Woodland (mn ha)	Harvested Land as % of arable land	Agri.Value as % of GDP	Agri lab as % of labor force
Burkina Faso	3.6	6.0	13.8	81.7	37.0	84.4
Chad	3.3	45.0	32.4	44.8	35.6	70.4
Gambia	0.2	0.1	0.3	44.0	23.0	79.6
Mali	2.5	30.0	6.9	98.0	45.3	78.6
Mauritania	0.2	39.3	4.4	98.0	20.2	62.7
Niger	3.6	8.9	2.5	97.0	40.9	85.4
Senegal	2.4	3.1	10.5	54.2	18.0	77.5
Sudan	13.0	110.0	44.2	73.0	34.7	72.7
Region Total	28.8	242.4	115.0	74.7	31.8	76.4
Africa Total	187.9	852.6	760.8	42.52	21.1	60.7
Region % of Africa	15.3	28.4	15.1	26.9	1.3	12.7

Source: Compiled from FAO 1994 Production Yearbook, vol. 48 and 1995 African Development Report of ADB.

(a):mn ha stands for million hectares.

The ecology of the region and lack of appropriate yield-enhancing production techniques are mainly responsible for the low agricultural productivity, as the natural vegetation of the region is dominated by savannah vegetation, bordered in the south by open woodlands and in the north by steppes and desert vegetation. The region is largely arid and semi-arid, and the woodlands have been subjected to desertification as well as grazing and farming pressures. The challenge, then, is to find farming technologies that are suitable to the ecological conditions of this zone. The most important activity is nomadic and semi-nomadic pastoralism, which is adapted to the arid ecological conditions dominating the region. Yields of most agricultural products of the region are lower than Africa's average yields and well below world averages. There are, however, profound differences within the zone with regard to natural resources, climate, and agricultural systems. In this regard, a number of questions will have to be addressed with respect to what to invest in and where. For instance, should the northern part of the zone specialize in livestock production? Should agricultural investment focus primarily on increasing productivity in the south of the zone, where technical possibilities are greater, or should it focus more on the higher risk northern areas?

Despite low yields, the region has enormous agricultural potentials in the form of unutilized pasture lands and water resources.[18] In this regard, the zone has scope for increasing its productivity through development of appropriate production techniques that are both user-friendly and environmentally sound. Regional cooperation within the zone and/ or with the northern bordering region could help it to improve farming through, say, irrigation techniques and insect control. As stated earlier, the significant differences across countries in the zone with respect to yields of various agricultural crops reveal that there is an opportunity for specialization within the region and a scope for increasing regional trade and exchange.

The Niger River's waters, for instance, are underutilized compared to those of the Nile in Egypt. Regional cooperation in efficiently utilizing the Niger's water resources could increase agricultural production in the Sudano-Sahelian zone. Moreover, this zone could specialize in livestock development, since its ecology seems to be suitable for rangeland management. But above all, this is the region in which agriculture must enable people to feed themselves, since more than 75% of the region's total labor force is employed in the agricultural sector. This is also one of the regions in which poverty seems to be pervasive, and agricultural structural transformation should address the delicate linkage between population growth, food security and natural resources management.

C) Humid and Sub-humid West Africa

This agro-ecological zone includes the following ten countries: Benin, Cote d'Ivoire, Equatorial Guinea, Ghana, Guinea Bissau, Guinea, Liberia, Nigeria, Sierra Leone, and Togo. In 1994 the region's population for the region was estimated at 163.5 million (with 100 million for Nigeria alone) representing about 23% of Africa's total population. Table 4.4 below gives some selected indicators for the zone. For instance, the zone has about 47 ma ha of arable land or one-fourth of Africa's arable land, but only one-third of this land is under cultivation. In 1994, the GDP for the region is estimated at US$138 billion, accounting for about 27% of Africa's GDP. Value added in agriculture is estimated at US$48 billion (at constant 1985 dollar), which represents 9.5% of GDP for Africa, 35% of agriculture value added to the region's GDP, and about 10% of Africa's agricultural value added as percentage of GDP.

Table 4.4: Some Selected Agricultural Indicators for Humid and Sub-humid Zone, 1994

Country	Total arable land (mm ha)	Pasture Land (mn ha)	Forest & Woodland (mn ha)	Harvested Land as % of arable land	Agri. Value as % of GDP	Agri lab as % of labor force
Benin	1.9	0.4	3.4	35.8	39.0	57.6
Cote d'Ivoire	3.7	13.0	7.1	35.1	33.0	51.7
Equ. Guinea	0.2	0.1	1.3	-	60.0	51.3
Ghana	4.3	5.0	7.9	30.0	37.0	47.5
Guinea Bissau	0.3	1.1	1.1	42.0	47.0	77.0
Guinea	0.7	5.5	14.4	42.0	22.0	71.1
Liberia	0.4	5.7	1.7	na	32.0	68.0
Nigeria	32.4	40.0	11.3	33.3	35.0	63.4
Sierra Leone	0.5	2.2	2.0	-	37.4	59.2
Togo	2.4	0.2	0.9	27.9	55.0	68.1
Region Total	46.8	73.2	51.1	33.3	35.0	60.0
Africa Total	187.9	852.6	760.8	42.52	21.1	60.7
Region % of Africa Total	24.9	8.6	6.7	19.5	9.9	23.3

Source: Compiled from 1994 FAO Production Yearbook, Vol. 48 and 1995 African Development Report of ADB.

(a): mn ha stands for million hectares.

In the northern part of this region vegetation consists of open woodlands, while closed evergreen forests are found in the south. Between the two is a transition zone of mixed forest/savanna vegetation. The tropical moist forests and the open woodlands have been mined for industrial timber, extensive logging, and the expansion of agriculture, leading to large-scale encroachment on the natural forest. Closed forests now cover less than 10 % of the wooded area. The region also has extensive tracts of mangrove forests along the coast (African Development Bank, 1995). The rate of deforestation is on the increase, especially in Cote d'Ivoire and Nigeria, mainly due to commercial logging and not through cultivation of new lands, since the percentage of arable land in each of these countries is below 40% (see table 4.4).

The humid/sub-humid countries of West Africa are rich in agricultural resources, such as forestry and fisheries. The relatively high rainfall and warm temperatures permit 200% to 300% cropping intensity and therefore the opportunity for year-round production of rice, tropical fruits, and vegetables. However, data from FAO shows that the region's 1994 average rice yield of 1,666 kg/ha is below the African average (2,166 kg/ha) as well as the world average (3,554 kg/ha). Other crops grown in the region include cocoa, coffee, palm oil, millet, groundnut, and cotton. Similarly, low comparative yields are shown for millet. Both rice and millet are important staple foods for the population of the region.

Production of forest products, cocoa, coffee, and palm oil accounts for a large percentage of the GDP and the bulk of the value added in agriculture for the region. However, Deng et al (1995) has observed that "in the last five years most countries in the region have seen little or no change in total production or area planted. Between 1990 and 1994, for example, the total sawn-wood production declined from 6 billion to 5.7 cubic meters. Increases in coffee, palm oil and cocoa were marginally small at 2% per annum. With an annual population growth rate for the region estimated at 2.8%, more will need to be produced if the per capita and surplus required to sustain production are to rise above the current levels" (1995:21-22). Given the relatively abundant agricultural labor, land, and adequate rainfall in the region, the sluggish performance can be attributed to the lack of appropriate technology and lack of access to markets both domestic and regional. There are, however, seasonal labor bottlenecks that may call for selective labor-saving technologies. In addition, African farmers — of which the majority are women — do more than farming. They have non-farm enterprises and often migrate (especially men) seasonally. Hence, the opportunity cost of another farm operation is often not the return to another cropping or livestock activity, but what s/he can earn from her/his non-farm activity. Seen in this "opportunity cost" light, I may not be totally right here in assuming agricultural labor to be in abundance in this region.

Nevertheless, the region's agricultural value added is about one-half (47%) of Africa's total value added in agriculture, even though it has only one-fourth of both Africa's total population and arable land. In this regard, I would think that this agro-ecological zone has the greatest potential of achieving an agricultural-led sustainable development, especially when what I call the "sleeping giant" of Africa — Nigeria — wakes up. However, external debt is becoming a serious problem for potential stars of development in the region. For instance, out of the highly indebted 19 countries that have more than 80% of Africa's total external debt, three are in this region. These are Cote d'Ivoire, Ghana, and Nigeria, with a combined total external debt of about US$58.4 billion or 20 percent of Africa's total external debt.

Furthermore, regional integration and the empowerment of farmers would enable this region to achieve sustainable agriculture-led growth by the IFPRI's year 2020. And in particular, harmonization of macroeconomic and trade policies should substantially enhance the role of traders (especially market women who are already active) and processors in the region. In addition, both agricultural research and infrastructure (especially roads connecting most of the countries) are relatively developed in this region. There are no available official trade statistics from the region showing significant trade with other African regions to the North, East or South. However, there is a substantial unrecorded trade in livestock, cola, and fish between West African coastal countries and the Sahel region.

d)   Humid Central Africa

This agro-ecological zone is predominant in the following five countries of Central Africa: Cameroon, Central African Republic (C.A.R), Congo, Gabon and Zaire. The population of this zone is estimated at 62.3 million, constituting about 8.8% of Africa's total population. The humid Central Africa agro-ecological zone has the largest remaining closed tropical rainforest in Africa, covering about 70% of the land area (African Development Bank, 1995). The remaining areas consist of open woodlands and high-altitude forests and savannas. Population density is much lower than in the other sub-regions. Forestry is an important part of the economy of all the countries in the region, but high infrastructure costs limit the extent to which the forests are exploited.

Table 4.5: Some Selected Agricultural Indicators In The Humid Central Zone, 1994

Country	Total arable land (mm ha)	Pasture Land (mn ha)	Forest & Woodland (mn ha)	Harvested Land as % of arable land	Agri.Value as % of GDP	Agri lab as % of labor force
Cameroon	7.0	2.0	36.0	11.6	27.0	57.4
C.A.R.	2.0	3.0	46.7	5.7	48.0	58.4
Congo	0.2	10.0	21.1	15.0	9.0	58.4
Gabon	0.5	4.7	19.9	3.0	6.0	64.2
Zaire	7.9	15.0	173.8	25.0	32.2	63.6
Region Total	17.6	34.7	297.5	16.8	24.4	60.4
Africa Total	187.9	852.6	760.8	42.52	21.1	60.7
Region % of Africa	9.4	4.1	39.1	3.7	1.0	8.6

Source: Compiled from 1994 FAO Production Yearbook, Vol. 48 and African Development Report, ADB.

(a): mn ha stands for million hectares.

Table 4.5 above shows that the region has about 300 ma ha of forest and woodland representing about 40% of Africa's total forest and woodland, and 18 mn ha of arable land, of which only 17% is under cultivation. This region is endowed with both renewable and non-renewable natural resources which can advance the objective of sustainable development without necessarily focusing on increasing agricultural production. The main problem in the region is endemic economic mismanagement. All the countries of the region with the exception of C.A.R are among the highly indebted 19 African countries. Cameroon and Zaire are frequently unable to service their debts, as oil and mineral export earnings are being pocketed by the ruling elite while the civil society sleeps. The priority concern in this region is definitely political reform and the empowerment of the civil society, before one can talk of a meaningful framework for sustainable development.

e)   **Sub-humid and Mountain East Africa**

This agro-ecological zone is exhibited in the following nine countries: Burundi, Djibouti, Eritrea, Ethiopia, Kenya, Rwanda, Somalia, Tanzania and Uganda. The population for the region is estimated at 157 million, representing about 22.2% of Africa's total population. The combined GDP for the region is around US$34.2 billion or about 6.8% of Africa's GDP. Value-added in agriculture for the region is about 44.5 and 3.0 % of the zone's and Africa's value-added in agriculture respectively (see table 4.6).

With the exception of Kenya, Tanzania, and Djibouti (to some extent), most of these countries have been at war with themselves. The internal conflicts and civil wars in this region have reinforced, in my view, the current "Afro-pessimism" that prevails within the international development community. In this regard, the road to the year 2020 is a rocky one. Yet, there is hope that the voices of reason and rationality will prevail, as has occurred in Uganda and Ethiopia, and that the region can put its act together by harmonizing its political, social, and trade policies and strategies. This is a region in which a regional approach to its economic, political, and social problems will require concerted efforts on the part of regional leaders as well as from friends of the region in the other parts of Africa and the rest of the world.

Table 4.6: Some Selected Agricultural Indicators In The Sub-humid and Mountain Zone, 1994

Country	Total arable land (mm ha)	Pasture Land (mn ha)	Forest & Woodland (mn ha)	Harvested Land as % of arable land	Agri.Value as % of GDP	Agri lab as % of labor force
Burundi	1.4	0.9	0.08	12.4	56.0	90.6
Djibouti	0.2	0.0	0.0	--	na	na
Eritrea	1.3	4.8	2.0	7.7	31.0	na
Ethiopia	13.9	45.0	27.3	35.8	55.0	73.3
Kenya	4.5	21.3	16.8	41.2	25.3	75.2
Rwanda	1.2	0.5	0.6	13.0	38.5	90.6
Somalia	1.0	43.0	16.0	na	na	na
Tanzania	3.5	35.0	33.5	86.3	53.0	78.6
Uganda	6.8	1.8	5.5	19.1	52.5	78.5
Region Total	33.8	152.3	101.78	34.3	44.5	79.2
Africa Total	187.9	852.6	760.8	42.52	21.1	60.7
Region % of Africa Total	18.0	17.9	13.4	14.5	3.0	31.8

Source: Complied from 1994 FAO Production Yearbook, vol. 48 and 1995 African Development Report of ADB.

(a): mn ha stands for million hectares.

f)   Sub-humid and semi-arid Southern Africa

This region includes all the Southern African countries of Angola, Botswana, Lesotho, Malawi, Mozambique, Namibia, South Africa, Swaziland, Zambia, and Zimbabwe. The total population for the region stands at about 104 million or 14.7 % of Africa's total. Its combined GDP represents approximately 27.6 % of the total GDP for Africa, with South Africa alone accounting for about 21% of

Africa's total GDP. Agricultural value-added as percentage of Africa's GDP is 3.7% (see table 4.7).

Table 4.7: Some Selected Agricultural Indicators in the Sub-humid and Semi-arid Zone, 1994

Country	Total arable land (mm ha)	Pasture Land (mn ha)	Forest & Woodland (mn ha)	Harvested Land as % of arable land	Agri. Value as % of GDP	Agri lab as % of labor force
Angola	3.5	29.0	51.9	32.1	8.8	68.2
Botswana	0.4	25.6	26.5	32.3	6.0	59.6
Lesotho	0.3	2.0	0.0	50.0	11.0	76.3
Malawi	1.7	1.8	3.7	72.5	38.8	71.3
Mozambique	3.2	44.0	14.0	47.5	57.2	80.4
Namibia	0.7	38.0	18.0	18.6	10.3	32.0
South Africa	13.2	81.4	8.2	45.7	4.9	12.4
Swaziland	0.2	1.1	0.01	30.5	11.2	63.5
Zambia	5.3	30.0	28.7	11.9	14.0	66.2
Zimbabwe	2.9	4.9	8.8	63.4	14.8	66.2
Region Total	31.4	257.8	159.81	40.9	6.5	60.0
Africa Total	187.9	852.6	760.8	42.52	21.1	60.7
Region % of Africa Total	16.7	30.2	21.0	16.1	3.7	12.5

Source : Compiled from 1994 FAO Production Yearbook, Vol. 48 and 1995 African Development Report of ADB.

(a): mn ha stands for million hectares.

Information in table 4.7 indicates significant declines in the share of agricultural value-added in GDP for Botswana and Lesotho due to the increasing dominance of other economic sectors. In the case of Botswana, the rapid expansion of the mining sector over the years has led to a precipitous fall in the share of agriculture in the economy. Lesotho, on the other hand, has limited potential for agricultural expansion due to lack of adequate arable land. In the case of Angola, Mozambique, and Zambia, agricultural value-added in GDP has actually increased over the years, even though the share of agricultural labor in the total labor force continues to decline.

The Southern African region is endowed with large expanses of arable land, most of which has yet to be exploited. To realize the full agricultural potential for the region, the policy environment will need further consolidation in favor of agriculture. This will include the streamlining of institutional reforms in such areas as marketing, credit provision, research, and extension. Further improvements of the incentive structure regarding such policy areas as exchange rate regimes, pricing structures, trade and tariff policy would also be required. With the end of *apartheid* in South Africa and the restoration of peace and tranquility to Angola and Mozambique, the prospects for regional economic integration are very good indeed, and this region is likely to achieve the status of a relatively developed region by the year 2025. This is based on the assumption that South Africa will take a more proactive economic and political role in leading the region toward full economic integration during the next decade.

Social Integration

The third key element in the proposed African model of sustainable development is social integration. This should be conceived at two general levels. The first level concerns the social dimension of development, that is, integration of social concerns into macroeconomic frameworks. The second level of social integration calls for integrating various communities (ethnic groups) with varied convictions into a single national multiple-identity, on the one hand, and blending traditional African values and institutions with the imperatives of modernity, on the other. The two levels of integration would be achieved through a broad-based political authority such as that found in Mandela's South Africa or Museveni's Uganda. These two levels of social integration are intertwined and positively reinforcing. For instance, the social dimension of development presupposes and reinforces harmonious integration of various ethnic groups into what political scientists call a nation-state. It is in this respect that two of the leading issues in African development — reducing poverty and resolving internal conflicts — can be meaningfully addressed. Moreover, those who are responsible for the design of macroeconomic frameworks must be sensitized to the social dimension of development, so as to appreciate the fact that the art of macroeconomic policy formulation is to use available exchange rate, fiscal, and monetary instruments not for their own sake but for the sake of the community as well as in the service of the person-in-community. For instance, a well-trained economist should know a priori the likely effect of, say, devaluation of a local currency, on producers of tradeable goods, of non-tradeable goods, and/or on those with fixed income.

Macroeconomic frameworks that ignore social institutions and the structures of the society/community would essentially undermine one of their main objectives — enhancing the capacity for generating investable domestic savings. This is because the likely gains from, say, macroeconomic adjustment, accruing to some individuals in a given community would probably not be saved or reinvested, but used to support other members of the community to cope with hardship. The inability to assist other members of the community at the hour of their need can induce social tension and violence, which in turn could wipe out what one has accumulated. As shown by P.C. Lloyd in his study of Nigeria, "social and economic change — at least of the type experienced in Abeokuta — does not result in any great increase in individual tension, and contemporary Yoruba society manages to assuage this tension with a high degree of success, so that the health of the majority is not significantly impaired " (1967:248). There is no rule of thumb for integrating social concerns into macroeconomic frameworks, but those responsible for their design are envisaged to be knowledgeable about the fundamentals of African traditional societies.

The call for the social dimension of development can be romanticized in phrases, such as poverty-sensitive macroeconomic frameworks (Deng, 1995). In this regard, a development policy formulator must know that the economic problem facing an African community is "not merely a problem of how to allocate given resources,' but "rather a problem of how to secure the best use of resources known to any of the members of society for ends whose relative importance only these individuals know. . . .it is the problem of the utilization of knowledge not given to any one in its totality" (Daly and Cobb, 1989:45). This is basically in line with what I think to be the core of *ujamaa* philosophy. As I have quoted it earlier from President Nyerere's seminal work, one of the basic principles runs as follows: "In our African traditional society we were individuals within a community. We took care of the community, and the community took care of us. We neither needed nor wished to exploit our fellow men." Such a community is worth fighting for, as it provides the security of living in dignity and self-respect. Of course, some people will laugh and ask, How come *ujamaa* has not delivered Tanzania out of underdevelopment? This, to be sure, is a legitimate question. However, I will argue that Tanzania has, thanks to *ujamaa*, achieved social cohesion, stability, and harmony. As shown in the preceding section, all the countries (nine of them) in the sub-humid and mountain agro-ecological zone of East Africa, except Kenya and Tanzania, had been (some are still) at war with themselves. In fact, Kenya has witnessed ethnic tension for some time now. In this regard, Tanzania might not have achieved economic growth, but it has attained a reasonable level of social integration, which is unmistakably reflected in tolerance and social stability.

Jan Tinbergen consoles us that: "Economic history is a history of struggle and of failures as well as successes. But failures are not completely negative since they may teach us what not to do" (1958:67). Gunnar Myrdal forewarns us, however, of the "danger in economists carrying on their research while remaining ignorant of how they are conditioned by the surrounding society — and also, of course, by tradition and their personal inclinations'"(1970:441). Moreover, Herman Daly and John Cobb strongly advise us to "leave GNP alone as the proper measure of economic success and seek to counterbalance its influence by pointing to social and ecological indicators as of equal or greater importance" (1989:371). And Pierre Landell-Mills, describing various attempts at development by African leaders, concurs that: "With the exception of Nyerere's *ujamaa*, these models can be viewed more as attempts by African leaders to rationalize their authoritarian regimes, than genuine efforts to construct nation states on the basis of the communal and participatory principles found in traditional societies. These leaders failed to articulate a process for nation building, understood by ordinary citizens, that could effectively mobilise them around a shared vision" (1992:2). We must, therefore, revisit *ujamaa* to guide us in the process of social integration and in the fight against poverty. People must be allowed to make their choices freely and should not be grouped into villages, as was attempted in the case of *ujamaa*, and which does not mean villagization anyway.

The tendency has been essentially to view social structures and institutions as main obstacles to 'modernization,' which were therefore to be eliminated in the name of nation-building and development. I have argued elsewhere that "modern traditionalism is the 'transitional integration' which is the analytical framework in which modern science and technology are supposed to utilize the traditional institutions and values in bringing about a guided change towards the future well-being of the Dinka community. A society dethroned from its basic human values and institutions is like a bird stripped of its wings — it cannot move or fly to its desired destination. Science and technology, though necessary, are not sufficient by themselves in achieving a development that is based on human dignity and self-respect as reflected in the Dinka institution of <u>cieng</u> (unity and harmony)" (Deng, 1984:168-69). This statement, although it was made more than a decade ago now, has in my view become more valid and relevant to the prevailing general situation of development in Africa.

The knowledge of both worlds — traditional and modern — should be sufficient, as articulated by P.C. Lloyd, in the process of social integration:

> The continuance of strong ties with the extended family is frequently described as an impediment to the modernizing process and to economic development. In the West African context this assertion needs considerable qualification. The extended family, it is claimed, leads to a dispersal of savings which might otherwise be productively employed. . . .But much of the assistance given by the affluent is to the genuinely poor and needy, for whom the state provides no support; indeed, the governments of West Africa could not possibly afford elaborate social security services. And, as we have seen, family savings are often aggregated and invested in education, thus benefiting the whole society. It is argued, furthermore, that the drain on his income disinclines the prosperous man to seek wealth. . . .Yet the West African does not see the issue in this light. The expectations of his family can be a spur to further effort; the respect and allegiance of those supported provide rewards in themselves for many who maintain such traditional values. (1967:191)

The institutions of giving aid and charity from Europe and North America, which have flourished with the intensity of natural disasters and man-made crisis in Africa, are not necessarily unique to these societies. The above epigraph clearly demonstrates that giving and charity are embedded in the African social value systems. It also confirms the centrality as well as validity of the basic philosophy of *ujamaa*, in the economic, political and social institutions, structures, and processes of African traditional societies. These institutions, structures, and processes defined roles for both the community and person-in-community as well as set of rules of behavior that were strictly adhered to and enforced. However, things started to fall apart — to rephrase Chinua Achebe's *Things Fall Apart* — when these rules began not to be respected, as alien norms emphasizing individualism were being imposed on African traditional structures and institutions. This point is articulated by Arthur Lewis as follows: "In Africa the European capitalists and governments have acted in opposition to, and with contempt for the established customs, religions and ways of life, wherever these conflicted with European interests, with the result of more extensive disintegration" (1955:146).

The revival of the principles of individuals taking care of their community, and the community taking care of them, should be appreciated within the current global consensus on the prominence of the civil society. And since about half of Africans are poor and are economically, socially, and politically excluded, their integration into the development process requires that communities be *empowered* to initiate, design, execute, and manage their own priorities. This would in turn enable the communities to take care of their individual members and vice versa, as articulated by the core principle of *ujamaa*. That is, issues of poverty reduction are better handled by the communities themselves. For this to be achieved, appropriate mechanisms for political, economic, and social empowerment will have to be in place. This could be done through the identification and creation of appropriate instruments and institutions of community empowerment as well as persons-in-community. In agreement with Pierre Landell-Mills, "Africa will only emerge from its current difficulties if it can progressively remodel its institutions to be more in tune with traditions, beliefs, and structures of its component societies. The challenge is to build on the elements that are compatible with modernisation and development, rejecting those that are not and, where necessary and appropriate, borrowing wittingly from foreign models, Western or Eastern. The nurturing of civil society through the development of its associational life is critical for success — to both deepen and broaden popular participation in and control of its institutions" (1992:3). In this regard, I have identified three — political, social and economic — mechanisms through which Africa can begin to remodel its institutions by empowering the people. This will, however, require an active role by African intellectuals, so as to enhance this empowerment by providing alternative scenarios from which various groups or stakeholders in a community can select. The social responsibility of intellectuals is articulated by Nzongola-Ntalaja as follows:

> Given his characteristic formalism and idealism, Plato is unwittingly raising a point that has become a cornerstone of materialist epistemology. This is the view that, to be able to capture reality and to know it fully, one must at the very least interact with it and at best attempt to transform it. It is a view that rejects the empiricist position, which consists in taking the immediate appearance for the whole truth, while neglecting the underlying factors and processes determining it. Truths are neither ahistorical nor 'given' in nature. Knowledge of the real world is of knowledge itself being intimately associated with the material and historical conditions of its production. It is a process that is closely linked with politics. Laying intellectual hands to concrete social tasks means concretizing the dialectical unity of theory and practice not only in the production of scientific knowledge, but also in the practical involvement of intellectuals in society. (1987:122)

I strongly believe that knowledge is power, which must be used for the benefit and advancement of the community. One of the roles of African intellectuals is to contribute toward the accumulation of this knowledge, which has been accumulated by the community over several generations, by bringing into it comparative perspectives. Knowledge in this context is a commonwealth of the community, which also includes the concept of "social capital," or cultural capital which I have referred to earlier. In addition, the sense of community itself is a treasured wealth as elucidated by Julius Nyerere: "I would add that while Africa is poor in material wealth, it is still comparatively wealthy in the sense of community and of 'belonging.' I believe it would be a grave mistake for that kind of wealth to be thrown away in the search for more material possessions, important as they can be" (1993:22). As I have shown in a policy matrix discussed earlier, commonwealth (accumulation) is one of the six imperatives of the state, which a broad-based political authority is expected to use in advancing the general welfare of the people. A state with a narrowly based political authority does not have the legitimacy and hegemony to effectively utilize such a commonwealth. Moreover, this knowledge is a product of communal investment in the education of a majority of these intellectuals. It's a point well illustrated by Lloyd: "Usually one son alone has been to secondary school or university; the financial resources of his parents, and perhaps of his entire community, may have been invested in him as he won admission to successive educational establishments" (1967:186). I should now turn to the three mechanisms of community empowerment that I have stated above.

Political Empowerment

This is one of the difficult areas of empowerment, since participation in the political system essentially presupposes an economic power–base. However, participation in the political process does not necessarily mean that the poor will have to be elected to the national legislative institutions of their countries. It simply means that they must have a voice and the right to vote for those whom they think would adequately represent them and reflect their interests on the national political agenda. But nothing should really prevent them from being elected to the national legislative bodies if the "rules were right." And they seem to be right in the case of the Resistance Councils (RCs) of Uganda, as observed by Pierre Landell-Mills: "Because the RC Executive Committees are elected from an assembly of all the people in a village, the prospects seem favorable. The experience to date with RC systems has been very encouraging. Elections to the RC Executive Committee are held every two years and have been hotly contested, officially on an individual, non-partisan basis, although old political parties are in practice quite active. . . .by giving political roles to hundreds of thousands of people, the system has stimulated an immense growth in social responsibility" (1992:15). And it is this social responsibility that is the key to tranquility, cohesion, and harmony in traditional African societies. The instruments of political empowerment would consist of (i) public administration institutions; (ii) village and neighborhood councils; (iii) voter registration; and (iv) political parties. I will only examine the first two, since voter registration and participation in political parties/organizations would normally presuppose the existence of such empowerment. Voter registration and mass participation in the political movements are, in my view, the backbone as well as the defining features of a broad-based political authority. The state derives its sovereignty and other attributes from the people through mass participation in its affairs; — in the absence of which there is no political authority in the real sense of the word. This is because without local-level participation and responsibility in the political movement by the ordinary people, there will be no real democracy at the state/national level.

1) <u>Public Administration Institutions</u>: These institutions must be democratized and restructured so that they are in

tune with the social value systems of the community being served. By way of ensuring both efficiency and equity, public administration institutions, which are basically the intermediaries between the community and national government institutions, must be based on proportionate representation of various groups, such as women, farmers, youth, "tribal" chiefs, age-set, teachers, and so forth. This also applies to management structures of development projects. For instance, in the case of the Abyei Development Project Authority (ADPA) for the Ngok Dinka people of Sudan, I have conceptualized the participation of the beneficiaries in the management of the project as follows: "The ADPA is to be headed by a commissioner appointed in the interim by the President of the Republic and to be assisted by a director who will have a counterpart (co-director) representing the expatriate personnel. The Ngok Dinka chiefs (9) and their representatives in both People's Regional and National Assemblies are to be members of ADPA, in addition to heads of the units (or sectors) comprising the project as well as the Assistant Commissioner for Abyei People's Rural Council. . . . Thus, traditionalism is embodied in ADPA through the membership of chiefs who are symbols of local organizations, Dinka judicial system, set of values and social relations as well as fair tenure conditions that foster positive change for development of the traditional society. Also, modernism is reflected in ADPA through the membership of professional and technical personnel both national and foreign that symbolize technical knowledge, effective administration, infrastructure, and effective pest control and water management" (Deng, 1984:87-8).

2) <u>Village and Neighborhood Councils</u>: These are what I call community-based organizations (CBOs), which have multiple roles and perform varied functions. The CBOs, in my view, are the most appropriate vehicles for enhancing the awareness/consciousness of members of the community about their basic political, economic, and social rights,

individually and/or collectively. They are also, if properly used and empowered, instruments for horizontal integration of various ethnic groups into conscious political entities with national vision, instead a "tribalistic" outlook. In this regard, political empowerment of CBOs is an imperative of nation building as well as of sustainable human development. However, empowerment cannot take place in a setting where individuals and/or communities are not aware of their basic rights. The first step, then, should be a critical examination of basic social structures and institutions, such as household, age-set, secret societies, fraternities, and so forth, before any empowerment is exercised. Such an examination should lead to the identification of existing social structures, highlighting their weaknesses and strengths. A brief description of the social structure and its institutions of a typical Dinka society is given below as by way of illustrating this point.

One can describe the Dinka philosophy of *cieng* (unity and harmony) as being guaranteed through a well-defined social system that consists of four main units or institutions. These are *wut, dhien, macthok,* and *hot-thok.* Each *wut* (clan) is composed of *dhian*[19](lineages), each *dhien* consists of *mecthook* (families) and each *macthok* is comprised of *hot-thok* (households). The chain of authority, codes of conduct and behavior, and social relations are explicitly defined for each of these institutions. Moreover, these institutions in turn produce social, spiritual, military, and political structures and organizations, such as the age-sets, warrior groups, headmen, and chieftaincy. I consider these to be institutions and structures of governance of the Dinka political system, which is founded on the participation of ordinary Dinka people in the management of their affairs. This system of governance may not resemble every aspect of Pierre Landell-Mills' "British system of governance — an elected parliament, independent judiciary, and a professional and politically neutral civil service," but is based on the Dinka social fabric embedded in the philosophy of *cieng*.

Political mobilization and empowerment can therefore be made through the four structures/organizations of age-set, warrior groups, headmen, and chieftaincy. These structures will in turn utilize the social institutions described in the preceding paragraph to disseminate information about their basic rights *vis-a-vis* the nation state. They will also utilize them in their participation in the development process by taking part in the various elections and in political parties. In light of these structures and institutions, empowerment through voter registration and political parties will be greatly enhanced. In this regard, political empowerment constitutes a solid foundation for social integration, which is one of the key elements of an African model of sustainable development. This can be further illustrated by a passage from my study of the Ngok Dinka:

> The affairs as well as the destiny of the Ngok community is more or less determined within the institution of age-set. The authority of the paramount chief or any chief, for that matter, lies within this institution. The chief, as a symbol of society, is usually praised in various war songs. The British Colonial Administration effectively made use of the institution of age-set in performing many public-work schemes, such as roads and other public buildings. The Ngok Dinka were quick to compose war-like songs in building these public schemes on a voluntary basis. To complete a public project (road) on time is similar to defeating an enemy. (1984:90 - 91)

Social Empowerment

There is now a general consensus within the development policy community that education is one of the key instru-

ments for combating absolute poverty. Hence, social empowerment would require (i) greater access to education
and health services; (ii) respect for positive traditional values, the structure of a civil society, and religious organizations; and (iii) community organizations (e.g., women associations, youth, and labor unions) that foster principles
of social integration, harmony and stability. From the perspective of the Dinka people, "empowerment for them is
simply a matter of survival with dignity" (Sandbrook,
1993:9).

Again we can find guidance in the basic principles of
ujamaa in our concerted efforts to ensure a living with dignity for ordinary African people. In this regard, provision of
secondary basic needs, especially education and health,
would go a long way to improving the productivity of ordinary people, and thereby guaranteeing a more dignified living. Recent studies by the World Bank (1991b), Ojo and
Oshikoya (1994), and so on, have shown that investment in
education has higher returns to both individuals and society. "There is evidence," according to Ojo and Oshikoya,
"that human capital, as proxied by literacy rate and mean
year of schooling, significantly affects growth" (1994:17).
Summers (1991) has also shown that "a two tenths of one
percent increase in total factor productivity in developing
countries would do more for their living standards than an
additional $100 billion of capital invested at historical rates
of return" (1991:1). Generally speaking, as productivity increases, households desire for larger family sizes (that is more
children) diminishes. Moreover, access to education by poor
households is likely to contribute to the reduction of fertility
rates, in that female education would delay early marriages
(Deng,1992; Dasgupta, 1993; Deng and Fadayomi, 1994).

I have shown earlier how the Dinka social institutions and
structures were effectively made use of by the colonial administration in the Sudan to build roads and other public
infrastructures. Social empowerment in this respect will not

necessarily focus on the allocation of resources to the community, but more on the recognition of social institutions and their integration into the development processes. The role of government and its agencies, then, is to facilitate the smooth functioning of social institutions by emphasizing the positive aspects of traditional cultures. For instance, CBOs, Non–governmental organizations (NGOs), private voluntary organizations (PVOs), and other community–based and grassroots institutions should fully be involved in the design and execution of development projects/programs that concern these communities. And since poverty in Africa is essentially a rural phenomenon, these organizations act as the most effective institutions of empowering the poor and other vulnerable groups to take active part in the conceptualization and preparation of multisectoral interventions at the community level. With social empowerment, the community can now begin to take care of its individual members, and the individual members in turn can take care of the community. It is also important to note that agriculture is not only the engine of growth for many African economies, but the key sector in the reduction of poverty and a vehicle for ensuring equity–enhancing policies. The underlying assumption in this book is that equity and efficiency are not incompatible when it comes to rural Africa. In fact, they need not be when viewed in the context of my definition of sustainable development, given earlier in this chapter.

Traditional cultures that hinder and frustrate the social rights and roles of women in the community must be reformed and/or discarded if they are not reformable. In this regard, the education of women is critical to a comprehensive social empowerment. Partial empowerment — that is, recognizing only male social organizations and/or sending only boys to school — is insufficient to alleviate poverty, on the one hand, and to achieve a sustainable human development, on the other. Furthermore, and as reflected by Julius

Nyerere, "membership of a community is still a very strong element in the life and culture of people. In Africa, human rights groups, and groups concerned to extend people's civil power, will not be capable of helping to `empower the people' unless they give greater emphasis to this cultural dimension than is customary in Europe and North America; in our circumstances we need to put as much emphasis on social duties as on social rights. There is plenty of work left in this field" (1993:19). Among the work left in this field is the urgent need to design mechanisms for the social empowerment of African women, which I think to be one of the major obstacles to economic and political empowerment. And this will require African women intellectuals to take the lead in this endeavor, so as to ensure that gender analysis in the African context would go beyond the usual activism and toward a real social empowerment of women. It is a challenge that I believe the present generation of African intellectuals, men and women, should be able to meet.

Economic Empowerment

I will start this section with a dialogue that took place in January 1983 between a group of headmen (most of them my uncles) and myself. I was on a short holiday from my graduate studies in the United States of America, and so the elders of Dacuek clan wanted, as it is customary, to know about the way of life in America. We were seated under a tree, which was the court of my late cousin, Chief Reec Deng. We exchanged views on economic, social, and political life in America, but the most interesting and relevant part, which I wish to reproduce some excerpts from here, was the one dealing with *hakuma* (government) and their perception of it:

My uncle Deng Herkeer (his praise name): Father Bany Dorjuur,[20] *hakuma (government) has been collecting taxes from us since the time 'turuk'* [21] *touched our land. What does it do with our taxes, and when is it going to be rich, so that it does not bother us anymore?*

My response: *Uncle Herkeer, let me first inform you that to the best of my knowledge, all governments in the world collect taxes from their citizens in one form or another. Then, to come back to your difficult question, hakuma in our case collects taxes to build schools, hospitals, roads and to provide security in the form of army and police. So, it will continue to collect taxes for-ever.*

Assembly of elders: *Laughter! Followed by a song in praise of my grandfather. Then a follow-up question from the same uncle: But, father Ajerbeek, you are the only son of Dacuek clan who had been to the university; we build and maintain all the time the section of the road that is allotted to Dacuek between Bor town and kongor district; the hospital is in Bor town, which you know is far (about 70 miles) from Wangkulei court center; we do not know what the army does for us, it only came here in the year of Macoot to kill most of our chiefs and burned villages and we do not have anybody from Dacuek in it now after Numeiri and Abel Alier brought peace; as for the police, yes police, those stationed in Kongor – they run away when the Murlei tribe attacks us with guns, even our women do not run away, but the police run away. So we think, oh son of my brother Acuek Majongthon[22] – we think that hakuma should stop collecting taxes from us until the time we have more children in schools and universities; until the time po-lice start protecting us from the Murlei; and until the time a hos-pital is built here in Wangkulei.*

The above excerpts will suffice to provide us with a point of entry for analyzing economic empowerment within the overall framework of social integration. The relevance of the cited dialogue to the discussion here is that economic empowerment should be seen in a wider context of village economy or what I would call "community economics."

Communities and/or villages should be allowed to raise revenues (taxes) and spend them according to their priorities in pursuit of their own well-being. It is my conviction that most villages and communities in Africa can improve their own economic situations rapidly, and contribute to the growth of the national economy, if they were allowed to do what they think is good for themselves, with minimal assistance from outside and at their request.

For the ordinary African people to fully participate in the productive activities of their national economies, they must have easy access to economic resources and institutions. But, such access would only be feasible if the communities are provided with basic economic assets, so as to improve their initial conditions. The government should not only come to the ordinary people when it is collecting taxes out of their meager resources, but should be there when they need it. However, it must be emphasized that provision of basic assets: equity–enhancing land reform measures, micro–credit, physical infrastructure and extension services, and so forth, should be done in consultation with the concerned communities. This implies that interventionist actions would be undertaken not only in response to market failures, but more importantly in empowering the communities so that they can take care of their poor and other vulnerable groups in the society. In this regard, three measures are central in the process of economic empowerment of the ordinary African people. These are centered on: (a) skill development; (b) provision of credit; and (c) small–scale enterprises.

a) Skill development: The most valuable asset that ordinary people have is their labor. Hence, skill development should be central to any empowerment policy, for it is an important instrument to enable communities to combat poverty in their societies. For instance, in my study of the Abyei area I advocated that: "The role of women will be more significant in cooperative management and primary health care units. Traditionally, Dinka women are good managers of their households, in that all decisions pertaining to household production and consumption are typically made by the housewife. In addition, women can also be trained in other skills just as men; this is because most of the real productive activities of the Dinka economy are performed by women. Most of the development projects are biased against women, hence the ADP-model is designed to integrate the importance of the role of the Dinka women into the process of transition from traditional mode of production to modern mode of production that utilizes science and technology" (1984:91-2). I have also shown the importance of skill development in the case of the Zimbabwe social development fund (SDF) under the Economic Structural Adjustment Program (ESAP), where retrenched and laid-off workers from both the public and private sectors were first given intensive short-term courses in basic skills required in the sectors of the economy that were likely to absorb them. As of July 1995, the SDF in Zimbabwe has generated employment for about 5,000 people, most of whom were self-employed mainly in micro-enterprises.

b) Provision of credit: I strongly believe that the most appropriate vehicle for provision of credit to either individuals or groups-in-community is the SDF. As pointed out by Stern (1994), to "be impoverished is to lack ability or power to change one's situation. It is thus imperative that for poverty alleviation efforts to be effective and sustainable, the strategies employed have to be internalized by poor people in a way that they themselves will be able and motivated to continue to improve the quality of their lives" (1994:28-29). In recognition of this fact, social development (or action) funds have been set up in a number of African countries to address the likely short-term effects of structural adjustment programs. These are now evolving into instruments for financing poverty reduction projects and programs, and could therefore be replicated as vehicles for provision of credit. A brief description of the SDF is given below, so as to illustrate the point being made here.[23]

The SDF is usually a quick–disbursing instrument for financing pilot schemes (or micro–projects) that aim at improving the social situation of the poor and vulnerable, in the short–to–medium term, and hence enable them to fully participate in meaningful and rewarding economic activities of their choice and design. In the Central African Republic, Malawi, Mozambique, Somalia, Zambia, and Zimbabwe, targeted interventions have been financed through SDFs. These targeted interventions, in my view, would serve as models for systematic and replicable assistance to the poor and vulnerable groups in Africa, especially where similar conditions exist. They are, therefore, the most appropriate instruments for empowering ordinary people and their communities. The focus of the SDF is the financing of activities in the three broad areas that make macroeconomic frameworks more poverty–sensitive. These are actions to protect the poor and vulnerable groups in the short run; compensatory measures to minimize the transitory costs of economic reform; and measures to empower the poor and vulnerable groups to participate in meaningful and productive activities. And they can be extended as measures of economic empowerment of the community.

Actions to protect vulnerable groups in the short run normally focus on the economic and social infrastructure. Experience from the Somali social action fund (SAF) shows, for instance, that ten micro–project proposals were on water supply— drilling wells. Moreover, a 15–Km long small irrigation canal was constructed and was functioning smoothly before the collapse of the Somali state. It is conceivable that these interventions would not have been possible if the SAF was not established. This is especially true given the relatively low cost of each intervention. Both donors and governments would normally find it costly to be involved in such micro–projects. For instance, the cost of the canal was about US$40,000 and was constructed over three months. Provision of water in the framework of actions to protect vulnerable groups is important in three ways. The first is that it minimizes chances of getting sick through unclean water, thus preventing a person from falling into a situation of defenselessness, insecurity, and exposure to risk, shocks, and stress (Chambers, 1985). Secondly, easy access to water reduces both the distance and time spent by women to fetch water for household consumption. This would enable the household to utilize time saved in productive activities, thereby increasing the income–generating capacity of the household. A third important aspect of providing water as a protective measure is to protect vulnerable households from the rising cost of water due to the liberalization of prices in the context of economic reform. The importance of water as a basic human need is quite obvious and cannot be overemphasized.

Compensatory measures to minimize the transitory costs of an economic reform are normally in the form of subsidies, food–for–work, feeding centers, and school lunches. Food–for–work is an important component of the Malawi poverty reduction strategy. In some instances as in Somalia food is provided to teachers in some of the rural areas as a supplement to their salaries. This direct supplement of teachers' salaries has two major positive implications. Most, if not all, of the teachers in rural areas could be categorized as vulnerable, to the extent that they are being protected and/ or prevented from falling into poverty. Furthermore, the children who are being taught by these teachers would not be attending school if the teachers were not given additional incentives to stay. The children are, therefore, being protected indirectly.

As regards provision of credit to the vulnerable groups in Somalia, three proposals for group–lending were presented to SAF. One was a small–scale credit scheme targeted at vulnerable women in Mogadishu. The women beneficiaries were to pay the prevailing market–determined interest rate. This credit scheme was managed by an indigenous PVO (i.e., Aadamiga) focusing only on women. There was a three-month grace period, after which the loan (principal and interest) was paid over a period of 15 months. The rationale behind charging a market–determined interest rate was to maintain the revolving nature of the credit, to the extent that many women benefitted from this facility. It was also meant to motivate efficient management of micro–projects financed by the revolving credit scheme, as these funds were not a 'free lunch.' Thus, this ensured that pilot interventions were not providing a new window for reintroducing distortions to the economy under the pretext of helping the poor. Another example of group–lending was the village revolving credit fund. This was managed by an international NGO (Save the Children — USA) operating in Somalia at the time. The main objective of the revolving fund was the establishment of an appropriate mechanism to efficiently administer US$50,000 that was lent by SAF to a group of small farmers in Qoryooley. My discussions with both market women and small farmers (in Malawi and Somalia) revealed that the problem facing these two groups is not the inability to pay the market–determined interest but rather the access to the financial market, where accessibility is a function of credit-worthiness based on collateral.

c) Small-scale enterprises: A number of small–scale enterprises are being financed through SDFs in Malawi, Zambia and, Zimbabwe, as part of empowering the poor and vulnerable groups to fully participate in productive activities. These persons have varied skills in craft making and carpentry. Other examples of micro–enterprise are grain grinding and oil millings, fishing gears, shoe–making factory, a bakery, and soap–producing factory. These projects, from our perspective, are good illustrations of how an African government could empower its poor and vulnerable groups to participate in the design, execution, and management of micro-projects which are too small for either government agencies or the international donor community to be involved in their identification and formulation. Table 4.8 below gives examples of complementary micro-projects within the overall framework of the Zimbabwe ESAP. One of the main objectives of the SDF in Zimbabwe is the promotion of income-generating and employment-creating micro-projects. The first group in poverty to be targeted by the SDF was the retrenched public sector employees. A total number of about 25,000 employees were envisaged to be laid-off by the end of the ESAP (1992-95). In this regard, micro-projects/programs were to be formulated to assist the retrenched workers to be "recycled" into productive activities of the economy. The drought of 1991/92 delayed the process of retrenchment, and it was only toward the end of 1992 thet the implementation of the retrenchment policy was resumed. As of 31 May 1994, a group of retrenched workers that have opted for micro-enterprises were engaged in 549 projects in 8 sectors with a total cost of about Z$35 million, and about 2,005 new jobs.[24]

Five out of eight sectors have the highest number of projects. These were service (209), manufacturing (121), agriculture (68), and transport and retail with 64 microprojects each. The same sectors, with the exception of the transport sector, created more jobs: manufacturing (819), service (570), agriculture (324), and retail (290). It is interesting to note that mining and construction appear to be labor-intensive compared to the other sectors. However, a close examination of the data shows that manufacturing enjoys labor-intensive micro-projects, which ranges between 3 (welding) and 45 (clothing) workers. Moreover, this sector (manufacturing) has created a higher number of jobs with more than 50 percent of activities concentrated in six major areas. These are: welding (36), clothing (12), oil pressing (11), leather (9), furniture (6), and bakery (5).

Table 4.8: Zimbabwe-SDF funded Micro-Projects by Sector, Total Cost and Number of Jobs Created.

SECTOR	NO. OF PROJECTS OF PROJECTS	TOTAL VALUE Z $"000"	NO. OF JOBS	AVE. VALUE Z $	AVE NO. OF JOBS/ PROJECT
AGRICULTURE	68	4,657	324	59, 662	5
MANUFACTURING	121	7,896	819	62,257	7
TRANSPORT	64	5,002	130	78,153	2
MINING	09	600	153	63,989	13
CONSTRUCTION	13	818	169	62,962	13
SERVICE	209	11,501	570	55,028	3
RETAIL	64	4,388	290	68,563	5
SPORT	1	80	3	80,000	3
TOTAL	549	34,942	2,458	63,647	4.5

Source: compiled by the author from SDF records as of 31 May 1994.

The service sector is second to manufacturing with respect to employment–generation, though the leading sector as far as the number of projects is concerned. More than 50 per-cent of micro–projects in this sector are grinding mills. These micro–projects appear to be spread throughout the country in sharp contrast to those in the transport sector, which are concentrated in the capital city, Harare. In fact, more than two–thirds of micro–projects in the transport sector (mainly mini–buses) are located in Harare. In addition, the service sector has the lowest average cost per project of about Z$55,000 compared to Z$80,000 in the sport and transport sectors. The average cost of a micro–project in the service sector varies between Z$10,000 (barber shop) and Z$150,000 (tillage). Agriculture is the third sector with respect to both the number of micro–projects and jobs created. About three-quarters of agricultural activities are concentrated in three out of nine areas: market gardening (22), pen fattening (17), and poultry (14). The cost of a micro–project in this sector ranges between Z$5,000 (poultry) and Z$120,000 (farm-ing). The number of employees per micro–project varies be-tween one worker (poultry) and 27 (fish farming) workers. The fourth major sector with respect to job creation is retail. Here, micro–projects are concentrated in general dealership (19), butcheries (7), restaurant (6), and fast–foods, i.e., take–away (6). The cost of a micro–project varies between Z$21,000 (tuckshop) and Z$143,000 (restaurant).

The purpose of reproducing some examples from the SDF in Zimbabwe is to make a case that ordinary people in most African communities can take care of themselves if sufficiently empowered. The words of my uncle spoken under a tree several years ago always haunt me. In retrospect, he foresaw what was coming, as current events in southern Sudan as well as the rest of Africa have proven him right. The positive elements of African value systems outweigh their negative aspects. We must blend these positive aspects with what we might have learned from other cultures. This is what I am calling social integration. Without it there will be no sustainable development in Africa.

Ecological Harmony

This is the fourth and final key element of what is being referred to in this book as an African model of sustainable development. As I have stated in the preceding chapter, it is my conviction that African economic 'man' was at peace with his ecology in the distant past. This peace was characterized by a symbiotic relationship. As the "mother of all continents," it would seem to me that ordinary African people are conservationists by intuition, otherwise Africa would not still have one-third's of the world tropical forest cover, when its land area is only one-fifth of the world (WRI, 1995). In a recent New York *Times* article,: "One Common Ancestor Of All Men Discovered," John Noble Wilson reported that,: "Earlier analysis of the DNA of the mitochondria, the tiny structures within each cell that generate its energy and that are transmitted only by the mother, indicated that all humans have as a common ancestor one woman who lived in Africa some 200,000 years ago — and inevitably has been stuck with the name Eve."[25] But the ecological harmony in the "mother of all continents" is increasingly coming under stress from "economic systems that developed in the West in conjunction with the Industrial Revolution as well as new political systems reinforced the lack of concern for conservation of nature. Industrial production systems divorced men from nature and their dependence upon it" (Tisdell, 1990:12).

The problem, however, is that ordinary African people still very much depend upon nature. Hence, the search for a development model that would improve the well-being of ordinary people, through environmentally sustainable production techniques, while ensuring a harmonious coexistence between African economic 'man' and his entire ecological system. Some analysts think there is generally a trade-off between the goal of economic well-being, on the one hand, and the goal of conservation, on the other. Such a trade-off is being advanced by two opposite views — mainstream economics and greenpeace activism. According to Tisdell, "The mainstream economic viewpoint remains that sustainability of natural resource use, even renewable resource use, is not a worthwhile goal in itself and, indeed, may reduce human welfare rather than add to it"[26] (1990:28). There is, however, a middle road between these two extreme opposite views. I believe that the two goals of human welfare and conservation can be achieved simultaneously, through sustainable development, which I have defined earlier in the chapter. In this regard, the call for ecological harmony and balance is a clear recognition of the need to maximize economic well-being subject, among other things, to rational utilization of natural resources. And as shown by Robert Riddell:

Human beings, the dominant predators and most comprehensive omnivorous, are totally dependent for life on other components in the living biomass. The egocentricity of human exploitation has ignored this interdependency and the need for balance. The point here is that mankind cannot go on indefinitely drawing resource needs from a finite larder and must learn to reciprocate with the environment in order to survive. Industrial pollution of riverine and ocean waters leads to new aquatic ecosystems with coarser and more poisoned inhabitants; whole-sale clearances of tropical forests induce irreversible soil erosion; and abstraction from aquafers at rates which exceed their replenishment ensures permanent water restrictions. Imbalance will serve to shrink the resources of nature, which means a lower level of atmospheric and hydrological purity and a reduced variety of flora and fauna available for people to live upon. (1981:40)

The message contained in the above passage is, in my view, simple and clear — production techniques and consumption patterns that are inharmonious with the natural resource base are likely to bring great sufferings to future generations. It should be emphasized at this point that ecological harmony very much depends on the other key elements of sustainable development — a consensus-based democratic system, agriculture-led economic growth, and social integration. This essentially calls for a multisectoral approach to the integration of environmental concerns into development strategies in Africa. Moreover, ecological balance requires a true partnership among all the stakeholders, including donors, in the African environment. For instance, African tropical rain forests are contributing to the global ecological balance through their absorptive capacities of greenhouse gases, which add to global warming. But this is not to romanticize them in the "global commons" of Daniel Bromley and Jeffrey Cochrane (1994). They stated that "the global commons consists of, for example, the earth's atmosphere, the oceans, the international tropical forests (especially the Amazon), biological diversity, and Antarctica" (1994:1). It is interesting to note that ecological problems manifested in recurrent droughts and land degradation in Africa were often attributed to the African communal system of land ownership, and became popularly known as the "tragedy of the commons," as advanced by Garrett Hardin (1968). But this notion is now being turned upside down by Bromley and Cochrane (1994), who eloquently show that the "tragedy of the commons" is a misplaced concept, for it confuses open access property regimes with common property regimes. This distinction is very important — and overdue — for the hypothesis of the so-called "tragedy of the commons" has led to many misguided policy prescriptions as well as ideologically loaded strategies that have of late advocated individualization of the land tenure system in Africa on economic efficiency grounds. Bromley and Cochrane have further provided a useful framework for those African countries that are endowed with tropical rain forests, to seek appropriate compensation packages for the role of these resources in absorbing greenhouse gases produced by the developed economies in Europe, Japan, and North America. The arguments of both sides are vividly illustrated by the following passage:

> Those in the North want to protect tropical forests as a means to process the large and increasing production of greenhouse gases. People in the North have one primary interest with two implications. Their primary interest is to maintain their lifestyle and their fossil-based energy system. They want to find a way to: (1) maintain tropical forests to process greenhouse gases and (2) discourage those living in the tropics from increasing production of greenhouse gases. People in the South have a primary interest in achiev-

ing economic development. This seems to imply: (1) cutting down tropical forests to earn foreign exchange or to clear land for agriculture and (2) building factories and buying automobiles for the newly prosperous masses. We could not have a more pronounced conflict of interests between the two regions. (Bromley and Cochrane, 1994:6)

The view taken here is in line with Barry Commoner's: "root cause of environmental crisis is not to be found in how men interact with nature, but in how they interact with each other and that to solve the environmental crisis we must solve the problem of poverty, racial injustice and war."[27] These three issues — poverty, injustice, and civil strife — were addressed in the context of agriculture-led economic growth, social integration, and a consensus-seeking democratic system of government. I would argue, however, that it is the interaction between human beings among themselves which in turn determines their interaction with nature. This takes us back to the important concept of a person-in-community, as used by Daly and Cobb (1989). I have shown in the section dealing with social integration that the core of the *ujamaa* philosophy is that the community takes care of its individual members, and these individuals in turn take care of the community, thus ensuring social harmony and stability. Put differently, social harmony would create an enabling environment for poverty reduction; social, economic and political justice; and peace and tranquility. Such a community should normally be at peace, as well as in a reciprocating relationship with its physical environment, thereby attaining ecological balance and stability. And in light of the fact that a typical African state consists of multi-ethnic groups as well as multi-stakeholders with respect to the environment, ecological harmony requires an all-embracing environmental policy. The main objective of this environmental policy should be integration of ecological principles into macro-policy frameworks.

According to Bromley and Cochrane, "environmental policy is about rights and duties. It is also about benefits and costs to various interests" (1994:7). These various interests are what I call multi-stakeholders, and what is at stake here is ecological harmony with poverty reduction and economic growth. In a typical African traditional community/society, rights and duties govern what in my view is the "goodness of the commons," in which individual well-being is synonymous with that of the community. This "goodness of the commons" is not restricted to natural resources, for example, land forests, and water, but it includes social values such as trust, self-respect, dignity and so forth. The benefits of the "goodness of the commons" are, in my view, embedded in social harmony and ecological balance, with all the multiple gains that subsequently arise from them. Its costs would very much depend on diverse perspectives. There are those who believe that the "tragedy of the commons" is the ultimate cost of the "goodness of the commons." But I would think that the costs are in the form of resources used in the observance of rules and regulations that are in place to ensure the flow of benefits, on the one hand, and performance of duties toward these benefits, on the other. In this regard, the design and implementation of environmental policy would involve a two-way communication process between three layers and/or centers of decision-making: micro, meso, and macro levels. This two-way process would facilitate horizontal and vertical integration of ecological principles into meso and macro-policy frameworks. Decision-making is used here loosely to include policy formulation, management, and implementation, and policy management is to be understood as meaning monitoring and evaluation.

The first layer or center of this policy formulation is the micro level, which is the community. The community is assumed to consist of socially homogeneous individuals with defined rights and duties. The individuals are also assumed to have identical preferences, but their wealth/income is a function of their personal characteristics and the initial re-source (for example, livestock and labor) endowment of the family. Moreover, community institutions and structures — CBOs, NGOs, household, age-set, secret societies, fraterni-ties — are the main instruments for accessing resources (use-rights) and for enforcing obligations (duties) to protect the "goodness of the commons." Farming households, for in-stance, have the right to choose what they want to produce on their land, using production techniques of their choice. However, they are obliged to select and use sustainable pro-duction methods that do not lead to the depletion of a natu-ral resource-base of the community. In this regard, the focus of the environmental policy would normally be on natural resources management at the community level for a given agro-ecological zone. This would in turn, as argued earlier, enable African agriculture to help people feed themselves, on the one hand, and lay the basis for sustainable economic growth, on the other.

This view is also supported by a number of policy ana-lysts and development agencies. For instance, the United States Agency for International Development (USAID) as-serts that "sustainable use of the natural resources base — soils, forests, range, water — to produce an improved liveli-hood is critical to the economic future of millions of African families" (1993:24). USAID also recognizes that Africa is a large continent which is rich in diversity and varied farm-ing systems, but "some characteristics are common to sus-tainable agriculture across sub-Saharan Africa" (1993:24). It points out four common characteristics that are relevant to our discussion here: (i) sustainable agriculture is not syn-onymous with subsistence agriculture; (ii) the diffusion of sustainable agricultural system is a multidimensional pro-cess; (iii) sustainable agricultural systems often incorporate forage crops and trees; and (iv) sometimes the diffusion of sustainable systems is linked positively to demographic pressure.

By way of enhancing natural resources management at the community level, it is imperative that environmental impact assessment (EIA) be performed on all the new production techniques before they are introduced for adoption by the farming households. It should be stated here that a farming household can be involved in multiple production activities, such as herding, cropping, fishing, woodcutting, and so forth. This would make the household the unit of analysis with respect to environmental management and policy formulation. The household would normally receive the best natural resources management practices from its participating members in various structures and organizations within the community. For those communities, such as the Dinka, that still maintain age-set structures and initiation rituals, new environmentally sustainable production techniques are likely to be adopted faster through these organizations. The role models and example-setters are logically found in each of these social structures, which can be targeted as agents of better natural resources management practices. A practical example from USAID of a pilot farmer in Mali may help to illustrate this point:

> He began by agreeing to be a pilot farmer, a status that enabled him to receive special training, gain access to new technologies, and receive on-farm help in trying new practices. Through the years, his example has inspired many others to try new practices that increase yields while maintaining the productive capacity of the land. Since 1980, yields on Coulibali's farm have increased dramatically. Average yields for millet are now 1,400 kilograms per hectare (kg/ha), up from 400 kg/ha. . . .In his diversified operation, he also grows maize, cotton, ground-

nuts, forage legumes, cowpeas, and pigeon peas —
and he maintains a tree plantation, harvesting poles
at regular intervals and selling them for use in construction. . . .group of farmers visit Coulibali's farm
and others like it to see new ideas in practice. These
farm visits are encouraging the transfer of technology. Estimates suggest that 80 percent of the 10,000
farmers in the region have adopted one or more new
practices to improve productivity. (USAID, 1993:25)

From the above passage, it is obvious that there are many
good examples at the micro level that hardly get the attention of a macro-policy formulator, simply because of lack of
communication between the various levels of policy formulation. The inability to understand and appreciate local
knowledge of natural resources management by those responsible for national public policy is one of the factors that
is threatening the stability of ecology and associated ecosystems in many African countries. The case study of the
Machakos in Kenya by John English et al. (1995), cited in
chapter three, is one of the examples in support of the argument that considers local knowledge as power. That is, when
local communities are empowered to manage their own natural resources, they usually do it in a sustainable way, which
in most cases defies the perceived conventional wisdom at
the meso and macro levels. My case study of the Rashiyida
Arab in eastern Sudan in 1980 illustrates a tragic situation of
how a community can lose its rights on pasture land through
policies designed in the name of national development advanced by bureaucrats who are ignorant about the local conditions. Another example, is the Jonglei canal in Southern
Sudan, where a top-down approach was adopted by policy-
makers with good intentions, but with very limited knowledge about and appreciation of its environmental consequences, including human suffering in the surrounding areas. Fortunately, the project was never completed, thanks to

the civil strife in that part of the country. All these examples illustrate one thing — the necessity of having a two-way communication between policy actors at the micro, meso, and macro levels.

The second level of policy formulation with respect to the environment is meso. Environmental policy is, however, more complex at the meso level than at the micro level. The complexity of environmental management and policy formulation arises from the fact that the policy formulator is dealing with different sectoral issues, on the one hand, and varied communities, on the other. My view would be to adopt national/global sectoral and/or sub-sectoral guidelines on the integration of environmental concerns into the design of projects/programs for all the relevant sectors at this level. For socially heterogeneous communities, the most appropriate strategy would be to harmonize rights and duties and integrate them into coherent institutional arrangements for social responsibility at the meso level, which would in turn ascertain ecological harmony. But I would argue that the basic systems of property rights of natural resources of each community be kept intact, as much as possible. A word about the meso level of policy formulation is needed here, so as to avoid any likely confusion that might arise. The meso level is analogous to the provincial, regional, or state level for countries that have such political systems and administrative structures.

In most African countries, the state nominally owns the land, forests, and other natural resources. And given weak administrative state structures in a large number of countries, this type of ownership has essentially evolved into an open access regime, where "there is no authority system to enforce behavioral norms among participants concerning the natural resource" (Bromley and Cochrane, 1994:10). In this regard, I would advise against state ownership of resources when it cannot enforce compliance with respect to proper natural resources management. As shown by Bromley and

Cochrane, it is important to have an authority system that "can meet the expectations of rights holders. Private property would be nothing without the requisite authority system that makes certain the rights and duties are adhered to. The same requirements exist for common property. When the authority system breaks down, management of natural resource fails, and common property degenerates into open access" (Bromley and Cochrane, 1994:13). This should be a powerful reminder against any attempt by the state to own all the natural resources in the country, as has been the tendency in the post-colonial era. Moreover, when the known authority system breaks down, it is not only natural resources management that degenerates, but communities also tend to disintegrate, which can sometimes have relentless ramifications on the nation-state. In addition, social irresponsibility reinforces the degeneration of natural resources management and consequently ecological imbalance, which leads to further impoverishment, thus producing a vicious cycle of poverty, rapid population growth and environmental degradation. An appropriate strategy then, would be to empower communities to manage, on user-rights basis, those natural resources that are likely to fall into "no man's land." However, if there is a relatively functioning market on, for example, land then a normal evolution of a private property regime should not be prevented from emerging. But, the most important point about environmental policy formulation and management at the meso level is the processing of information and its timely communication (more than dissemination) within the meso layer, that is, between its socially heterogeneous communities, on the one hand, and to the other two centers of decision-making — the macro and micro levels — on the other.

The third level of environmental management and policy design is the macro or national layer. This has been the level at which policies, environmental and otherwise, have been formulated without substantial inputs from the other two

— meso and micro—centers or points of decision-making. Moreover, this level has unduly benefitted from external support, both in material and intellectual resources, which have not been passed on, in most cases, to the other layers. Since the Rio Earth Summit in 1992, the number of environmental plans, such as National Environmental Action Plans (NEAPs), has increased. In addition to environmental plans, a number of studies are being conducted with a view to enhancing environmental management and policy design. Among these studies are, for example, the Country Environmental Profiles (CEPs) being undertaken by the African Development Bank for all its Regional Member Countries (RMCs). There are also numerous efforts at institutional strengthening and capacity building in the area of environmental management and policy formulation. All these efforts are genuine attempts, which are aimed at making macroeconomic frameworks more pro-nature. However, these efforts and plans will not, in my view, lead to any significant improvement in the quality of the African physical environment if they continue to focus on influencing macro-policy without due regard to the other two important layers of policy formulation. Hence, the need for a two-way communication between the three levels of environmental policy and decision-making. This kind of two-way communication would only be possible when the political authority begins to derive its legitimacy through mass participation in the affairs of the state at all levels of governance. As it has been mentioned earlier, the emerging African model of democracy is likely to produce such a system of governance in which ordinary people are sovereign.

Conclusion

By way of recapitulation, I have shown in this chapter that the main purpose of public policy is the enhancement of the general welfare of the people. This general welfare, from an economist's point of view, is an optimization problem which needs to be solved by the state subject to the six leading issues in African development. Furthermore, an expanded Human Development Index (HDI) of the UNDP is used as a proxy for the policy objective of general welfare or human progress and betterment. An African model of development is then conceptualized and presented as the most appropriate framework for solving the leading issues in African development discussed in chapter three. In this regard, I consider the state as the hub of an African model of development around which the other key elements — agriculture-led economic growth, social stability, and ecological harmony — depend. This is because the state is treated in the proposed model as an endogenous factor, whose characteristics (attributes and imperatives) are determined by a development policy formulator. For instance, a policy analyst under this model must first address the political element as a point of departure for prescribing development strategies. The underlying assumption here is that one should not prescribe policies for a state whose face is unknown to the prescriber. I believe that part of Africa's development problems are due to our designing economic policies in isolation from the state, as if it does not matter. We must have a clear idea of the sources of state attributes and imperatives to design and recommend an appropriate development strategy. That is, development policy formulation must go beyond prescribing/packaging policies and begin to address itself to the political dimension of development.

I have argued in this chapter that the emerging African state, symbolized by South Africa and Uganda, derives its attributes and imperatives from the mass participation of various segments of the community/civil society in its governance at differing levels. This in turn provides the new state with a broadly based political authority, which is necessary for the implementation of the key elements of the proposed African model of development. The new state has, for example, the legitimacy and power to carry out economic reform by implementing requisite measures that would create a sustained enabling environment for the mobilization of domestic savings (private and public) and foreign private capital for investment in the leading sectors of the economy, especially the agricultural sector. It also has the legitimacy and power to pursue a regional economic integration strategy as a way of ensuring a sustained economic growth with initial focus on the agricultural sector. A growing economy would enable the state to get out of the debt trap. Moreover, a conducive macroeconomic environment resulting from a broad-based support for economic reform would in turn enable the poor and other vulnerable groups to fully participate in the productive activities of their respective national economies. Thus, the new state would be able to tackle simultaneously all the six leading issues in African development, through a consensus-seeking system of governance as a dominant strategy for achieving agriculture-led growth, social integration, and ecological harmony.

NOTES

1. The generation of African leaders who brought about
    political independence were also intellectuals who
    devoted their thinking to the liberation struggle and
    issues of Pan-Africanism. Their success then was inher-
    ent in their unity. It was the intellectuals of the post-inde-
    pendence era who failed to achieve the second indepen-
    dence through their inability to adapt development para-
    digms to the objective conditions of Africa.

2. I should here qualify the notion of economic independence,
    so that it is not misunderstood. I am not at all calling for
    Africa to de-link from the global economy, as was often
    done by the dependency school. By economic indepen-
    dence, I mean internalization of economic policies and
    strategies, so that economics is made more relevant to
    public policy, more sensitive to social suffering, more in
    harmony with the environment, and more focused on
    raising the well-being of ordinary African people. All these
    concerns cannot be achieved if Africa were to disengage
    from international trade. By designing economic strate
    gies that are in harmony with her history, values, and
    institutions, Africa can effectively compete in the global
    economy.

3. From "Free From Royals," an article published in the
    Financial Times of May 6, 1996, page 14.

4. I recently came across this useful terminology in a
    presentation by Professor John Toye of the Institute of
    Development Studies (IDS), University of Sussex, at a
    Workshop on "Sub-Saharan Africa — Looking Ahead,"
    organized by the Institute of Economics, University of
    Copenhagen during 1-2 November 1995. According to
    John Toye, social capital is "trust, norms and `horizontal'
    networks which provide the social context of institutional
    performance." In African traditional societies people do
    invest in trust and social norms, and in this regard, it is

social capital. The various references to Nyerere, Soyinka, Platteau, and to Serageldin and Taboroff in this book illustrate this fact.

5. Some observers think that this is unrealistic! But nothing should prevent us from dreaming and aspiring to such a public policy goal. I do not believe in Afro-pessimism, I subscribe to Afro-optimism.

6. The International Food Policy Research Institute (IFPRI) has set an agenda for the year 2020. It is known as A 2020 Vision Food, Agriculture, and the Environment. It is an appropriate framework for situating the development policy objective of an African 'consensual democratic state.'

7. *Brackets in the original text.*

8. The call for cultural values to be respected and reflected in the public policy of a country is not unique to African scholars. President Clinton of the United States of America is reported by the New York *Times* (Internet edition of 26 October 1995:3), to have said: "If the Republicans plunge ahead and pass this budget, I will veto it and demand a budget that reflects our values."

9. Brackets and inverted commas in the original text.

10. The government of Siad Barre collapsed while a joint mission from ADB and the World Bank was in Mogadishu discussing with the "government" implementation of an Agricultural Sector Adjustment Program. ADB is the only multilateral development institution currently giving loan to Sudan, which is at war with itself. And of course our children will pay back the ADB and IMFs the debt that was used to kill their uncles and cousins!

11. Quoted from the National Bureau for Economic Research (NBER) Report, Winter 1994/5, page 72. I am not of course implying the return of a relatively small elites of Euro pean descent to re-colonize Africa. The point being made is to show the importance of initial conditions for growth.

12. Quoted from John M. Staatz. (1994). *The Strategic Role of Food and Agricultural Systems in Fighting Hunger Through Fostering Sustainable Economic Growth.* Michigan State University (MSU), Agricultural Economics Staff Paper #94-39

13. The new technological revolution in information brought about by the electronic "super highway" should enable farmers to have easy access to global technology, without necessarily waiting for researchers in African research stations to produce the needed technology. The focus now may well be shifted to roads and farmers' education in the use of new information technology, i.e., how to access and utilize information from the electronic super high way, through the Internet.

14. The six country islands are not included: Cape Verde, the Comoros, Madagascar, Mauritius, Sao Tome & Principe, and the Seychelles. They together have about one-fifth (17.6%) of Africa's total arable land.

15. From a background paper for an international conference organized by PAPA on *The Future Face of Post Cold War Africa: Building Inter-African Solutions to Urgent Needs,* held in Leiden, The Netherlands on 22-24 November 1996.

16. The Lagos Plan of Action (LPA), which was adopted in 1980 by the Organization of African Unity (OAU) envisioned an African common market to come into being by the year 2000. According to Onwuka the objectives of the common market were: "to promote development, co-operation and integration among its member states, in all economic, social, and cultural fields for the purpose of fostering closer relations among its member states towards accelerated collective self-reliant and endogenous economic, social and cultural development of the African continent to raise the quality of standard of living and dignity and respect of its people" (1985:60).

17. This should not be surprising, given the fact that these are oil producing countries.

18.   For example, Sudan, which is the largest country in Africa, is well endowed with natural resources, but they cannot be fully utilized because the country has been at war with itself for 31 years out of 41 years of political independence. In fact, many experts and policy analysts in the 1970s and early 1980s thought that Sudan was a potential "bread-basket" for Africa and the Arab world. The current war in southern Sudan has discarded such hopes.

19.   Dhian is plural of dhien, with two main usages. Dhien either is lineage, which is the meaning used here, or hearth.

20.   I am named after my grandfather, Lual Deng, so all my uncles and aunts normally address me, especially on happy occasions, as if they were talking to their father. Bany Dorjuur is one of several praise names of Lual Deng, this particular name literally meaning "chief that reconciles many races." The story goes that Lual Deng was given a bull in marriage from a distant clan and possibly "tribe," and since marriage is a symbol of harmony and living in peace, I guess, this was the logic of his praise name after that bull.

21.   Turuk refers to Turkish-Egyptian rule of the Sudan during the Ottoman Empire.

22.   Praise name of my father.

23.   Most of this section has appeared in some of my recent publications (cf selected references at the end of this book).

24.   Latest figures, obtained by a recent African Development Bank mission to Zimbabwe in June/July 1995, show that about 10,500 persons have been trained in how to start and run their own enterprise; some 1,290 micro-projects have been approved for a total loans amount of Z$98.8 million.

25.   From The New York Times, Internet edition of 23 November 1995.

26.   The (in)famous internal memorandum of Lawrence Summers, former vice president of the World Bank,

in which he proposed migration of "dirty" industries to Africa, is a good example of this thinking.

27.   Quoted from Robert Riddell. (1981)

CHAPTER FIVE

THE BASIS FOR HOPE
AND OPTIMISM

◆

Africa has 23 of the world's land; yet less than 25 percent of arable land is actually cultivated, and only 2.8 percent of the cultivated land is irrigated. Merely 1 percent of Afica's approximately 4,500 cubic kilometers of annual internal renewable water resources are currently being put to use. Only a tiny fraction of Africa's rangeland is being managed as improved pasture. And Africa's forests, including almost a third of the world's tropical forest cover, could yield significantly more timber and other forest products.

-Peter Veit et al. (1995:2)

The above epigraph provides an important point of departure for concluding this book. In spite of the complexity and resource implication of the six leading issues in African development that are likely to dominate Africa's policy agenda in the 1990s and beyond, I still think the time has come for the so-called Afro-pessimism to give way to Afro-optimism. There is always a turning point in the history of nations, and the year 1994 is a historical moment for Africa. This turning point is characterized by three emerging themes: new realities in development assistance; the rediscovery of Africa's resource endowment; and Africa's rebirth. I will examine each of these themes in the rest of this chapter, by way of concluding the book.

New Realities in Development Assistance

The year 1994 marks a new era with respect to development aid, as the Republicans recaptured control of both chambers of the U.S. Congress. This has in turn triggered a heated debate on foreign aid, especially with respect to Africa, in the U.S. Congress and the rest of the developed world. This debate is opportune from two important points. First, it is a last "wake-up call" for Africa to disentangle herself from the vicious circle of underdevelopment on the one hand, and from foreign-aid addiction and the dependency mentality on the other. The condition of dependence, according to Rajni Kothari, "has in many respects been far worse than that of colonial subjugation. Moreover, paradoxical as it may sound, it is a dependence that has become more real with growing aid, transfers of technology and assistance for furthering economic development of the so-called developing countries" (1993:85). And in agreement with the Washington-based Global Coalition for Africa (GCA), "aid dependency, not inadequate external financial support is, the problem.[1]" This is particularly true in light of emerging empirical work, which tends to show that foreign aid normally benefits the politically powerful groups in the recipient countries (Bjorvatn, 1995; Pedersen, 1995). In this regard, aid recipient countries may not have incentives to address the root causes underlying the pervasive poverty afflicting a majority of their citizens. On the contrary, the argument goes, some of these countries use poverty as an instrument for seeking more aid; and more aid tends to widen the gap between the ruling elite and ordinary people. But a broadly based political authority will use foreign aid

to advance the general welfare of its people. Mass participation at various levels of governance is inherent in the
Mandela's/Museveni's model of African democracy.

Furthermore, Karl Pedersen argues that "since aid is allocated to countries where the need is highest -- where consumption of the poor is lowest -- recipient governments may
find it advantageous to keep the consumption of the poor
down" (1995:1). Jakob Svensson has also found some evidence that "aid induces weak fiscal discipline and that increased fiscal difficulties lead to higher inflow of aid"
(1995:28). All these arguments, combined with budgetary
difficulties in the donor countries, are beginning to exert
pressure for a drastic reduction in the volume of aid on the
one hand, and more stringent conditions attached to its utilization on the other. This also is affecting the so-called soft-
loan-window of the multilateral development institutions,
such as the African Development Fund (ADF) of the African Development Bank and International Development Association (IDA) of the World Bank. According to the *New
York Times*, the U.S. under President George Bush's leadership "committed itself to contributing about $1.3 billion next
year to the International Development Association...As part
of its deficit reduction program, the House and Senate want
to renege on that commitment and reduce the contribution
to between $577 million, the House figure, and $775 million,
the Senate's figure. Neither figure makes fiscal or ethical
sense...Every dollar in American contributions leads to $4
or $5 more in contributions from other industrialized coun-
tries.[2]" The effect on the ADF will be more drastic than that
on IDA, as the U.S. is likely to reduce its contribution by
more than 50 percent[3]. In this regard, the focus should now
be on how to enhance the marginal productivity of foreign
aid, rather than wasting scarce resources in attempting to
increase its volume. This would make every dollar of foreign aid more significant in combating absolute poverty in
Africa, and thereby generating for the poor an effective de

mand, which will in turn create, other things being equal, its own supply of goods and services.

Secondly and most importantly, the debate has reconfirmed the strong conviction of many researchers and policy analysts that Africa has great strengths, both human and material, to develop. This point is particularly articulated by Peter Veit, Tanvi Nagpal and Thomas Fox: "Although the natural resource base has been severely exploited in the past by colonial powers, indigenous political and military leaders, and foreign interests-often with U.S. support during the Cold War -- it (Africa)[4] can still meet the basic needs of Africans and contribute to the growth of the global economy" (1995:1). Moreover, friends of Africa have eloquently argued, together with those having a stake in foreign aid, that the donor economy stands to benefit most from development assistance.

But more interestingly, foreign aid is the most effective instrument for ideological indoctrination as observed by the *New York Times*: "The loan program is also politically effective. By inviting poor countries to open their economies to trade and adopt market reforms, I.D.A. loans are a cheap way for Congress to spread capitalism.[5]" There is nothing wrong with capitalism as long as it aims to improve the economic well-being of all the people in a given African economy. And for Africa to participate effectively in the new global economy, she must invest in the education of her people, so that they become more productive and competitive. This should in turn attract some of the labor-intensive industries to Africa, in search of cheaper factors of production. Hence, the new realities with respect to foreign aid may actually help African development in the long run; it is creating a new positive attitude of inward-looking and political will to do better than before in the service of Africa and her ordinary people. And as the saying goes -- where there is a will, there is a way. Moreover, Sara Berry (1993) reminds us of an ancient African proverb -- no condition is permanent. Furthermore, Benno Ndulu has, along this line of reasoning, stated:

> One also sees considerable change towards diversi-
> fication of channels of assistance to encompass a
> larger set of players in the recipient countries in keep-
> ing with the broader trend of enhanced local owner-
> ship and democratization of the political systems. The
> implication of the above changes are mainly two.
> First, domestic resource mobilization and the effort
> of diversifying sources of external finance attain a
> central position in development efforts and with them
> required domestic policy changes. Second, the effi-
> cacy of resource use, particularly under public
> programmes, become imperative. The upshot of
> these two implications is that SSA countries have now
> to set in motion changes and mechanisms that will
> allow them to survive with much less external assis-
> tance as they raise efficiency and their own resource
> mobilization. In this context enhanced local owner-
> ship and accountability are means for achieving
> greater efficacy in the utilization of dwindling exter-
> nal resources. (1995:5)

Resource Endowment

Economic theory postulates that production of goods and
services is a function of four factors of production -- land,
labor, capital and entrepreneurship. The first two factors are,
generally speaking, in relative abundance in Africa, while
the last two are in short supply. The cited passage at the
beginning of this chapter illustrates the extent of Africa's
natural resources -- land, water, and forests -- and their level
of utilization. Africa is also endowed with renewable resources (for example, solar energy) and non-renewable resources, such as gold, copper, uranium, oil, and so forth.

As argued by Robert Riddell, "fuel for mankind in low-income countries will always be available in ways that are hardly mysterious. First, there is the eternal sun and its direct warmth. Second, there is the very efficient solar-based creation of carbohydrate energy through photosynthesis. Future tropical-living people will be comfortable, and can always have the use of fuel adequate to their needs" (1981:31). In addition to these natural resources, Africa's peoples and their indigenous knowledge are now being recognized as among the most important ingredients of African development. The African woman is a critical resource that has been neglected for too long in the conceptualization and design of macroeconomic frameworks in the continent. Moreover, the current global trend toward political pluralism and subsequent empowerment of the civil society should enhance the important role of women in the economy. African women, it will be recalled, are intuitive entrepreneurs -- an important factor that has been often overlooked in the past. I would also think that the new macropolicy environment will facilitate the return of African talents from the rest of the world to Africa. Edgar Pisani has shown that "a large number of teachers, researchers and scientists from the South fill and enrich the universities and laboratories of the North. Very few return home, because they do not find there the conditions for intellectual growth and for a life in keeping with the requirements of their work" (1993:98-9).

The challenge, then, is how to design production techniques that will make optimal use of Africa's resource endowment. There is an urgent need to produce, for instance, technologies that will generate food surplus from the unutilized three-fourths of Africa's arable land, while maintaining harmony between African ecology and economy[6]. It will require, however, a careful and delicate mix between labor-intensive and labor-saving technologies. But above all, it will require a leading role for African women in the conceptualization and design of these production techniques. I would think that this approach goes beyond the self-defeating concept of women in development (WID) which paradoxically reinforces the marginalization of women in the development process instead of including them in it. African women should, therefore, be seen not from the perspective of WID, but rather as managers of resources, initiators and nurturers of development. This should in turn enable Africa to adopt an agriculture-led economic growth strategy at the turn of the century. In this regard, the role of African institutions, such as ADB and ECA, is to ensure adequate investment in female education on the one hand, and effective utilization of foreign aid (capital) and its complementarity to the other factors of production on the other. In fact, Africa's agriculture is the most un-protected and least subsidized in the world. Yet, we expect Africa's agriculture to perform wonders with little investment and no protection. Recent events in the developed world tend to indicate that agriculture and natural resources management will be at the center of the coming debate on international trade in the context of a liberalized global economy. The following passage illuminates this point:

> To leave agriculture to forces of the free market will not work. For thousands of years, governments have safeguarded food production with price interventions and subsidies, for both political and economic reasons. The factors of production in agriculture, such as climatic variations, can never be fully controlled, so some safeguards are essential. What has been gained on the one hand - the incentive to produce in an ecofriendly way - must not be lost on the other, through irresponsible surrender to the overwhelming forces of free trade. Wouter van Dieren (1995:2)

Africa's Rebirth

The establishment in 1994 of a democratically elected Government of National Unity (GNU) in South Africa, led by President Nelson Mandela, marked the end of *apartheid* and the beginning of a new era, not only for South Africa, but for Africa as a whole. It marks the rebirth of Africa and symbolizes her long walk to freedom, liberty and above all, to human dignity. I would also hope that it is the beginning of the end of the repeated humiliation and indignation that Africa has been subjected to, over the years, if not centuries. But, will Africa -- especially African intellectuals -- seize this opportunity and start a serious process of soul searching and of rethinking the formulation of her development policy? From the perspective of an African intellectual, I would think that we must first rediscover our mission and our role in making Africa's rebirth a reality. In the words of a great African revolutionary scholar:

> Each generation must out of relative obscurity discover its mission, fulfill it, or betray it. In underdeveloped countries the preceding generations have both resisted the work or erosion carried by colonialism and also helped on the maturing of the struggles of today. We must rid ourselves of the habit, now that we are in the thick of the fight, of minimizing the action of our fathers or of feigning incomprehension when considering their silence and passivity. They fought as well as they could, with the arms that they possessed then; and if the echoes of their struggle have not resounded in the international arena, we must realize that the reason for this silence lies less in their lack of heroism than in the fundamentally different international situation of our time.
> Frantz Fanon (1963:207)

There is now a tendency to forget and/or ignore the work of African writers during the Cold War era, as being too radical or because the demise of the Soviet Union and death of communism have rendered it irrelevant.[7] But our analysis would be incomplete if we were not to revisit and make use of the work of the preceding generations of African scholars. Their work is an integral part of our intellectual heritage and knowledge - a treasure which we must replenish and pass on to the next generations. We are in a better position than our ancestors, who in most cases passed down wisdom and knowledge to us and the preceding generations through the oral tradition. Moreover, it would be recalled that Africa was a battleground between capitalism and communism during the competitive politics of the Cold War era. This had in turn hindered the process of critical thinking within the community of African scholars. Africa's contribution to knowledge and human betterment was often disregarded as either "unscientific" and/or "primitive." It is therefore our duty to pay homage to the past generation of African scholars -- progressive and reactionary -- who stood up against humiliation, even though their thinking was essentially conditioned by the prevailing geo-politics of the cold war world. The ideological conflict in Africa had inevitably produced a conducive environment for mediocrity.

Tah Asongwed has, for instance, articulated such an environment in his autobiography of a life president of a fictitious country, yet reflecting some realities of the competitive security politics of the Cold War: "For the moment, I am Life-President, Commander-in-Chief of the Armed Forces, National President of Mandzah National Union Party, Chancellor of the National University, Keeper of the Till, Custodian of National Wisdom, Depository of Talent, Most Exemplary Paramount Chief, and so many titles" (1993:226). A careful reading of Crawford Young's seminal book, *The African Colonial State in Comparative Perspec-*

tive, will vindicate the point being made by Tah Asongwed. Asongwed's adjectives of a life-president demonstrates how African scholarship was utilized to flatter leaders instead of guiding African development. This, in my view, led to intellectual poverty in Africa, which I have alluded to in chapter three of this book. For example, in Numeiri's Sudan, such phrases were written and chanted by many intelligent people who put their scholarship in the service of a dictator instead of the country. Some became prisoners of their own ideas, so as to avoid any conflict with the dictator and his gang of self-conceited and mediocre intellectuals. And others challenged the system after they have left it. Mansour Khalid, who was a Minister of Foreign Affairs for some time during Numeiri's Sudan, has elucidated this point in his two books -- *Numeiri and The Revolution of Dis-May* and *The Government They Deserve*[8]. His analysis confirms the point being made here: "If Numeiri's regime had survived for sixteen years it was neither because that was predestined by Allah nor only made possible through external championship; the sixteen-year panorama of unmatched successes, peremptorious tyranny and self-indulgent decay was the creation of the Sudanese elite, civilian and military, progressive and conservative" (1990:243).

The international situation of our time has, however, created new circumstances that have facilitated the challenging of systems of life president and/or the like that perpetuate misery and indignation in Africa. Nevertheless, Africa's "strong men" seem to be defying the logic of the new global consensus on freedom of expression, liberty, and *glasnost* as basic human rights. In this regard, challenging African dictators is proving to be fatal, as illustrated by the heroic death of Ken Saro-Wiwa, who was one of the leading environmental scholars in Africa. His brutal execution is a clear reminder of the kind of sacrifice that an African intellectual may be forced to make. Ken Saro-Wiwa has set a difficult standard for some of us who are willing to sacrifice their lives in pursuit of truth in the defense of the dignity of ordinary people and in the **service of Africa**. I hope his sacrifice will awaken the sleeping giant of Africa -- Nigeria -- and lead Africa's rebirth. In fact, the Global Coalition for Africa (GCA) has warned that "Nigeria, the largest African nation, is experiencing an alarming deterioration of governance and threatens to destabilize the region at enormous cost.[9]" Ken Saro-Wiwa's blood has reignited the fire on the shrine of African heritage, which is full of struggle and sacrifice. His blood will turn into a precious spring, an internal renewable resource that will continue to water the green grass of African scholarship forever. We must be ready to die for our convictions with respect to African development, or else Africa will continue to be marginalized and humiliated perpetually.

At the institutional level, the 1995 Annual Symposium of the African Development Bank on Socio-political Approaches and Policies for Sustainable Development in Africa could be seen as a kick-off for the process of soul searching as well as of rediscovering our mission. The soul-searching aspect of this process essentially calls for a critical assessment of development strategies tried by Africa during the last thirty years (1965 - 1994). Such an assessment is intended to provide a point of entry in the rethinking process of African development policy formulation. All the stakeholders in Africa's economic progress, political stability and social well-being should fully participate in both the assessment of the past efforts at development and in the determination of the most appropriate strategy for the future. The involvement of all the stakeholders -- government, business community, civil society, donors, and so forth -- in the process of policy formulation, would in turn, ensure sustainability of development in Africa. In this regard, African intellectuals are particularly called upon to lead this process, so as to guarantee its conformity with African thought and culture. This has been the underlying premise of this book.

One important point needs to be made before concluding this book. That is, Africa's rebirth will not be realized without a comprehensive reform of the governance of African institutions, such as the African Development Bank (ADB), ECA and the Organization of African Unity (OAU). For the ADB, the turning point was also 1994, a year in which the Bank initiated its own reform through an internally inspired process of self-examination and soul searching of what is wrong with the Bank in **its service of Africa**. But this was in reaction to what I call Gorbachev's *glasnost* and *perestroika* that had finally hit the multilateral financial and development institutions, after having hit countries first. These institutions started their own internal self-examination through formation of task forces to review portfolio management with respect to quality. The World Bank was the first to go public, admitting that its investment projects in the developing countries have not been 100 percent successful. This was made in the Wapenhans report, *Effective Implementation: Key to Development Impact,* issued in November 1992. The Wapenhans report was produced by a portfolio management task force. Subsequently, the three regional development banks -- Inter-American Development Bank (IDB), the Asian Development Bank (AsDB) and the African Development Bank (ADB) -- established their own task forces on portfolio management. The IDB report, *Managing for Effective Development,* was released in October 1993 and it is known as the Qureshi report. The AsDB report was issued in January 1994, while the ADB released its report in April 1994.

For the African Development Bank, the reform comes after thirty years of existence. By any standard, thirty years in the life of a public institution, especially a financial one is a very long time indeed. During this period the Bank has made outstanding contributions to economic development and social progress of the African continent. Although there have been shortfalls in achieving some of the goals, this is expected in the evolution of any institution. President Julius Nyerere has once stated: "For too long we in Africa -- and Tanzania as part of Africa -- have slept, and allowed the rest of the world to walk round and over us. Now we are beginning to wake up and to join with our fellow human beings in deciding the destiny of the human race. By thinking out our own problems on the basis of those principles which have universal validity, Tanzania will make its contribution to the development of mankind. That is our opportunity and our responsibility" (1968:32). It was with this understanding in mind that Mr. Babacar Ndiaye, president of the African Development Bank at the time, commissioned a study "to critically analyze Bank's portfolio with respect to quality." The task force to undertake this review consisted of eminent experts in the field of development, assisted by senior Bank staff[10].

The team was to review four major areas of the Bank: its performance over the years; lending policies and practices; resources and organization; and culture and governance. As stated earlier, the report of the task force on Project Quality was released in April 1994, with shocking findings. The report does not mince words -- it calls a spade a spade, both praise and criticism are given where and when due. The issues raised by the Knox report are relevant to the main theme of this book -- rethinking African development. In this regard, I will summarize its main findings below. But I will first state the following seven key points that are highlighted in the report:

a) Africa needs a Bank that is fired with imagination, ideas and flexible and innovative approaches to development[11];

b) The Bank does not have a comprehensive reporting system to assess the quality and status of its portfolio;

c) The Bank aims for volume but does not have the capacity to supervise;

d) The Bank tries too much with too little;

e) Fundamental changes in attitudes are needed if efforts to improve the quality of lending are to succeed;

f) There must be unity of policy and purpose throughout the Bank; and

g) Finding an African solution to Africa's problems depends on the Bank reforming itself.

On Performance: At the outset, the report recognizes that the Bank, to a greater degree than other sister institutions, is operating in a continent racked by civil unrest, poverty, famine, corruption, and with soaring populations, on the one hand, and declining levels of quality of life, on the other. These problems are compounded by weak institutional and analytical capacities and a low level of human development in the Bank's Regional Member Countries (RMCs). With this difficult working environment in mind, the report nevertheless points out that the Bank lacks a comprehensive reporting system to assess the quality and status of its portfolio. The task force supported this finding by stating the following five points:

a) Sector goals were often ill-defined or simply implied.

b) Project terminology is imprecise, inconsistent and often ambiguous. Words (such as goals, objectives, aims, and purposes) meant different things to different readers and. . . .different authors of reports.

c) Monitoring is not systematic and so does not allow management control and oversight by the Board.

d) There is no reporting system in the Bank to alert management and the Board to potential problem projects. Of the Bank's 630 completed projects, only 200 (31.7 percent) have been the subject of completion reports. Even when written, such reports are prepared in haste and often incomplete.

e) Disbursement is handled slowly in all sectors and spread over longer periods than initially provided for. This is especially noticeable in public utilities (water and sanitation) and agricultural projects.

All of the above points are factors that determine the quality of operations on the one hand, and their impact on economic development and social progress on the other. In this regard, the findings of the task force were of great concern to all the Bank's stakeholders, and not only its shareholders. They also strengthened the internal call for institutional reform and adjustment

On Lending Policy and Practice: The report confirmed that the Bank's lending policies and procedures on project development were "generally sound," but observed that they were "not applied with consistency nor with the required knowledge of country, sector and project." Specifically, the report draws attention to (i) inadequate understanding of RMCs as reflected in the weakness of the Bank's economic strategy papers and the absence of comprehensive sector studies; (ii) reliance on RMCs in identifying investment projects despite their institutional weakness to do so within a comprehensive development framework; (iii) inadequate allocation of time and resources (human and material) to preparation, appraisal, supervision, and post-evaluation, leading in turn to problems with respect to disbursement, repayment, and eventually indebtedness. The report asserts that the way out of this problem would be strict adherence to quality, which "must be ensured at all stages of the project cycle -- from programming and identification, through appraisal, supervision, post evaluation and the collection and feedback experience."

The findings of the report in this area also confirm the thinking of the reform-minded professional staff within the Bank. This is illustrated by the following passage from my internal memorandum:

> The rationale for a more integrated country focus results from a fundamental observation about the institutional structure of the operations departments. At present, the institutional layers separating sector

specialists on the one hand, and economic and programming analysts, on the other, do not encourage
or facilitate comprehensive country analysis. Country analysis is the foundation of a viable lending program and the major tool is Economic Prospect and
Country Programming Paper (EPCP). The EPCP
does indeed contain country analysis, but it is normally prepared by a macroeconomist and a program
officer. While sector specialists are in theory expected
to participate in the preparation of the EPCP, they
hardly take part in practice or do so only from a
distance. You will recall that economists and program officers are in the Country Programs Departments, while sector specialists are in the Projects
Departments. This institutional arrangement is, to
my mind, one of the major constraints to our understanding of the borrower's needs and to the
elaboration of appropriate country programming
based on a comprehensive country analysis supported by rigorous sectoral studies. I would, therefore, think that the time has come for some institutional restructuring of our own with the view to
enabling the Bank Group to finance economic development and social progress in Africa more effectively as we approach the twenty-first century.
(March 1994)[12]

On Resources and Organization: The report gives considerable time and space to allocation and use of the resources at
the Bank's disposal, particularly human. It confirms that the
Bank has a competent and qualified professional staff. This
staff, however, are either under-utilized or shackled by the
system -- a system which either duplicates or suppresses
responsibilities. For instance, "There are officers doing too
much while others do virtually nothing." Moreover, the general criticism of this section of the report focuses on the Bank's

tendency to try to do too much with few resources. This observation is supported by the following six specific points: (i) regionalization of the Bank's operational task fragments its vision of African development issues; (ii) operational staff lack the right mix of skills to accomplish their tasks; (iii) the work load of operational staff at the ADB is substantially greater by a factor of three than at similar financial development institutions; (iv) operational managers lack the authority to manage resources or allocate funds; (v) Bank professionals spend too much time doing administrative jobs and routine paperwork; and (vi) regional offices lack a clear mandate and the appropriate technical staff to resolve problems in the field.

On Governance: The report calls for a fundamental change of attitude and a new culture in the Bank. Specifically, the report points out four aspects of the present culture to be changed. These are (i) the emphasis on quantitative targets over quality; (ii) a reluctance to delegate authority and refusal to accept responsibility; (iii) lack of transparency in decision-making; and (iv) suspicion and distrust among management and staff at all levels. It cites the position of the President as an outstanding paradox. The President is described as one with "authority but with no power." The report qualifies this statement as follows: "He makes virtually all Bank appointments, yet he cannot appoint his Vice Presidents. He is more overleap [*sic*] by governors but can be suspended by the Board." That is, the Board of Executive Directors (EDs), which consists of 12 regional (that is, Africans) and six non-regional EDs.

Recommendations: On the face of it, the report was a damning indictment of what the Bank stands for and what it has been doing during the 30 years of its existence. This was, however, not the case. The report, with the appropriate title "Quest for Quality," portrays warts and all in order that "the Bank can be strengthened to produce quality lending. If strengthened, it will contribute even more effectively

than in the past to Africa's economic and social development. If not strengthened it may end up by destroying itself." A tough warning, but not pessimistic. The report rec-
ommends that the Bank give more powers to office holders
and an equal amount of accountability which provides
advancement to the best and weeds out those who have
become a liability, which the report sums up in these words:
"The Bank must strive to strengthen its personnel management and improve the motivation of its staff."

There were several reactions to the report both within and
outside the Bank. I will not, however, address them here,
since they deserve a proper analysis within the overall framework of institutional adjustment. This essentially calls for a
separate research project. Moreover, a number of recent studies have analyzed the Knox report (see for instance, English
and Mule, 1996; Mistry, 1995). Nevertheless, I will cite the
view of the Bank's staff that believed then and now in the
urgent need for reform within the Bank as articulated in my
internal memorandum, which I have mentioned earlier. This
view was represented in an editorial comment in the Eco-
Afrique newsletter on environment and social policy that I
founded in September 1992. It used to be published quarterly by the Environment and Social Policy Division in the
Central Projects Department of the Bank, where I was its
managing editor. The comment was as follows:

> The Knox report must be read in its proper context.
> It is a product of an internally inspired process of
> self-examination that the President of the Bank initi-
> ated a year ago, when the terms of reference for a
> task force on project quality were prepared and ap-
> proved by the Board of Directors. It was in the spirit
> of constant search for excellence in the service of Af-
> rica that the task force was established, with the view
> to enabling the Bank to institutionally adjust its struc-
> tures in the face of changing circumstances. The point

of departure for this institutional adjustment must be a critical examination of some of the Articles of the Agreement Establishing the Bank, specially those concerning its functioning. The Bank has evolved *over* the years from a US$250 million institution to a US$33 billion Bank that is standing tall with an impressive triple-A credit rating in the international financial markets. The ADB has also evolved from a ten-staff institution to a 1,400-staff Bank; a high-calibre staff with dedication, knowledge and professionalism. However, there could be very few deadwood that might have out-lived their usefulness with the passage of time and during the long march toward excellence. But it should be pointed out that they have also contributed to the great achievements of the Bank. Through self-adjustment, this institution shall remain standing tall and those few free-riders shall wither away, but their contribution will be well-remembered. This Bank, this premier pan-African financial institution, shall not destroy itself. To state it otherwise is a wishful thinking, for its many stakeholders will not allow this to happen. Nairobi, you are the leap point. (April 1994)[13]

A new organizational structure for the ADB was approved in January 1995. It was the beginning of the rebirth of African institutions, though it was unfortunate that a Canadian consultancy firm was later asked to assist in the implementation of the new structure, which was conceived and designed by the staff of the African Bank themselves without any outside help[14].

Africa has depended for so long on foreign experts in the design and implementation of her development policies and strategies. The time has come for Africa to formulate her own strategies and policies for sustainable development. The relevant question, then, is whether or not there exists an institutional capacity to make Africa's rebirth a reality. A typical economist's answer to this question, would be "it depends." From an African perspective, one would argue that there is adequate capacity in Africa to internalize sustainable development policies that aim at improving the social well-being of ordinary African people. However, many people in the donor community would say that there is inadequate institutional capacity, to the extent that they will require technical assistance as an element in their loans and/or grants. Moreover, structural adjustment programs have further reinforced the dependency on foreign experts, on the one hand, and enhanced the World Bank's intellectual hegemony with respect to Africa's development, on the other. In describing the role of the World Bank in coordinating the Special Program of Assistance (SPA) for Africa, Percy Mistry has recently articulated this point as follows: "One unintended consequence of SPA is that the WB now tends to exercise a monopoly over adjustment issues and development assistance to Africa. As in the case of monopolies, this one has unfortunate consequences in depriving African countries from the benefit of countervailing views and of building up their own intellectual capacities" (1995:33). Hence, dependency on foreign experts is essentially a by-product of development assistance itself. It should be pointed out that the overall aim of technical assistance in the short-term was to provide institutional capacity to implement a given development project/program, while a national was being trained in the requisite skills.

There was, and still is, a mental malady that seems to have afflicted a number of African policy-makers and some intellectuals: not trusting their own ability to shape the destiny of Africa. This in turn, I would argue, perpetuates an inferiority complex and further reinforces stereotypical stories. Africa must discover that knowledge is the most valuable asset and the key to sustainable development. This knowledge asset has significantly depreciated during the

macroeconomic adjustment programs of the 1980s, especially
the austerity measures embedded in the stabilization programs. This situation has forced some of the highly qualified nationals to migrate in search of greener pastures, as
the purchasing power of their salaries was eroded by the
economic crisis and subsequent corrective measures that
further aggravated their hardships. General Olusegun
Obasanjo elucidates this:

> Africa has world-class scientists who could make
> meaningful contributions to the development of this
> continent. Some of our best brains have been disillu-
> sioned and frustrated and they are out of the conti-
> nent for political or economic reasons and are help-
> ing to strengthen Europe, North America and Pacific
> Asia that are already developed. They are giving
> world-class performance out there while we are un-
> der-performing at home with truncated and dis-
> tressed capacity left[15].

Furthermore, depreciation of the African knowledge asset
is associated with the pathetic state of social services, especially education and health, in the 1980s. In desperate situations of budgetary belt-tightening and public expenditure
reductions, social services in most of the African countries
were often the first to be affected. Rural areas, where most
Africans live, were usually affected more than the urban centers. Education is now seen as an important element in enhancing human capital formation in Africa, which would in
turn strengthen the capacity of African intellectuals in the
design and implementation of sustainable development
strategies. In this regard, the role of African scholars in the
process of self-examination and reformulation of development policy was vividly demonstrated by Claude Ake, when
he led the debate at the African Development Bank's Symposium in 1995. This Symposium was indeed opportune, as

it provided a true dialogue between African scholars, on the one hand, and policy-makers, on the other. His assessment of Africa's development during the last three decades was very critical.

Claude Ake's appraisal should be viewed within a proper context, for it is likely to be misunderstood as part of the growing pessimism with respect to African development. His critical assessment of the past performance was meant to generate serious thinking among the African scholars and policy analysts. It was also a prelude to his prescription for the endemic malaise of African development. Moreover, this approach is different from the one usually adopted by some analysts who see Africa as a terminally ill patient who therefore does not need any additional treatment (for example, foreign aid), for this would be a waste of efforts. U.S. Senator Jesse Helmes has recently described foreign aid to Africa as "pouring money down a rathole[16]" Others have romanticized this through provocative statements, on the one hand, and sympathetic expression, on the other. For instance, Basil Davidson (1974) out of sympathy pondered: Can Africa Survive? While Axell Kabou (1993) wondered, why does Africa refuse to develop?

The answer to the first question is in the affirmative, for Africa has survived the brutality of slavery as well as the grave humiliation and indignity of colonialism. In fact, Africa is the only continent that had been subjected to unprecedented massive exploitation and degradation of its human and natural resources by the evil forces of racism and colonialism. Yet, it has miraculously weathered them away and made substantial contributions to global progress and development. This historical fact is often ignored by prophets of doom, who are usually quick to paint a gloomy picture of Africa. However, the graphic pictures of "man-made" catastrophes from Ethiopia, Liberia, Somalia, Sudan, and Rwanda in the recent past have provided sufficient munition to cynics and pessimists to write off and erase Africa from the development map of the world. Moreover, the growth of humanitarian relief assistance as an important industry for the international charity organizations and their unaccountable employees has contributed to the so-called Afro-pessimism. Furthermore, recent developments in global communication, for example Cable News Network (CNN), have instantly brought into TV rooms the world over the shocking images of starving children from those African countries that are at war with themselves. And, in a sense, one is tempted to say that Africa is the enemy of her own self. These CNN pictures have reinforced the negative image of Africa in the minds of ordinary people the world over, and in turn perpetuated the usual stereotyping of Africans.

On why Africa refuses to develop, I must agree with Peter Veit, Tanvi Nagpal, and Thomas Fox (1995) that such questions essentially "reflect faulty reasoning and a flawed assessment" of the past as well as of present efforts at development in Africa. It will, nevertheless, take courage, vision, and hard thinking on the part of Africans and their friends the world over to dispel and put to final rest the kinds of stereotypes about Africa embedded in the so-called Afro-pessimism. One of the negative consequences of the current pessimism on African development is the inferiority complex and passiveness that it has inflicted on a sizeable number of African intellectuals. Very intelligent Africans have withdrawn from the ensuing discourse on Africa's economic development and social progress. This has, in turn, allowed policies and strategies to be formulated and applied with little regard to the objective conditions of Africa. But when these policies and strategies fail, many analysts and cynics are quick to blame Africa. In this regard, it should be stated at this juncture that Africa has historically contributed to the world economy, especially to Western Europe (Britain and France) and America, by providing human and material resources.

That contribution was, in most cases, through force and enslavement and not trade. It is interesting to note that these resources contributed substantially to the creation of the initial *conditions for growth in Europe and America (Rodney, 1974;* Engerman and Sokoloff, 1994). Yet, Africa still has the requisite resources that could substantially improve the social well-being of her people, if these resources were used wisely. And there is every reason in the world to believe that they will be utilized rationally for the betterment and social progress of ordinary African people. My optimism is particularly strengthened by the current political will of African leadership, on the one hand, and by the courage and determination to speak out loudly on issues of Africa's development by African scholars, on the other. There is, therefore, a good chance for the realization of an African model of development, one that integrates economic, political, social, and ecological concerns into a single framework. This would in turn lay the foundation for Africa's renewal and eventually lead to human betterment and progress in Africa in the 21st century. Our mission then, as Africans and intellectuals, is to put science and technology in the **service of Africa**. The time has come to tell our people the truth of their underdevelopment; yes, nothing but the truth of their misery amidst a world of plenty. Look at Asia, Latin America, and the Middle East; then look at Africa. What do you see? I see nothing wrong with Africa and nothing wrong with us either other than being afraid to tell the truth to our people, to the world around us, and to say no to mediocrity within us. The truth is this: Nobody will bring lasting solutions to Africa's problems through critical thinking and systematic analysis other than ourselves -- we, the African scholars and people! What a noble mission.

NOTES

1. From Closing Statement of the GCA co-chairmen, GCA Plenary, November 27-28, 1995, The Hague, The Nether lands. Page 4.

2. From a commentary on "Aid for the World's Poorest," by the New York *Times*, Internet Edition of October 18, 1995, page 8.

3. The contributions of the U.S.A. to ADF-VII is envisaged to be US$315 million, and if the U.S. reduces her contri- butions, say, by 50%, then the amount would be $157.5 million, which could in turn trigger an overall reduction by the other ADF contributors. ADF-VII negotiations have been concluded in May 1996 for an amount of US$2.5 billion without a contribution from the United States.

4. Insertion is by the author.

5. A commentary on "Aid for the World's Poorest," by the New York *Times*, Internet Edition of October 18, 1995, page 8.

.6. In chapter four of this book, I am arguing for an agricul- ture-led sustainable economic growth in Africa, without neglecting the importance of industry.

7. A recent cover story in The Economist (December 16th- 22nd, 1995) on the results of the December 1995 Russian elections to the Duma reminds us that Communism is not quite dead! It reads: "Communism II, it's alive! Just when you thought it was safe for democracy." It is interesting to note that Communism still sends waves of fear from its grave beneath the Kremlin!

8. I would think that the correct title should have been *The Government We Deserve!* We, the Sudanese elite, especially the scholars — past and present — including Dr. Mansour Khalid himself.

9. From a closing statement of the GCA co-chairmen, GCA Plenary, 27-28 November 1995, The Hague, The Netherlands.

10.   The task force was chaired by a former World Bank vice president for Latin America and the Caribbean, Mr. A. David Knox.

11.   This point is one of the factors that motivated me to undertake this research project. But more importantly, I was encouraged by the response of the president of the Bank Group to my internal memorandum on the need for institutional adjustment, with emphasis on a country-focus approach to operations. My memorandum was written on 25 March 1994 before the release of the Knox report, when I did not have prior knowledge of its content. Moreover, it was in reference to the point I made during a meeting between the president and division chiefs on 9 March 1994.

12.   EPCP stands for Economic Prospects and Country Programming paper, NCPR and SCPR refer respectively to country program departments for North and South regions. The Bank's lending operations were organized into two main regions — north and south. NARD & SARD stand for agriculture and rural development departments, and NISI and SISI stand for industry and infrastructure departments.

13.   This was supposed to be a special edition of Eco-Afrique on the occasion of the 30th anniversary celebrations of the Bank, which coincided with the annual meetings of the Bank Group in Nairobi, Kenya, in May 1994. However, my immediate supervisor was alarmed by the find ings of the task force and subsequent hostile reaction to these findings from a number of "powerful" African EDs. In fact, the reaction of my supervisor was a clear valida-tion of the findings of the task force, as it illustrated clearly "a reluctance to delegate authority and refusal to accept responsibility," on the one hand, and "suspicion and dis-trust among management and staff at all levels," on the other. When this issue was censored and banned, I de cided to discontinue the publication of Eco-Afrique. The

new structure has taken into account recommendations
of the Knox report, but more importantly it is a product
of the internal work of the reform-minded professionals
within the Bank. In this regard, 1994 was the year when
the Bank rediscovered its most valuable asset — its human capital.

14. For more of this, see Lual A. Deng, *My Nine Years with the
African Development Bank: A Professional Aide Memoir* (forth-
coming).

15. From a statement at a conference organized to launch the
African Fund for Research and Development (AFRAND),
Nairobi, Kenya, in May 1993, and quoted from ADB
Today, a newsletter of the African Development Bank
Group.

16. Quoted from Peter Veit, Tanvi Nagpal, and Thomas Fox
(1995), "Africa's Wealth, Woes, Worth," in *Issues and
Ideas*, by the World Resource Institute.

APPENDIX

◆

As stated in the main body of chapter four, the state is treated as an endogenous factor in the proposed African model of development. This implies that we can address the political dimension of development by determining *ex ante*, the features of the type of the state that we would like to prescribe policies for and which we believe would be in a position to implement them. In this regard, a policy matrix is constructed from Crawford Young's attributes and imperatives of the state. I call it a policy matrix because of the simultaneous interaction between attributes and imperatives of the state on decision variables and whose values are unknown to us and hence the focus of our model. This approach, I believe would enhance our understanding about the role of the state in the process of development management. Let us then examine the concurrent interaction between attributes and imperatives on decision variables and their envisaged (desired) outcomes. We first construct a matrix of these interactions, which will become the coefficients of the decisions variables. This is given in Table A.1 below.

Table A.1: A Policy Matrix Showing The Likely Interactions Between Attributes and Imperatives of State

attribute\ imperative	Hege- mony	Legi- macy	Auto- nomy	Secur- ity	Reve- nue	Acum- lation
Sovereignty	a_{11}	a_{12}	a_{13}	a_{14}	a_{15}	a_{16}
Power	a_{21}	a_{22}	a_{23}	a_{24}	a_{25}	a_{26}
Nationhood	a_{31}	a_{32}	a_{33}	a_{34}	a_{35}	a_{36}
Idea	a_{41}	a_{42}	a_{43}	a_{44}	a_{45}	a_{46}
Law	a_{51}	a_{52}	a_{53}	a_{54}	a_{55}	a_{56}
International -Actor	a_{61}	a_{62}	a_{63}	a_{64}	a_{65}	a_{66}

From the table A.1 above, we can determine the value of each cofactor a_{ij}, i=1,..., 6 and j=1,..., 6, which is a product of the interaction between an attribute (i) with an imperative (j) on a decision variable, say, economic reform for a given state. For instance, a_{11} is the interaction between sovereignty and hegemony of a given state, which is a coefficient of a decision variable, say, reforming the economy in order to achieve a growth rate of 4 percent (which is an output). That is, how can the state use its sovereignty and hegemony in taking reform measures (policies) that would restore growth to the economy. But this is not the whole story, for there are other interactions -- a_{12}, a_{13}, a_{14}, a_{15}, and a_{16} -- that affect concurrently the six decision variables and not just only on economic reform, but combined with it so as to achieve the desired rate of growth of the economy. To get the whole picture, we have to bring in the decision variables and the desired outcomes (or parameters).

Let us, for instance, assume a column matrix B comprising the six leading issues in African development as the decision variables: b_1, b_2, b_3, b_4, b_5 and b_6 respectively standing for economic reform, democratization, protecting the environment, reducing poverty, controlling indebtedness, and resolving internal conflicts. These will constitute a system of six simultaneous linear equations, with six unknown decision variables. We further assume a column matrix C comprising six desired outcomes (outputs/parameters) from solving this system of six simultaneous linear equations. These are: $c_1, c_2, c_3, c_4, c_5,$ and c_6 respectively denoting the rate of economic growth, civil liberty, ecological balance, equity, balanced-budget, and social harmony. The system of simultaneous linear equations is now complete and can be written in a matrix form as a system of three matrices: **AB=C,**

$$
\begin{array}{cccccc}
a_{11} & a_{12} & a_{13} & a_{14} & a_{15} & a_{16} \\
a_{21} & a_{22} & a_{23} & a_{24} & a_{25} & a_{26} \\
a_{31} & a_{32} & a_{33} & a_{34} & a_{35} & a_{36} \\
a_{41} & a_{42} & a_{43} & a_{44} & a_{45} & a_{46} \\
a_{51} & a_{52} & a_{53} & a_{54} & a_{55} & a_{56} \\
a_{61} & a_{62} & a_{63} & a_{64} & a_{65} & a_{66}
\end{array}
\quad
\begin{array}{c}
b_1 \\ b_2 \\ b_3 \\ b_4 \\ b_5 \\ b_6
\end{array}
\quad
\begin{array}{c}
c_1 \\ c_2 \\ c_3 \\ c_4 \\ c_5 \\ c_6
\end{array}
$$

Where **A** is a 6 by 6 matrix of coefficients (a_{ij}) giving the interactions between attributes and imperatives of the state; **B** is a 6 by 1 matrix of the six unknown decision variables; and **C** is a 6 by 1 matrix of development policy outputs or parameters. The six parameters of a development policy are constant, so their values can also be determined *ex ante*, by a policy analyst as the desired outcomes of a development strategy. We have stated earlier that the coefficients resulting from the simultaneous interaction between attributes and imperatives, were constant --their numerical values known to a policy analyst. In this regard, the value of each a_{ij} varies between 1.0 and -1.0, depending on the nature of the government of the day that is managing the affairs of the state and the country. An example of three extreme cases may help illustrate how this can take on different values along the scale: +1.0 to -1.0. For instance, the

36 coefficients will take on 1.0 each in a Mandelaist-Musevenist African state; -1.0 in Bula Matari state; and 0.0 (zero) when the state disintegrates and ceases to exist (withers away) as previously known. These coefficients are subjective, since their values are determined by a policy analyst. They are however useful in the conceptualization of the role (behavior) of the state in the development management process.

BIBLIOGRAPHY

◆

Adelman, Irma and Cynthia T. Morris. (1973). *Growth and Social Equity in Developing Countries.* Stanford, California: Stanford University Press.

African Development Bank. (1992). *Poverty Alleviation Strategy and Action Program,* Abidjan, Cote d'Ivoire.

_____. (1994a). *Guidelines for the Implementation of the Action Program for Poverty Alleviation.* Abidjan, Cote d'Ivoire.

_____. (1994b). *African Development Bank and the Environment.* Annual Report, Abidjan, Cote d'Ivoire.

_____. (1995). *African Development Report.* Abidjan, Cote d'Ivoire.

Ahn, K. (1990). "The Sense of Relative Poverty and Its Effects on the Equity – Efficiency Trade Off," *Journal of Economic Development,* Vol. 15 (1), pp. 191–98.

Ake, Claude. (1995). *Socio-political Approaches and Policies for Sustainable Development in Africa.* Paper presented at the Annual Meetings Symposium of the African Development Bank, 23 May 1995, Abuja, Nigeria.

Ali, Abdel Gadir A. (1985). *The Sudan Economy in Disarray.* Khartoum (Sudan): University of Khartoum Press.

Amin, Samir. (1976). *Unequal Development: An Essay on the Social Formation of Peripheral Capitalism.* New York: Monthly Review Press.

Angelsen, Arild. (1996). "Deforestation: Population or Market Driven? Different approaches in modelling of agriculture expansion." Paper presented at CFOR and UNDP/WIDER workshop on Theories and Modelling of Tropical Deforestation, Bogor, Indonesia, 20 -23 January, 1996.

Angelsen, Arild, E.F.K. Shitindi and J. Aarrestad. (1996). "Causes of Deforestation: An Econometric Study from Tanzania." A paper presented at the Annual Conference of the Norwegian Association for Development Research (NFU), Christian Michelsen Institute, Bergen, Norway: 22-24 May 1996.

Anyang'Nyong'o, ed. (1990). *Regional Integration in Africa: Unfinished Agenda.* Nairobi: African Academy of Sciences.

Apter, David E. (1987). *Rethinking Development: Modernization, Dependency, and Postmodern Politics.* London: Sage Books.

Arnold, Stephen H. and Andre Nitecki. (1990). *Culture and Development in Africa.* New Jersey: Africa World Press.

Arrow, Kenneth. (1950). "A Difficulty in the Concept of Social Welfare." *The Journal of Political Economy,* 58:328-346.

Asongwed, Tah. (1993). *Born to Rule: A Biography of a Life President.* Silver Springs, Maryland (USA): Heritage Publishing Company.

Badiane, Othmane and C. Delgado. (1995). *A 2020 Vision for Food, Agriculture, and the Environment in Sub-Saharan Africa.* Washington, DC: IFPRI.

Balassa, Bela. (1983). "The Adjustment Experience of Developing Economies After 1973." In IMF Conditionality, edited by John Williamson. Washington, DC: Institute for International Economics.

Berg, Elliot. (1986). "Structural Adjustment Lending: A Critical View." Unpublished report for the World Bank
_____. (1988). *Policy Reform & Equity, Extending the Benefits of Development*. International Center for Economic Growth and Sequoia Institute Seminar, ICS Press.

Bergson, Abram. (1938). "Reformulation of Certain Aspects of Welfare Economics." *Quarterly Journal of Economics*, 52:310-334.

Berry, Sara. (1993). *No Condition Is Permanent*. Madison: University of Wisconsin Press.

Bjorvatn, Kjetil. (1995). "Rent-seeking and Foreign Aid." Paper presented at the Annual Development Economics Conference, Norwegian School of Economics and Business Administration, November, 1995, Bergen, Norway.

Bromley, Daniel. (1991). "Legal Foundations of Exchange: The Development Imperative." *In Democratization and Structural Adjustment in Africa in the 1990s,* edited by Lual Deng, Markus Kostner and Crawford Young. Madison, Wisconsin (USA): African Studies Program, University of Wisconsin.

Bromley, Daniel and Jeffrey A. Cochrane. (1994). *Understanding the Global Commons.* Environment and Natural Resources Policy and Training Working Paper No.13, Madison, Wisconsin (USA): University of Wisconsin.

Brown, Richard. (1992). "Migrants' Remittances, Capital Flight, and Macroeconomic Imbalance in Sudan's Hidden Economy," *Journal of African Economies*, Vol. 1 (1), pp. 86–108.

Chambers, Robert. (1985). *The Crisis of Africa's Poor: Perception and Priorities.* IDS
_____. (1993). *Challenging the Professions, Frontiers for Rural Development*, Intermediate Technology Publications.

Chenery, Hollis et al. (1974). *Redistribution With Growth.* New York: Oxford University Press.

Christian Michelsen Institute (CMI). (1995). *International Response to Conflict in Africa: Conclusions and Recommendations.* Bergen, Norway.

Cleaver, K.M. (1993). *A Strategy to Develop Agriculture in sub-Saharan Africa and Focus for the World Bank.* Technical Paper No. 203, Washington, D.C.: The World Bank.

Cleaver, K.M. and W. Graeme Donovan. (1995). *Agriculture, Poverty, and Policy Reform in Sub-Saharan Africa.* World Bank Discussion Papers, No. 280, Africa Technical Department Series. Washington, D.C. (USA): The World Bank.

Cooper, Richrad N. (1986). *Economic Policy in an Interdependent World - Essays in World Economics.* Cambridge, Massachusetts: The MIT Press.

Coplin, W.D. and Michael K. O'Leary, eds. (1991). *Political Risk Yearbook,* Vol. VI: Sub-Saharan Africa. Syracuse, NY (USA): Political Risk Services.

Cornia, G.& G.K. Helleiner (eds). (1993). *From Adjustment to Development in Sub-Saharan Africa.* London: MacMillan.

Cour, Jeane-Marie and David Nauget. (1996). "West Africa in 2020," in *The OECD Observer.* No. 200, June/July 1996, pp 20-26.

Daly, Herman E. and John B. Cobb, Jr. (1989). *For The Common Good- Redirecting the Economy Toward Community, The Environment and a Sustainable Future.* Boston, Massachusetts (USA): Beacon Press.

Dasgupta, Partha. (1993). "Poverty, Resources, and Fertility: The Household as a Reproductive Partnership," *Environmental Economics and Natural Resource Management in Developing Countries,* edited by Mohan Munasinghe. Committee of International Development Institutions on the Environment, The International Bank for Reconstruction and Development/The World Bank, Washington D.C., pp. 73–103.

Davidson, Basil. (1974). *Can Africa Survive?* Heinemann: London.
_____. (1992). *The Black Man's Burden: Africa and the Curse
of the Nation-State.* New York and London: Times Books.
_____. (1993). "Comments on Mamdani." *Monthly Review,* Vol.
45, No. 3, July-August, pp.49-57
De Melo, J. and S. Robinson. (1982). "Trade Adjustment Policies
and Income Distribution in Three Archetype Economies."
Journal of Development Economics. Vol. 10, pp. 67-92.
Deng, Francis M. (1971). *Tradition and Modernization: A
Challenge for Law Among the Dinka of the Sudan.* New
Haven: Yale University Press.
Deng, Lual A. (1984). "The Abyei Development Project: A Case
Study of Cattle Herders in the Sudan," Unpublished Ph.D
Dissertation. University of Wisconsin–Madison, USA.
_____(ed). (1985). *African Development Crisis: Looking for the
Way Out.* Processed Monograph. Madison, Wisconsin
_____. (1988). "Economic Recovery Program: An Overview of
the Adjustment Experience in the 1980s," in *Economic
Reform in Africa: Lessons from Current Experience.*
Edited by David Gordon and E. Wilson, Ann Arbor,
Michigan (USA): Center for Research on Economic
Development, University of Michigan.
_____. (1992). "Demographic Trends in Africa: Elements of a
Population Policy for the Bank Group," 1992 African
Development Bank's Annual Meeting's Symposium,
Dakar, Senegal.
_____. (1995). *Poverty Reduction: Lessons and Experiences
From Sub-Saharan Africa.* Environment and Social Policy
Working Paper No.6: African Development Bank, Abidjan,
Cote d'Ivoire.
Deng, Lual A. and Dan Mou. (1985). "African Development
Crisis, Structural Adjustment and Donor Community."
Nigerian Journal of International Affairs, Vol.11, No.1,
pp. 32-57.
_____. and T. Oshikoya. (1991). "Structural Adjustment
Programs in Africa in the 1990s: An overview of the

performance of restructuring economies." In *Democratization and Structural Adjustment in Africa in the 1990s,* edited by Lual Deng, Markus Kostner and Crawford Young. Madison, Wisconsin (USA): African Studies Program, University of Wisconsin.

_____. and T. O. Fadayomi. (1994). "Issues of Population Growth and Sustainable Development in Africa," *Population Growth and Sustainable Development in Africa.* African Development Bank, Abidjan, Cote d'Ivoire, pp. 12–35.

_____., Charles Mbwanda, Nadir Mohammed and Charles Lufumpa. (1995). *Agricultural Transformation in Africa: The Missing Link,* paper presented at USAID/ADB/MSU seminar on Agricultural Transformation in Africa, 25 - 27 September 1995, Abidjan, Cote d'Ivoire.

_____. and Elling N. Tjønneland, eds. (1996). *South Africa: Wealth, Poverty and Reconstruction.* Bergen, Norway: Christian Michelsen Institute and Center for Southern African Studies.

Dia, Mamadou. (1996). *Africa's Management in the 1990s and Beyond: Reconciling Indigenous and Transplanted* Institutions. Directions in Development Series. Washington, D.C.: The World Bank.

Dixit, Avinash and Barry Nalebuff. (1991). *Thinking Strategically.* New York and London: W.W. Norton & Company.

Dornbusch, Rudiger. (1988)."Balance of Payments Issues." In *The Open Economy: Tools for Policymakers in Developing Countries,* Rudiger Dornbusch and F. Lesile C.H. Helmes eds. New York: Oxford University Press.

Dorosh P. A. and D. E. Sahn. (1993). *A General Equilibrium Analysis of the Effect of Macroeconomic Adjustment on Poverty in Africa,* Working Paper 39. Ithaca, NY: Cornell Food and Nutrition Policy Program.

El-Affendi, Abdelwahab. (1991). "Out of Africa's Troubles." Comment: Africa and the West in Africa Events of August 1991, pp 36-37.

Elbadawi, I. (1992). *World Bank Adjustment Lending and Economic Performance in SSA in the 1980s: A Comparison of Early Adjusters, Late Adjusters and Nonadjusters.* Policy Research WPS No. 1001, The World Bank.

_____. (1995a). "Consolidating Macroeconomic Stabilization and Restoring Growth in Sub-Saharan Africa," paper presented at the Overseas Development Council Conference on Africa's Economic Future, Washington, D.C., April 23-25, 1995.

_____. (1995b). "Structural Adjustment and Drought in Sub-Saharan Africa," paper presented at a Development Studies Association Annual Conference, University College, Dublin: 7-9 September 1995.

_____. (1996). "Market and Government in the Process of Structural Adjustment and Economic Development in Sub-Saharan Africa," paper presented at Market and Government: Foes or Friends? a theme of an International Conference on the World Economy in Transition, held at the Institute of Economic Research, Hitotsubashi University, Tokyo: 8-10 February 1996.

Elbadawi, I. and Benno J. Ndulu. (1995). "Growth and Development in Sub-Saharan Africa: Evidence on Key Factors," invited paper for presentation at the 1995 World Congress of the International Economic Association (IEA), Tunis: 17-22 December 1995.

Emmerson, Donald K. (1991). "Capitalism, Democracy, and the World Bank: What is to be done?" In *Democratization and Structural Adjustment in Africa in the 1990s,* edited by Lual Deng, Markus Kostner and Crawford Young. Madison, Wisconsin (USA): African Studies Program, University of Wisconsin.

English, Philip and Harris M. Mule. (1996). *The Multilateral Development Banks: Volume 1 – The African Development Bank.* Boulder, Colorado (USA): Lynne Rienner Publishing.

Etounga-Manguelle, D. (1994)."Culture and Development:
    African Responses." *In Culture and Development in
    Africa: Proceedings of an International Conference.*
    Environmentally Sustainable Development Proceedings
    Series No. 1, by Ismail Serageldin and June Taboroff eds.
    Washington, DC: The World Bank.
Fanon, Frantz. (1963). *The Wretched of the Earth.* New York:
    Grove Press.
Food and Agriculture Organization (FAO) of the United Nations.
    (1994). *1994 Production Year Book.* Vol. 48. Rome: FAO.
Genberg, H. and A.K. Swoboda. (1987). *The Current Account and
    Policy Mix Under Flexible Exchange Rates.* Processed
    manuscript, the IMF.
Greer, J. and E. Thorbecke. (1986). "A Methodology of Measuring
    Food Poverty Applied to Kenya," *Journal of Development
    Economics,* Vol. 24.
Grubel, H.G. (1981). *International Economics.* Homewood,
    Illinois (USA): Richard D. Irwing.
Gulhati, Ravi and R. Nullari. (1990). *Successful Stabilization and
    Recovery in Mauritius.* The World Bank, Washington, D.C
Hardin, Garrett. (1968). "The Tragedy of the Commons." *Science,*
    162:1243-1248
Helleiner, G.K. (1986). *Policy-Based Program Lending: A Look at
    the Bank's New Role.* U.S.-Third World Policy
    Perspectives, No. 7. New Brunswick: Transaction Books.
Hettne, Bjorn. (1990). *Development Theory and the Three Worlds.*
    New York: Longman.
Hogan, Michael J. (1987). *The Marshall Plan.* New York:
    Cambridge University Press.
Hyden, Goran. (1980). *Beyond Ujamaa in Tanzania,
    Underdevelopment and Uncaptured Peasantry.* Berkeley
    and Los Angeles: University of California Press.
International Monetary Fund (IMF). (1987). *Theoretical Aspects
    of Fund-Supported Adjustment Programs.* Washington,
    D.C. (USA): The IMF Research Department, occasional
    paper No. 55.

Joseph, Richard. (1995). "The International Community and
        Conflict in Africa: Post-Cold War Dilemmas." Paper
        presented at a Workshop on The International Response
        to Conflict in Africa, organized by the Christian Michelsen
        Institute, Bergen, Norway: 7-8 September 1995.

Kaldor, N. (1955). "Alternative Theories of Distribution." *Review
        of Economic Studies,* **23**:83-100.

Khalid, Mansour. (1990). *The Government They Deserve.*
        London: KPI limited.

Killick, Tony. (1992). *Explaining Africa's Post-independence
        Development Experiences.* London: Overseas
        Development Institute, Working Paper.

_____. (1993). *The Adaptive Economy: Adjustment Policies in
        Small, Low-income Countries.* Washington, D.C.: The
        World Bank.

Klitgaard, Robert. (1994)."Taking Culture into Account: From
        'Let's' to 'How.'" In *Culture and Development in Africa:
        Proceedings of an International Conference.*
        Environmentally Sustainable Development Proceedings
        Series No. 1, by Ismail Serageldin and June Taboroff eds.
        Washington, DC: The World Bank.

Kofi, T.A. (1994). *Structural Adjustment in Africa: A Performance
        Review of World Bank Policies Under Uncertainty in
        Commodity Price Trends — The Case of Ghana.* Helsinki:
        WIDER.

Kothari, Rajni. (1988). *Rethinking Development: In Search of
        Humane Alternatives.* New Delhi: Ajanta Publications.

_____. (1993). "Towards a Politics of The South," in *Facing The
        Challenge.* The South Center. London and New Jersey:
        ZED Books.

Krueger, Anne O. (1991). *Ideas Underlying Development Policy
        in the 1950s.* Paper prepared for Institute for Policy
        Reform: Washington, D.C, USA.

_____. (1993). *Political Economy of Policy Reform in
        Developing Countries.* The MIT Press: Cambridge,
        Massachusetts, USA.

Landell-Mills, Pierre. (1992). *Governance, Civil Society and Empowerment in sub-Saharan Africa*. Washington, DC: Africa Region, The World Bank.

Leontief, W. (1983). "Technological Advance, Economic Growth and the Distribution of Income." *Population and Development Review*, Vol. 9, No. 3, pp. 403-410.

Lewis, W. Arthur. (1954). "Economic Growth with Unlimited Supplies of Labour." *Manchester School*, 22, 139-191.

_____. (1955). *The Theory of Economic Growth*. London: George Allen and Unwin.

Limqueco, Peter and Bruce McFarlane eds. (1983). *Neo-Marxist Theories of Development*. New York: St. Martin's Press.

Lloyd, P.C. (1967). *Africa in Social Change*. London: Penguin Books.

Lufumpa, Charles Leyeka. (1994). *The Nature and Magnitude of Poverty in Sierra Leone*. Environment and Social Policy Working Paper Series No. 1. African Development Bank, Abidjan, Cote d'Ivoire.

_____. (1995). *The Nature and Magnitude of Poverty in Uganda*. ESP No. 11. African Development Bank, Abidjan, Cote d'Ivoire.

Mackenzie, J.S.(1894). A Manual of Ethics. London: University Correspondance College Press

Mamdani, Mahmood. (1993). "The Sun Is Not Always Dead at Midnight," *Monthly Review*. July–August, Vol. 45, No. 3, pp. 27-48.

Mandela, Nelson. (1994). *Long Walk To Freedom: The Autobiography of Nelson Mandela*. New York and London: Little, Brown and Company.

Martin, W. and L.A. Winters. (1995). *The Uruguay Round – Widening and Deepening the World Trading System*. Washington, DC: The World Bank.

Meeks, Gay (ed). (1991). *Thoughtful Economic Man: Essays on Rationality, Moral Rules and Benevolence*. Cambridge: Cambridge University Press.

Meier, Gerald M. (1976). *Leading Issues in Economic Development*, 3rd edition. New York: Oxford University Press.

_____ed. (1987). *Pioneers in Development.* New York: Oxford University Press.

Meier, Gerald M. and D. Seers. (1984). *Pioneers in Development.* A World Bank publication: Oxford University Press.

Mehmet, Ozay. (1995). *Westernizing the Third World: The Eurocentricity of Economic Development Theories.* London and New York: Routledge.

Mistry, Percy S. (1995). *The African Development Bank (AfDB): An Agenda for Renewal (Lessons & Options).* A report prepared for the Governments of Denmark, Finland, Norway and Sweden.

Mohammed, Nadir A.L. (1993). "Defense Spending and Economic Growth in sub-Saharan Africa: Comment on Giymah-Brempong" Journal of Peace Research, 30(1) 95-99

Mundell, R.A. (1968). *International Economics.* New York: MacMillan.

Mwega, F.M. (1996). "Saving in Sub-Sahara Africa: A Comparative Analysis." Paper presented at the African Economic Research Consortium Plenary, May 1996, Nairobi, Kenya.

Myrdal, Gunnar. (1970). *The Challenge of World Development.* London: Allen Lane.

Naqvi, S.N.H. (1993). *Development Economics: A New Paradigm.* Karachi: Oxford University Press.

Ndisale, Brave. (1995). *Food Security and Nutrition in Africa: Some Proposals for a Policy Statement for the African Development Bank,* Environment and Social Policy Working Paper Series No. 10. Abidjan (Cote d'Ivoire) African Development Bank.

Ndongko, W.A. (1985). *Economic Cooperation and Integration in Africa.* Dakar: CODESRIA Book Series.

Ndulu, Benno J. (1995). "Africa's Development Challenges in a Changing World Economy," paper presented at a

conference on Africa: Looking Ahead in the Light of
Recent Thinking on Economic Development, held at the
Institute of Economics, University of Copenhagen: 1-2
November 1995.

Ndulu, Benno and Nicolas van de Walle (ed). (1996). *Agenda for
Africa's Renewal*. ODC Policy Perspective No. 21.
Washington, D.C: Overseas Development Council.

Nkrumah, Kwame. (1965). *Neo-colonialism: The Last Stage of
Imperialism*. London: Nelson.

Nyerere, Julius. (1967). *Freedom and Unity*. London: Oxford
University Press.

_____. (1968). *Freedom and Socialism*. London: Oxford
University Press.

_____. (1993). "Reflections on Empowerment," in
*Empowering People: Building Community, Civil
Associations and Legality in Africa*, edited by Richard
Sandbrook and Mohamed Halfani. Toronto (Canada):
Center for Urban and Community Studies, University of
Toronto.

Nzongola-Ntalaja, G. (1987). *Revolution and Counter-Revolution
in Africa*. London and New Jersey: Zed Books.

O'Boyle, Edward J. (1991). "On Justice and Charity," *Review of
Social Economy*, Vol. XLIX, No. 4 (Winter 1991),
Milwaukee, WI. (USA): Association for Social
Economics, Marquette University.

Ogbu, Osita M. (1993). *Setting Agricultural Research in
Sub-Saharan Africa*. Nairobi (Kenya): International
Development Research Center (IDRC).

Ojo, Oladeji and Temitope Oshikoya. (1994). *Determinants of
Long-Term Growth: Some African Results*. Abidjan (Cote
d'Ivoire): Economic Research Paper Number 19, African
Development Bank.

Onwuka, Ralph I. and A. Sesay, ed. (1985). *The Future of
Regionalism in Africa*. London: MacMillan Publishers.

Organization of African Unity (OAU). (1981). *The Lagos Plan of
Action for Economic Development in Africa: 1980-2000*.

Geneva: International Institute of Labor Studies.

Organization for Peace and Appropriate Development in the Horn of Africa (PADA). "The Future Face of Post Cold War Africa: Building Inter-African Solutions to Urgent Needs." Conference Background Paper (1996). Leiden, The Netherlands.

Pearce, David, Edward Barbier and Anil Markandya. (1990). *Sustainable Development — Economics and Environment in the Third World.* London: Earthscan Publications.

Pedersen, Karl R. (1995). "Aid, Poverty Alleviation and Incentives." Paper presented at the Annual Conference of Development Economics, Norwegian School of Economics and Business Administration, November, 1995, Bergen, Norway.

Pisani, Edgar. (1993). "Inventing the Future," in *Facing The Challenge*. The South Center. London and New Jersey: ZED Books.

Platteau, Jean-Philippe. (1991). "Traditional Systems of Social Security and Hunger Insurance: Past Achievements and Modern Challenges." In *Social Security in Developing Countries*, edited by E. Ahmad, J. Drèze, J. Hills and A. Sen. Oxford: Clarendon Press.

_____. (1993). *Sub-Saharan Africa as a Special Case: The Crucial Role of (infra)structural Constraints.* A paper commissioned by the FAO.

Potholm, Christian P. (1970). *Four African Political Systems.* Englewood Cliffs, N.J.: Prentice-Hall.

Preston, P.W. (1982). *Theories of Development.* London: Routledge and Kegan Paul.

_____. (1987). *Rethinking Development: Essays on Development and Southeast Asia.* London and New York: Routledge & Kegan Paul.

_____. (1994). *Discourses of Development: State, market and polity in the analysis of complex change.* Aldershot: Averbury.

Prong, Jan and Mahbub ul Haq. (1992). *Sustainable Development: From Concept to Action.*

Riddell, Robert. (1981). *Ecodevelopment: Economics, Ecology and Development.* Hampshire (England): Gower Publishing Company.

Rodney, Walter. (1974). *How Europe Underdeveloped Africa.* Washington D.C.: Howard University Press.

Rostow, W.W. (1962). *The Stages of Economic Growth: A Non-Communist Manifesto.* London: Cambridge University Press.

Rwegasira, Delphin G. (1987). "Balance-of-Payments and Structural Adjustment in Low-income Developing Countries: The Experiences from Kenya and Tanzania in the 1970s." *World Development.* Vol. 15, No. 10, pp. 1321-1335.

Sandbrook, Richard and Judith Barker. (1985). *The Politics of Africa's Economic Stagnation.* London: Cambridge University Press.

Sandbrook, Richard and Mohamed Halfani. (1993). *Empowering People: Building community, civil associations and legality in Africa.* Toronto (Canada): Center for Urban and Community Studies, University of Toronto.

Schmitz, J. and David Williams Gillies (1992). *The Challenge of Democratic Development: Sustaining Democratization in Developing Countries.* Ottawa: North-South Institute.

Scott, James. (1976). *The Moral Economy of the Peasant.* New Haven and London: Yale University Press.

Serageldin, Ismail. (1995). *Nurturing Development: Aid and cooperation in today's changing world.* Washington, D.C.: The World Bank.

Serageldin, Ismail and June Taboroff eds. (1994). *Culture and Development in Africa: Proceedings of an International Conference.* Environmentally Sustainable Development Proceedings Series No. 1. Washington, DC: The World Bank.

Shaw, Timothy M. (1985). "Towards a Political Economy of
    Regionalism in Africa," in Onwuka, Ralph I. and A. Sesay,
    ed. (1985). *The Future of Regionalism in Africa.* London:
    MacMillan Publishers.

Silberberg, E. (1978). *The Structure of Economics: A
    Mathematical Analysis.* New York: McGraw-Hill Book
    Company.

Skålnes, Tor. (1993). "The State, Interest Groups and Structural
    Adjustment in Zimbabwe." *The Journal of Development
    Studies,* Vol. 29, No.3, pp. 401-428.

Solow, Robert. (1956). "A Contribution to the Theory of Economic
    Growth." *Quarterly Journal of Economics,* 70:65-94.

_____. (1957). Technical Change and the Aggregate
    Production Function." *Review of Economics and
    Statistics,* " 39:312-320.

_____. (1970). *Growth Theory.* New York and London: Oxford
    University Press.

Soyinka, Wole. (1994). "Culture, Memory and Development." In
    *Culture and Development in Africa: Proceedings of an
    International Conference.* Environmentally Sustainable
    Development Proceedings Series No. 1, by Ismail

Serageldin and June Taboroff eds. Washington, DC: The
    World Bank.

Spencer, Dunstan S.C. (1995). "Past Trends and Future Prospects
    for Agricultural Development in Sub-Saharan Africa."
    Paper prepared for presentation at the Workshop on
    Agricultural Transformation in Africa, 26-29 September
    1995, Abidjan, Cote d'Ivoire.

Staatz, John M. (1994). *The Strategic Role of Food and
    Agricultural Systems in Fighting Hunger Through
    Fostering Sustainable Economic Growth.* MSU
    Agricultural Economics Staff Paper No. 94-39. Department
    of Agricultural Economics, Michigan State University,
    East Lansing, Michigan, USA.

Stern, Joseph B. (1994). *Poverty Reduction in Sierra Leone: A
    Framework for a National Action Plan,* Environment and

Social Policy Working Paper Series, No. 3. African
Development Bank, Abidjan, Cote d'Ivoire.

Summers, Lawrence H. (1991). "Knowledge for Effective Action."
A Keynote Address to The World Bank Annual
Conference on Development Economics, Washington,
D.C., April 25-26, 1991.

Svensson, Jakob. (1995). "When Is Foreign Aid Policy Credible?
Aid Dependence and Conditionality." Paper presented at
the Annual Conference of Development Economics,
Norwegian School of Economics and Business
Administration, November. . . ., 1995, Bergen, Norway.

Taylor, Lance. (1979). *Macro Models for Developing Countries.*
New York: McGraw-Hill.

_____. (1983). *Structuralist Macroeconomics: Applicable
Models for the Third World.* New York: Basic Books

Tinbergen, Jan. (1958). *The Design of Development.* Baltimore
(MD): John Hopkins University Press.

Tisdell, Clement A. (1990). *Natural Resources, Growth, and
Development: Economics, Ecology and Resource-scarcity.*
New York: Praeger.

Toye, John. (1987). *Development Theory and Experience of
Development.* New Brunswick: Transaction Books.

ul Haque, I. (1995). *Trade, Technology, and International
Competitiveness.* Washington, D.C.: The World Bank.

UNDP. (1992). *Country Human Development Indicators.* New
York: Oxford University Press.

_____. (1994). *Human Development Report 1994.* New York:
Oxford University Press.

_____. (1995). *Human Development Report 1995.* New York:
Oxford University Press.

UNEP. (1994). *An Environmental Impact Assessment Framework
for Africa.* Nairobi: Environment and Economics
Unit, UNEP.

_____. (1996). *The UNEP/World Bank Workshop on the
Environmental Impact of Structural Adjustment*

Programmes. Environmental Economics Series Paper No. 18, Nairobi: UNEP.

UNICEF. (1987). *Adjustment With a Human Face*. Edited by G. A. Cornia, Richard Joly and F. Stewart.

United States Agency for International Development (USAID). (1993). *Africa: Growth Renewed, Hope Rekindled*. A Report on the Performance of the Develoment Fund for Africa. Washington, D.C.: USAID.

Van Dieren, W. (1995). *Environmental News From The Netherlands*. No. 3. The Hague, The Netherlands.

Van Nieuwenhuijze, C.A.O. (1982). *Development Begins at Home: Problems and Prospects of the Sociology of Development*. Oxford: Pergamon Press.

Veit, Peter, Tanvi Nagpal and Thomas Fox. (1995). *Africa's Wealth, Woes, Worth*. Washington, D.C (USA): World Resources Institute.

Vogt, Margaret A. (1995). "Managing Conflicts in Africa: Evolving a Meaningful Partnership Between the United Nations and OAU." Paper presented at a Workshop on The International Response to Conflict in Africa, organized by the Christian Michelsen Institute, Bergen, Norway: 7-8 September 1995.

Washington, Sally. (1996). "Globalisation and Governance,"in *The OEACD Observer*. Number 199, April/May 1996, pp 24-27.

Williamson, John ed. (1983). *IMF Conditionality*. Washington, D.C.: Institute for International Economics.

Word Commission on Environment and Development. (1987). *Our Common Future.* New York: Oxford University Press.

World Bank. (1984). *Toward Sustained Development in Sub-Saharan Africa — A Joint Program of Action*. New York: Oxford University Press.

_____. (1989). *Sub-Saharan Africa: From Crisis to Sustainable Growth*. Washington, D.C.: The World Bank.

_____. (1990a). *World Development Report 1990*. New York: Oxford University Press.

_____. (1990b). *Making Adjustment Work for the Poor: A Framework for Policy Reform in Africa*. Washington, D.C.: The World Bank.

_____. (1990c). *Adjustment Lending Policies for Sustainable Growth*. Washington, D.C.: The World Bank.

_____. (1991a). *Assistance Strategies to Reduce Poverty*. Washington, D.C.: The World Bank.

_____. (1991b). *World Development Report, 1991: The Challenge of Development.*, New York: Oxford University Press.

_____. (1992a). *Poverty Reduction Handbook*. Washington, D.C.: The World Bank.

_____. (1992b). *Social Indicators of Development 1991–92*. New York: Oxford University Press.

_____. (1992c). *Skill Acquisition and Work in Micro–Enterprises*. Washington, D.C.: The World Bank.

_____. (1993a). "Poverty in Sub–Saharan Africa: A Role for SPA–3." Washington, D.C: The World Bank.

_____. (1993b). *Mali: Assessment of Living Conditions*. Report No. 11842–MLI. Washington, D.C.: The World Bank.

_____. (1993c). *Uganda: Growing Out of Poverty*. Report No. 11380–UG. Washington, D.C.: The World Bank.

_____. (1994a). *Adjustment in Africa: Reforms, Results and the Road Ahead*. New York: Oxford University Press.

_____. (1994b). *Status Report on Poverty in Sub-Saharan Africa: The Many Faces of Poverty.* Africa Technical Department, The World Bank.

World Resources Institute. (1991). *World Resources 1990–91*. New York: Oxford University Press.

_____. (1992). *World Resources 1992–93*. New York: Oxford University Press.

Young, Crawford. (1976). *The Politics of Cultural Pluralism*. Madison: The University of Wisconsin Press.

_____. (1982). *Ideology and Development in Africa.* New Haven: Yale University Press.

_____. (1991). "Democratization and Structural Adjustment:

A Political Overview." In *Democratization and Structural Adjustment in Africa in the 1990s,* edited by Lual Deng, Markus Kostner and Crawford Young. Madison, Wisconsin (USA): African Studies Program, University of Wisconsin.

_____. (1994). *African Colonial State in Comparative Perspective.* New Haven: Yale University Press.

_____. (1996). "Accountability and Transparency: Towards Stronger Governance in Africa." Paper prepared for presentation at the 1996 Annual Meetings Symposium of the African Development Bank.

Index

Kaunda, Kenneth 14
Klitgaard, Robert 133

Lagos Plan of Action 16, 33, 62,
    84-85, 87, 239
Landell-Mills, Pierre 18, 23, 75,
    203, 205, 208

Mamdani, Mahmood 13, 21, 78,
    139
Mandela, Nelson 58, 96, 127,
    132, 135, 250
Matari, Bula 162, 165
Megharib Union 99
Museveni, Yoweri 77
Myrdal, Gunnar 202

NAFTA 180
National Resistance Movement
    7, 77
Naudet, David 176
Ndongko, Wilfred 180
Neocolonialism 12
NGO 44, 121, 220
Nkrumah, Kwame 1, 130
Nyerere, Julius 29, 59, 74, 77,
    141, 143, 162, 207, 214,
    255
Nyerereism 29, 36, 58

OAU 33, 39, 63, 127, 129,
    131-132, 167, 168, 239,
    254
Onwuka, Ralph 180

PADA 178
Perestroika 57, 75, 254
Plato 206
Preston, W.P. 145
Prowse, Michael 73, 144

Robinson, Sherman 16

SADC 97, 99, 179, 181, 184
Sahel 196
SAM 113
Schmitz, Gerald 79
Scott, James 103
Shaw, Timothy 180
Smith, Adam 71
Sokoloff, Kenneth 169
Soyinka, Wole 29, 100-101,
    139, 145, 172

TANU 27-28
Tiffen, Mary 89
Tinbergen, Jan 202
Tisdell, Clement 83
trade and tariff 200U

UMOA 179, 181
UNDP 47, 64, 105-109, 112,
    147-148, 150, 153-
    154, 235
UNEP 83, 85-86
UNICEF 53, 112
USAID 112-113, 229-230, 231
U.S.S.R 25